FHM Presents…

THE BIGGEST BOOK OF

TRUE
STORIES

THIS IS A CARLTON BOOK

Text copyright © Emap Elan Network 2002, 2005
Design copyright © Carlton Books Limited 2005

This edition published by Carlton Books Limited 2005
20 Mortimer Street
London W1T 3JW

A CIP catalogue record for this book is available from the British Library.

ISBN 1 84442 465 0

The material in this book was previously published as
FHM Presents... The Best True Stories and FHM True Stories 2

Printed in the UK
Typeset by e-Type, Liverpool

www.fhm.com

FHM Presents...

THE BIGGEST BOOK OF

TRUE
STORIES

CARLTON
BOOKS

Thanks to FHM's readers for all their true stories

www.fhm.com

Dog goes airborne

This happened when I was a young gunner working in Canada, a few years ago. I was operating a Challenger Battle Tank on a live firing exercise one afternoon when we were told by our commanding officer to expect a visit from a high powered general, and that best behaviour was required. After a few hours of live firing, the order came through to cease fire, and the tanks rumbled out of the greenery to form a neat line for the General's arrival. He arrived by helicopter and, with a small white Scottish terrier under his arm, swiftly made his way along the tanks introducing himself to everyone. When he reached our tank he clambered aboard for a quick look around, patted us all on the back, said, 'Right ho, chaps,' climbed off the machine and walked back to his helicopter to get an aerial view of the tanks firing their guns at predetermined targets. As we advanced into position I saw my first target and shouted up to the loader to arm the gun. As he stuck his hand in the charge bag however, he suddenly withdrew it with a loud 'Ouch,' and I turned to see the General's dog with its teeth clamped to the hand of the burly Irish gunner. Angry beyond belief, the gunner suddenly pushed the dog into the barrel of the 120mm gun, slammed the breach closed, looked at me and bellowed 'Fire!' In the heat of the moment I nodded grimly and pulled the trigger; the slobbering canine left our Challenger at mach three, and the spotters radioed through that the General was impressed by our accuracy.

Royal takes charge

In the Seventies I was working out in the North Sea on the Claymore Alpha Oil rig. One day we were notified of an impending visit from Prince Charles, and the guy in charge of the deck, a Canadian and staunch Royalist – ran us ragged for weeks, taking us through the landing drill over a dozen times. Once the helicopter had landed, the heli-crew would have to wait for the pilot to switch off a flashing red light under the fuselage before they could open the doors. The big day came and it was a scorcher – beautiful sunshine and not a breath of wind. The RAF Sea King appeared and made a perfect touchdown, but although the engines started to slow, the fuselage warning light kept flashing. We waited and waited and then, realising that his drill was starting to fall apart, the Canadian began gesturing to the pilot to turn the light off. He pointed under the aircraft and twirled his fingers frantically, but the confused pilot shrugged his shoulders and shook his head. Furious, the Canadian grabbed the radio and yelled into it, 'Turn off your fucking red light so we can approach your fucking aircraft, you goddam fucking idiot!' The pilot gave an immediate thumbs up and the light went out. He then slowly removed his sunglasses and pulled off his helmet: Prince Charles had opted to fly the helicopter himself that day.

Out of the mouths of babes ...

It'd been a hard day at work, when my colleague Michelle asked me what the time was. "4.45,"
I replied. "Blimey!" she said. "It was six o'clock this time yesterday."

My girl was filling in an application for holiday work. "Are you a member of a professional organisation?" asked one question. "Does that mean the IRA?" said my girlfriend.

Blind man betrayed

I am a self-employed joiner who works away from home, and the following disaster happened to me last year when I was working at a hotel complex in London. I was using an angle-grinder and had a slight accident with a grinding disc. The disc shattered and left a really nasty gash just above my eye, an injury which needed 20 stitches. On the way to the hospital the ambulance medic bandaged both of my eyes shut and told me not to try to open them as this could result in more damage to my eye. After waiting on a hospital bed for over two hours I told my mate, who had come along to give me moral support, that I needed a pee, and he agreed to guide me to the loo. We walked aimlessly around the corridors for several minutes until I was really desperate. Finally, we walked through some doors and my friend positioned me in front of the bowl. I pulled out my cock and sighed, letting the hot gushing stream hit the pan. In seconds I heard howls of laughter and felt a hand on my arm. Then a woman's voice calmly asked me if I would mind not peeing in the wastepaper basket of the outpatient's department. My friend had calmly let me get my todger out in full view of over 20 other patients.

Orderly confuses paste

Many years ago I worked as a hospital orderly looking after elderly, senile patients. One particular woman didn't need much looking after, but understanding any of her requests was tricky due to her severe speech impediment, coupled with the fact that she wore cheap, ill-fitting dentures. One day, I decided to help her out by giving these stained gnashers a good clean, so I gently teased them from her chops and gave them a thorough scrub in the sink. I was proud to see that they looked absolutely gleaming when I had finished, and when I jammed them back in she had a true, gleaming, Hollywood smile. As I set about tidying the rest of the room, however, she suddenly started rolling around the bed and whimpering. There was also blood streaming out of her gob. Racing over, I grabbed her head, whipped out her dentures and dragged her over to the sink to wash her mouth out. It was only as the old dear was spitting down the drain that I saw the words 'Fungal Foot Cream' printed across what I had supposed to be the toothpaste tube.

Patient forgets amputations

Many years ago, I worked as an orderly in a local hospital. Although the sight of blood didn't bother me, I could never come to terms with the geriatric ward, where the old timers would continually cast aside blankets, offering me a display of their saggy breasts and greying, dilapidated pubic thatches. To make matters worse, one particularly senile woman mistook me for a wartime spiv, and demanded nylon stockings and bacon whenever I passed. Naturally I always ignored her, but one morning she changed her patter and asked me to fetch her slippers from under the bed. I got down on my knees and looked, but when I explained that they weren't there, she went berserk, shouting, 'What's wrong with you? Why can't you see them?', which was enough to convince me I simply wasn't looking hard enough. Just as it was getting to the stage where I was lifting the bed to look in the corners, the duty nurse tapped me on the shoulder and asked me what I was doing. When I explained I was hunting for the woman's slippers, she simply shook her head and through stifled laughter pointed at a gap in the bed – the precise gap where the old bat's legs should have been.

Word mix-up

As a fresh-faced member of the Metropolitan Police Force, I was once asked to deal with a case of an old Jewish lady who had tragically attempted to take her own life. My partner at the time was an officer with numerous years of experience, and when we arrived at the hospital he propped himself up outside the nurses' rest area and informed me that I would be conducting the interviews. But while he stood there with his chest puffed out, the distraught daughter of the Jewish lady walked up and proceeded to embark on a long tale of suffering and pain, describing in great detail her mother's third suicide attempt. Evidently my partner's concentration had been entirely focused on the young girls in uniform, because he suddenly leant forward and, with as much sincerity as he could muster, boomed, 'Yes – it's tragic, isn't it? It almost makes you believe there's a real case for genocide.' We all stopped what we were doing and a stunned silence followed, before the daughter managed, 'You mean euthanasia, surely?' Realizing his blunder, my colleague nodded, then silently shuffled out of the room, to spend the rest of the afternoon sitting shamefaced in the patrol car.

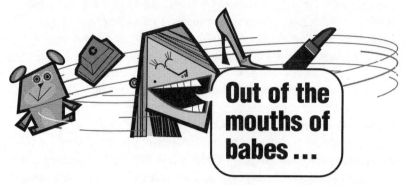

Out of the mouths of babes ...

One weekend, my sister's boyfriend announced that he intended to try out his new kite. "Don't be silly," my sister remarked, "it's too windy to fly a kite."

Playing Risk with my housemate's girlfriend, I complained about the low numbers I was getting. "Try rolling the dice one at a time," she told me in all seriousness. "That way they won't affect each other."

Watching a TV show about rhinos having their horns cut off to protect them from poachers, my lady housemate said, "That's terrible. How do they kill their prey?"

Road sign no use

This story dates back to when I worked at a parachute-training unit in Germany. We had a foreign skydiving team training with us, and at the end of their stay one of the lads was tasked with driving them to Hanover airport for their flight home. It was a three-hour round trip, and after six hours we started to worry. A quick call to the airport confirmed that he had dropped the team off, so we knew he was somewhere on the road back. Then the phone rang, and a rather panicky squaddie explained that he was lost and had run out of diesel for the van. To make matters worse, he only had one Deutschmark for the phone, and the pips were starting to go. Thinking quickly, we asked him if he could see any street signs to indicate his position. There was a brief pause, and then he excitedly replied 'I can see a sign for Rollsplitt. Oh thank

God, I'm in Rollsplitt...' before getting cut off. It sounded familiar, but none of us could place it, so we asked our German accountant. 'Rollsplitt?' he asked, completely deadpan, 'but that means loose chippings.'

Engineer inspects firearm

Several years ago I worked night shifts as an electrical maintenance engineer. To pass the time, the team started to devise stupid ways of producing the loudest noise possible. The best technique was to place a mixture of oxygen and acetylene welding gas into a crisp packet, and light it at arm's length, but I developed the idea and came up with 'The Spud Cannon'. Basically a steel pipe with two gas taps and a spark plug, the cannon's power was breathtaking, and could easily put a King Edward clear over the horizon. All was well, until someone stuffed in a soggy tea bag, soaking the spark plug. I loaded and reloaded several times, but to no avail. It was then I made a critical error and ignored the rule, 'never look down the barrel of a gun'. Peering in to see if a spark was being produced, I pulled the trigger. There was a deafening noise, I went blind, and for a split second I thought I had blown my face off. When I got to a mirror, I realized I had singed my eyebrows and hair, huge pieces of rust from the pipe were embedded in my bleeding nose, and red welts showed where bits of tea leaf had peppered me.

Alcoholic acts deceased

While on duty in the East Midlands, I was sent to an address following a report that the owner of the house had died. The tip had come from a well-known wino, who claimed that he had popped around to his mate's house and found him dead. Unable to stay in the house with the body, he said that he would wait outside the premises until I arrived. When I got there, a crowd of concerned locals, including the deceased's family were standing around, but the wino was nowhere to be seen. The door was firmly locked, but I could see that the upstairs window was ajar, and as everyone was becoming increasingly agitated,

I called the fire brigade. Some time later, with a large audience, including six firemen, I ascended the ladder. When I got to the window I could see the body on the sofa, tongue hanging out, and lifeless. But as I opened the window and climbed in he sat bolt upright and looked straight at me. Excitedly I stuck my head out the window and shouted, 'He's alive.' Oh how the family members cried, and the firemen cheered, as they all waved happily at me. And then I felt a tap on the shoulder. 'I suppose you've come for the dead guy in the bedroom,' the wino said. Sheepishly I stuck my head back out and said, 'Actually, he is dead. Sorry.'

In-flight terror

While on a flight across China to take up a post with a minerals exploration company, I was too busy enjoying the spectacular view to bother too much about the slapdash standard of service. It wasn't until a stewardess entered the cockpit shouting at the top of her voice that I realized this was no ordinary flight. After a bit of a barney on the flight deck, she emerged, followed by the co-pilot, and they carried on their heated discussion in front of the passengers.

When they'd finished, the co-pilot turned to go back into his cabin, only to realize that the door had jammed. After much rattling, shaking and knocking, the captain came out to demand what was going on. He stepped out of the cockpit and closed the door behind him in order to deliver a stern lecture to his subordinates. It was only when they tried to open the door again that they realized it had jammed once more. This time, there was no-one left on the flight deck to open the door from the inside, and the captain, his co-pilot and the stewardess were getting more and more frantic as the door wouldn't budge. The passengers were also going mad, and it wasn't until someone found an emergency axe that they chopped down the door and regained the cockpit. For the rest of the flight, we could see the two embarrassed pilots through the splintered hole in their door, glaring at each other like mortal enemies.

Officer's mess

While performing my duties as an Edinburgh police officer, my partner
Colin and I had reason to stop a motorist, who was driving somewhat
erratically. As I got out of the car to talk to him, two healthy young
blondes started chatting to Colin, who was still sitting in the passenger
seat. I spoke to the motorist, decided that he had been drinking, and
asked him to accompany me back to the squad car. As he climbed into
the back seat I couldn't help but notice that Colin had now exited the
vehicle, was flirting like crazy with the giggling blondes, and was even
showing them his handcuffs. I got in beside the worried motorist,
prepared the breathalyser for the breath test, and put on the sternest
face possible to read Section Six of the Road Traffic Act. However, no
sooner had I uttered the words 'Now then, sir' when Colin dived into
the front seat, slammed the door shut, turned to the pair of us and said:
'She's Swedish, and says if we give her and her a friend a lift up the
road, she'll suck my cock!'

We stared at Colin's beaming face in stunned silence, until the police
radio suddenly garbled a message. In a huge fit of laughter I told the
motorist that we had an urgent call to attend and he was free to go. His
bemused face, as he stood in the middle of the road and watched us
roar off, will stick in my mind for ever.

Fast tracks

While serving out in Africa many years ago as a regular in the army, a
mate of mine, Joe, found himself sitting on the roof of an old Bedford
bus, heading into the local town with the rest of his mates for what
promised to be an almighty piss-up. As they hurtled down the dusty
road, a great cheer suddenly went up from the front of the bus as it
pulled out and began to slowly overtake a ramshackle pick-up truck.
The little pick-up was being driven by an African family, and they were
loving the attention, smiling and waving and doing their best to get a
race going as the drunken squaddies slowly rumbled past. What was
really making the boys laugh, however, was the grandmother. Due to
the severe lack of space, she had been rolled up in a dirty red carpet and
strapped to the roof rack. With only her wrinkled face visible, she jutted

out about five foot in front of the truck, leading the charge with grim determination. Then, as Joe's bus inevitably pulled away, she emitted a banshee-like wail as she disappeared in a cloud of dust and diesel.

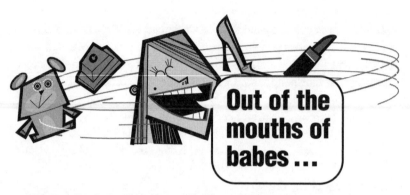

Out of the mouths of babes ...

Ordering drinks on holiday, my girlfriend asked for a Margarita. I suggested getting a pitcher. "I can't," she replied, "the camera's in the apartment."

Seeing a live penguin for the first time, my girlfriend was amazed how small it was. "I'd always assumed they were my height," she explained.

During the Golden Jubilee celebrations, my sister-in-law said what a shame it was that the Queen's dad had died just before she was crowned.

Local poultry

In 1995 I was in the Royal Navy serving onboard HMS Southampton in the West Indies. Visiting the islands in the Caribbean while doing our country's bit for the counter-drugs operation, one of our stops was the island of Montserrat. Our stay took the usual form of getting ashore and downing as much low-priced white rum as possible. Every bar seemed to offer much the same as the last: cheap booze and identical menus containing 'mountain chicken' and chips. After the fourth, we were starving and being adventurous we all opted for the chicken. When it came there only seemed to be chicken legs. The barman explained that because of the mountainous island, the legs of the mountain chicken were very big and the best part, so we tucked in. Two months later, when the island's volcano erupted, we were called back to aid in the disaster relief operation. We were erecting tents for the islanders to wait out the eruptions when, during a break, the biggest bullfrog we had ever seen – as big as a small dog – bounded across the field. We all laughed as this enormous amphibian hopped by. The laughter soon stopped when an old woman who was chasing it shouted, 'Hey, stop that mountain chicken!'

Early shout

I'm a member of the fire service, and recently had to have a vasectomy. The night before the operation I received a phone call from a nurse Smithers, confirming my appointment and reminding me to bring a pair of tight underpants and fresh urine and sperm samples. The urine sample did not prove a problem, but the sperm donation reduced my wife to hysterics as I struggled nervously – the morning of the operation – to beat my non-responsive member into action. Finally my pathetic secretions were bottled, and off I went to hospital. The operation was a success, but I was slightly annoyed when the medical staff ignored my hard-won samples – although by the time my wife arrived to take me home I was past caring. It was only when I returned to work that I discovered that 'nurse Smithers' was in fact a work colleague, and that, during the 09:00hr parade – just about the time I was beating my floppy member into oblivion – a full squad of 22 firefighters had performed a mass groan of sympathy.

Suspect device

I am presently on a tour with a rifle company, serving in Belfast. While out and about a few months ago I noticed something which I thought required my expertise as a Unit Search Advisor: near a large tree a plank had been put across a hole in the ground, and leaves had been scattered over the board in an attempt at concealment. I went over with a member of my unit. We pulled the plank clear, and bingo! I found a small box, eight inches by four inches, the same size as a TPU (timer power unit) – a component in many of the terrorist devices used in the province. On closer inspection I saw that the box was made of cardboard, and I gingerly removed the lid. Inside, I saw a package wrapped in a handkerchief, with what looked like a piece of string sticking out of it. I decided to uncover the device, and at this point my company commander suggested we call in the experts. I resisted, seeking the glory for myself. I gently lifted the string and the handkerchief fell away. At that moment, my place in battalion legend became secure: the string was in fact a tail. In the torch beams we stared at a dead hamster, ruthlessly plucked from its lovingly constructed grave.

Deterrent misused

This story dates back to when I was a police probationer, being shown the ropes by an experienced copper called Baz. We were on routine patrol one night when a call was received of 'intruders on the premises' at a local breaker's yard. Baz was all too aware that the place was guarded by a vicious Rottweiler named Sid, so when we arrived he pulled out his trusty Halon fire extinguisher – an exceptional deterrent when sprayed into an animal's eyes. Our shift sergeant duly arrived and confidently led the way into the dark yard. No sooner had we rounded the first corner when the slavering Sid confronted us, baring his teeth and growling with intent. Then he charged us. Rather than run however, the sergeant decided he was Crocodile Dundee and attempted to out-stare the beast. It didn't work, and when Sid was a mere 15 metres away, Baz grabbed the extinguisher and yelled 'Here, sarge, use this!' The sarge nodded grimly, took it and swung it high over his head, bringing it down on the leaping mutt's cranium with a massive thud, killing it outright. 'Not quite what I had in mind, sarge,' was all a bemused Baz could say.

Hair Loss

Some years ago, a mate of mine worked in the drawing office of a building company near Manchester. Every Friday they would go for a drink with the office girls, including a 40-year-old, size-18 receptionist, who habitually wore a white blouse which was virtually see-through. On this particular day they took their seats in the sun, and the receptionist sat opposite the newest draughtsman, who noticed that a hair had fallen down onto her shirt. Keen to appear friendly, he leaned over and gave a hearty tug, only to pull out possibly the world's longest, darkest nipple hair. It came out with such force that her whole boob lunged forward, and her scream brought the entire pub to a standstill. To top it all off, the surprised man dropped the hair in her pint, where it floated like a drowned worm, while all at the table tried to smother their guffaws of delight.

Welcome to Bosnia

My mate Norm is a copper who often had to work the night shift. To relieve the tedium, the bobbies devised a game: cowboys and Indians. They would stalk each other in the dead of night, while the town slept peacefully. Norm was a cowboy, but, being a bit slow, he was often subjected to vicious barrages of arrows. So, in order to exact revenge, he bought himself a blank-firing pistol. However, after two weeks of patrolling his territory, without seeing any Injuns, he began to wonder whether he was ever going to christen his peacemaker. One evening, having stopped in a doorway for a break, he could suddenly hear approaching footsteps. 'Ha!' thought Norm. 'This has got to be an Indian.' Out came the peacemaker and, with a devilish glint in his eye, Norm waited. Then, as the adrenalin pumped and the sweat dripped off his brow, Norm jumped into the street and shot at the Indian. But, to his horror, the victim was not an Indian. Norm vividly recalls watching his gun smoking, while an innocent member of the public lay sprawled on the floor, suffering a severe shock and involuntary urination and defecation.

Bucket contains surprise

Last summer I found myself refurbishing The King Solomon Hotel in
Israel with another Brit in an attempt to earn enough cash for a ticket
home. Our job was to rip the tables, mirrors and beds out of the rooms
and throw them 14 floors down into the skips below. In one such room
my fellow worker discovered a sealed 20-litre bucket of shit, which had
been used by previous labourers as a toilet. Not knowing what to do
with it, he hurled it over the edge, and we watched it plummet down to
the ground. To our surprise, it remained intact. We forgot about it until
four days later, when the whole team was led out to the courtyard to
empty the skips. Two lads climbed up onto the piles and started
throwing rubbish down to us – which was when, to my horror, I
noticed a familiar-looking bucket soaring through the air. With no time
to offer a warning, I bailed out of the way as the bucket hit with an
explosion of spicy gases, spraying everyone with a heady cocktail of
human faeces and urine. The result was a spontaneous vomiting
session, as grown men puked until they could no longer stand.

Road killer

One chilly winter's night, while serving with the army in Northern
Ireland, I was manning a vehicle checkpoint when a Ford Transit
screeched to a halt and an off-duty soldier jumped out. He was in a
state of extreme shock and, when he had finally calmed down, he
explained that he had been driving back from Lisburn when he'd seen
what he thought was a body lying in the middle of the road. Fearing a
possible terrorist ambush and unable to stop in time, he had put his
foot down and ran straight over it. I asked him where the body was,
and was shocked when he stammered that he thought it was stuck
under the van. My friend, Taff, looked at me in disbelief, and gingerly
bent down to look underneath the Transit.

 'There's a guy under there ...' he said as he got to his feet. 'Oh my
God! What have I done!?' cried the squaddie, falling to his knees and
bursting into tears. '... It's Guy Fawkes,' said Taff.

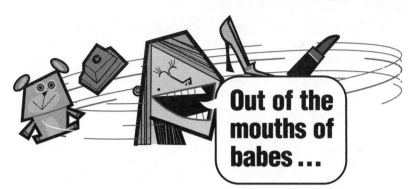

Out of the mouths of babes ...

My brother was cooking some munch when my girlfriend asked whether you could get "reverse-microwaves, to make things colder?" Er... like a fridge?

On a jolly to New Brighton, me and my good lady passed through the Mersey Tunnel from Liverpool to Birkenhead. My wife got all giddy. "This is good!" she said. "Is there one of these in Birkenhead as well?"

The missus was driving us home on the M1, northbound – except that when I glanced up from my newspaper I saw we were approaching the M25. When asked to explain why we'd gone 20 miles in the wrong direction, she sheepishly replied, "I thought we were going north because we were travelling uphill..."

Wheelchair deception

About five years ago I worked as a backstage tour guide for a well-known television station. Part of the tour included an explanation of the intricate details of the blue screen – where anything coloured blue fails to show up on camera. To do this properly, my group had to climb a near-vertical ramp and take their places in fitted seats, from where they could see themselves embarking on a magical journey via the screen in front of them. On this particular occasion I had a middle-aged lady in a wheelchair on my tour, who for obvious reasons could not get up into a chair, so I placed her at the front so that she could still see herself and enjoy the show. As the ride began, I explained that if anyone was actually wearing an item of blue clothing, it would look as if it had disappeared. Trying not to leave anybody out, I pointed at the lady at the front and said, 'Ladies and gentlemen, if you look you will see that this lady is obviously wearing blue trousers, as you cannot see her legs.' To my utter horror, she slowly turned towards me and replied, 'Actually, I don't have any legs.'

Little voice

I work in an impersonal building with around 500 people. I was therefore rather surprised one bright morning when a fellow employee – nonetheless a complete stranger – said 'Hi' as we stood at the urinals. I found this an odd time to be greeting anybody, but not wishing to seem rude I turned and said, 'Oh, hello.' I was then rather taken aback when he stared as if I was insane before muttering, 'Hello.' It wasn't until I sat back at my desk that it all became crystal clear. My new-found buddy's first greeting had simply been a fart.

Restaurant urination disaster

About ten years ago, while serving with the RAF, a few of my fellow airmen and I were on exercise near a village in North Wales. The end-of-exercise binge coincided with FA Cup final Saturday and a large contingent of RAF lads descended on the local hostelry. The landlord agreed to keep the pub open all day, only closing between 5pm and 6pm to clean up and replenish the shelves. As soon as he had closed the door on us at 5pm I felt the desperate need to urinate. The village was deserted and without public conveniences. I found an alleyway, which had a brick wall on one side and a large shop window on the other, which seemed to be painted from the inside with black paint. I was blissfully engaged in the most satisfying pee I had ever had when I was accosted in mid-stream by a burly Welshman who, in mixed English and Welsh, accused me of exposing myself and peeing against the window of a restaurant. Apparently, although I couldn't see in, 30 or 40 people, including a local landowner with his daughter and prospective son-in-law, and a contingent of nuns from a nearby convent, could see out! The worst part of the whole affair was that after the local police were called and gave me a good telling off in front of the locals, I was assured that no further action would be taken. On my return to base, though, I found that a summons had been served on my CO. I paid a £20 fine and lost several years seniority in rank.

Fire aid

While working as a military policeman, I was called to a hospital one evening to help move patients caught in a fire. With my partner 'Fez' Parker, I started to shift about 18 elderly folk, some of whom were ranting and raving. Fez and I would grab a gibbering old lady each, wrap them in blankets and jam them into wheelchairs, before threading our way through the inferno to the car park. We were making good progress when suddenly my passenger, obviously panicking, tried to dive out of the chair, forcing me to grab her and put her back. No sooner had we restarted when she gave a grunt and lunged forward. I tried to pull her back but her strength was phenomenal, forcing me to shout, 'Fez, stop! This one's trying to escape. We've got a jumper!' Fez simply burst into laughter. 'You've got her blanket wrapped around the front wheels,' he explained. Needless to say, she never thanked me.

Workman stuck

While working some time ago as a gasman in Manchester, I received a call on my radio asking me to assist another workman in the area. When I arrived at the house, I found the carpet rolled back and the head of my friend sticking out through a lifted floorboard. When he saw me, he shouted that he needed some extra pipe and nodded his head in the direction of his van. Unfortunately, the subsequent motion of his long hair and beard attracted the attention of the customer's poodle, who embarked on a sexual assault of such ferocity on my friend's head that his unthinking reaction was to try to stand up, jamming himself between the floorboards. With one paw covering his eye and another stuffed in his mouth, his furious head-shaking only served to excite the eager pooch to ever more energetic arousal: it was jerking away at breakneck speed, eyes crossed and tongue flapping wildly. Fortunately, just as it looked as if the dog was about to come in my mate's ear, the poodle's owner came flying in and booted the dog across the room. These days, my mate sports a crew-cut.

Trophy wives

About a year ago, I sold used cars for a city-centre dealer. We worked out of two huge Portakabins, one nice and clean for the customers, the other a 'snake pit' for eight salesmen. It was horrific, full of dirty magazines, men swearing and filthy mugs. Our favourite item, however, was what we called the Trophy Tree. Basically, whenever we delivered a car, we would ask to use the toilet. While in there, a quick root through the laundry basket was undertaken, and the dirtiest pair of knickers stolen. The offending item then went on the tree, points being awarded on a scale of sauciness, amount of material soiled and sex-appeal of the owner. One day one of the lads was lounging around in our private cabin when the door flew open and in walked a customer. 'What's that?' laughed the bloke at the door, pointing at our tree. 'It's a trophy tree,' my friend Mark answered sheepishly, explaining that the boys brought in knickers from the girls they had scored with over the weekend. The customer thought it was brilliant and recounted bawdy tales of his youth. As he left he pointed at a nasty grey pair and sighed, 'That's all my missus wears these days, though.' We never heard from him again, but the awful fact is that they were the dirty grots of his beloved wife. Mark had stolen them the previous week.

Tragic hair loss

Many years ago, while working as a care assistant at a nursing home, I had the pleasure of dealing with some lovely old people, several of whom, naturally, died while I was working there. We had one resident, Fred, who had a fine toupee, and it was his wish that when he died I made sure he was wearing his rug when he was laid to rest. Sadly, he did indeed die, and I was left with the task of preparing his body for the undertaker, and for his family to view. As I was preparing the old man I popped his toupee onto my head for 'safe keeping', and continued cleaning the body. Just as I was finishing, the phone in the corridor rang, and I ran out to answer it. While I was on the phone who should walk in but Fred's son, who instantly recognized his father's syrup on my head. So while Fred got his last request, I got the sack.

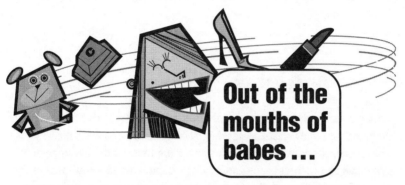

Out of the mouths of babes ...

Out for dinner at a smart Spanish restaurant, my girlfriend made sure we didn't come over as ignorant tourists when she deftly greeted the waiter with, "Buenos Aires, señor!"

On holiday in Woolacombe, my girl, noticing a small island off the bay, declared that it would be nice to walk there when the tide was out. The island in question, Lundy, was at least 30 miles off the coast.

Returning from Crete, I commented that my girlfriend's mate's suitcase was really heavy. Luckily she had a solution: "If you repack everything neatly, it'll weigh less."

Jungle boogie

During a break from patrolling the jungle in Belize, my platoon stopped to enjoy a quiet afternoon of drinking and sunbathing. Spotting a turtle in a storm drain, we brought it over for a closer look. Its immediate response was to extend its neck slightly and open its beak in a gesture designed to frighten away pissed-up squaddies. While most of us could recognize an angry snapper turtle when we saw one, one guy – Tam – was blissfully ignorant, and we cringed as he held the livid creature at waist level, took his member out and laughingly demanded oral sex. Suddenly there was a blur of movement – the snapper had stretched out and clamped down on the idiot's meat and potatoes. We were then treated to the sight of a screaming Tam, charging through the jungle with an angry green turtle dangling from his cock. Amazingly, both parties survived, but we never did manage to ascertain who emerged most traumatized.

Plumbing gaff

While relaxing after an enormous roast dinner one Sunday afternoon, the telephone rang. I am a plumber, so it is not unusual for me to get emergency call-outs, and sure enough, it was one of my elderly and more snooty customers. Apparently, her boiler was making unusual noises and she was worried it might explode. So, with much regret at having had my day off interrupted, I agreed to go over to her house. She met me at the front door and I asked her where the boiler was located. She informed me it was a wall-mounted boiler in the kitchen, over the worktop, so I walked through to the kitchen, thinking the old lady had stayed in the hall. In the kitchen, I climbed onto the worktop to inspect the boiler, but as I did so, I let out a fart of epic proportions. I was mortified, therefore, to find the lady of the house standing behind me with a look of contempt on her face. Thinking it would be too rude and obvious to simply apologize, all I could say was, 'Is the boiler making a noise similar to that?'

Financial farrago

A few years ago, I was working in Southampton for a national bank as a trainee manager. Every couple of months or so, my boss would poke his head out of his office and despatch one of his boys off to some remote branch for 'a taste of the real world'. That's how, one rainy October morning, I found myself standing on a deserted railway platform far away in the Cheshire countryside. After wandering through the peaceful hamlet, I located the branch of my bank, where I was royally greeted and shown into a huge room – the regular manager was on holiday, and I could use his office. The assistant manager saw me settled in, then shut the door, screening off from my sight the bumpkins queuing up to cash their EC subsidies. I unpacked my briefcase, shuffled a few papers, and realized I didn't have a clue what to do next. Glancing around, I found a nice big button under an old copy of the FT. 'Tea!' I thought, and buzzed the assistant. I couldn't hear a thing, so I gave the buzzer another good old push. But my daydreaming was interrupted by a banshee wail. Rushing out, I was greeted by the sight of a middle-aged lady teller collapsed in tears in the street. I'd been pressing the silent alarm, and the poor woman I'd terrified had just been transferred to the bucolic village. She had been held up at the Wolverhampton branch two weeks earlier.

Fireman framed

It was my third day as a fireman. My station was in two parts – one for the appliances, the other for tools and admin. My boss asked me if I could take some gear to be serviced at the second part of the station. I was wearing full kit – boots, orange trousers and black donkey jacket and they loaded me up with breathing apparatus (helmet on, as my hands were full). One of the guys handed me an old pickaxe handle which needed reheading. As I walked out of the station our office clerk handed me a deposit envelope, asking me to drop it into the bank on the way past. At the bank I attracted a few odd looks as I waited in the queue. Eventually I gave a cashier the envelope. She asked me to wait for my receipt. I leaned on the counter, leafed through a brochure and waited. And waited. Thinking she was taking her time, I looked up and she'd gone. Well, not exactly gone, but standing with the rest of the staff in a far corner looking past me at the bank's entrance. I followed her gaze and nearly shit myself. An armed policeman in a crouched firing position told me very firmly to drop the axe handle. As I did so another one grabbed me and handcuffed me. Only when we reached the station did they let me see the bank deposit envelope. On it was written: 'Give me all your money or I'll smash in the screen!'

Birds blunder

I work as an air traffic controller for the RAF, and we occasionally get people ringing up to complain about low-flying jets 'going under my washing line' or 'in between my hedges'. One night at work the switchboard lit up with people complaining about nine Tornadoes flying incredibly low. One call in particular has kept the entire fast jet community in stitches for months. A local farmer who kept ostriches called to say the jets were playing havoc with his birds. It's a well-known fact that ostriches stick their heads in the sand at the first sign of danger and it seems that they'd been so scared by the jets they'd instinctively tried to bury their bonces. Sadly, the farmer had the flock standing on concrete at the time, and five of his beauties had rendered themselves unconscious trying to hide.

Rude corpse

While on a peacekeeping mission in Kosovo, I found myself leading an army patrol in the capital, Pristina. As soon as we arrived, my team of three was called to a block of flats where an Albanian had shot his Serb neighbour. On arrival we found that the victim lived on the 12th floor and weighed at least 20 stone, which posed the real problem of getting the bull-sized corpse outside. I got on the radio and asked if we could throw the whale out of the window, and received a prompt ear bashing, so we lugged him out to the knackered lift. Unfortunately, after dragging him in, neither of us could reach the buttons, and it was then that I was struck by true genius. The body was in the later stages of rigor mortis and, with Herculean strength, I managed to snap his middle finger up into a 'pointy' position and got him to press the ground floor button. He was taken to hospital 'flicking the bird,' and months later a medical friend told me of a mysterious case that his team had to deal with. They dubbed it 'The phenomenon of the pointy finger.'

Art appreciation

Some years ago, I worked as a bus driver for a local company. One beautiful summer's afternoon a very attractive young lady boarded my bus and, as she rummaged in her purse, a magnificent rose tattoo – located just at the top of her cleavage – was revealed to me in all its splendour.

As I took her fare, I thought that I would try my luck and make a compliment about her great body art. Looking her straight in the eye I gave my most engaging smile, leaned up to the glass and shouted, 'I like your tits!'

All explanations that what I had meant to say was 'tattoo' fell on deaf and somewhat angry ears as I was loudly harangued as a 'pervert' and 'dirty sod' in earshot of every other passenger on the bus.

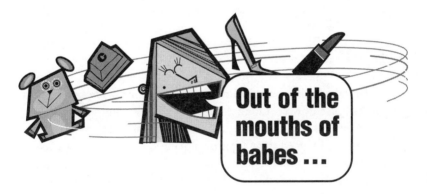

Out of the mouths of babes ...

While driving to work, my partner looked out at the local school's all-weather hockey pitch, before turning to me and asking, "How often do you have to cut Astroturf?"

Watching an ad for Appletise, the missus piped up with, "I like Appletise, but it would be so much nicer if there was a non-fizzy version." That'll be apple juice.

Watching Big Brother with a female friend, we wondered where Cameron came from. I said he was from the Outer Hebrides. "Aren't they in space?" she said, puzzled.

Service suspended

One Sunday morning about ten years ago, I went with my road-gang to resurface a road in Seaford. We turned up early, hoping to beat the traffic, but were somewhat dismayed to find a large number of cars parked exactly where we needed to work. There was a large church nearby, and as I was the new boy, I was sent along to see if any of the worshippers owned any of the vehicles. Inside, the vicar was right in the middle of his sermon, so I stood at the back to try to catch his eye. Just as everyone knelt down to pray, my two-way radio burst into life: 'Holy shit! What the hell are all those cars doing here?' hollered one hairy-arsed pal. 'I bet it's those bastards in the church!' came the grumpy reply. As one, the angry congregation spun round to see a red-faced lad staggering out of church, fumbling with a radio. Needless to say we waited for the service to end before we started resurfacing the road.

Dumb driver

Last year, I was driving to work in the morning when I noticed a man spread out face-down on the pavement. I slowed right down and watched him for a few seconds, and he appeared to be completely still. Worried, I parked the car and watched for a minute or so, but he remained absolutely motionless. I decided he must have either been knocked over or collapsed from a heart-attack, so I jumped out of the car and ran across to the pavement, screaming and shouting for help. When I got to the bloke, I grabbed him under the arms and tried to turn him over, just as a small crowd began to assemble around me. It only took me a few seconds to realize that he was, in fact, a workman with his arm down a manhole. He wanted to give me a panning for 'tickling' him while he was trying to work, but I eventually convinced him I was simply trying to be a good Samaritan and save his life.

Rural rage

I'm a farmer in a quiet, scenic part of south Yorkshire. There are rolling fields surrounded by lakes and woods – it really is a beautiful part of the world. However, as the school summer holidays coincide with harvest-time, we do have a problem with kids. They seem to delight in setting fire to 6ft-round bates of straw and rolling them downhill, so when I spotted a group of people gathered in a field I had baled earlier I was pretty angry and tore towards them on my tractor. The sight of a ten-tonne machine hurtling across a field must be pretty frightening, and it's usually enough to send the little terrors scarpering off. But as I got nearer they refused to budge. I blared my horn and shouted at them to get the hell out of my field. By the time I was right upon them I was furious. It was only then that I realized they were all in their forties and fifties and all wearing suits. Then an elderly lady said: 'I'm sorry, we're observing a minute's silence. We've just scattered my husband's ashes here as he loved this place so much.'

Hole puncher

In 1974 I was serving in Cyprus with the RAF. I was sent for a week's firing practice near Famagusta. On our first evening, a long convoy of trucks, laden with Greek builders, drove up the hill past our camp. As they went by us, the tailgates dropped and, jeering, they all started urinating on the road, pointing at their members to imply that they were hung like donkeys. This happened each day, and by the third day we had seen enough. I found a long piece of hose that had been bleached white in the sun. As their ritual began I walked towards them, causing almost deafening levels of insults, and a mass display of swarthy penises. Then I pulled out the pipe and, with my own willy tucked inside it, began to pee onto the road while swinging it from side to side. The visual effect was stunning, my RAF chums went ballistic and three Greeks fell off the back of the truck. We never saw a single open tailgate again.

Kitchen cock-up

While working as a kitchen assistant in a bistro in Australia I formed a mischievous friendship with the chef. He and I were working one New Year's Day, when the bistro took record business. In the midst of a particularly panicky period, I was trying to set up an 'avocado cheese melt' open sandwich. I laid out two slices of bread and sliced the avocado at blur speed. But in my haste, I cut myself from thumb to wrist, splattering blood all over the meal. In shock, I ran off to put a plaster on. When I came back, the sandwich had disappeared, so I just got on with the next order. Later on, when we finally had a quiet spell, I commented how quickly the chef had finished making up the meal. He confessed: he'd just turned the avocado over and melted the cheese on top. Hey presto! Avocado cheese melt. Morbid laughter filled the kitchen area. We went to the dining area and identified the unsuspecting 'vampire', a beautiful blonde lady. Strange morbid laughter once more. A waitress came to inquire what the joke was. We recounted the tale, still hysterical. She replied, rather sternly, 'That's my best friend.' Ouch. Incidentally, the unsuspecting vampire left a big tip.

Sausage surprise

After ten years, I feel ready to make this confession. While serving in the Gulf back in 1991, I found myself alone in the back of my wagon on night-watch duties, while my two crewmates slept under the stars. It was about 5.30 in the morning and I was thinking about my fiancée when I struck upon an idea. Warming up a tin of sausages in the kettle, I removed the middle three, popped the can over my knob and proceeded to give my little fella a good thrashing. When I had finally finished, it was 6am, and time for breakfast. I dutifully cooked up a culinary delight of beans, bacon burgers, eggs and, obviously, the spunky sausages. My crewmates wolfed the whole lot down and thanked me for the wonderful morning meal. I've not seen Keano or Skell for nine years, and if they are reading this, I hope I never see them again.

Break errand

A few years ago, my father came home from work killing himself with laughter. Apparently a young guy had been taken on as part of a Youth Training Scheme to run the daily errands for the workers. On that particular day he had been given a list of requisites from the workmen, including Dave's, which was, 'Get me 20 Benson & Hedges, and if they don't have those, get me anything else.' When the teen returned he shared out all the goods, approached Dave, and said 'Sorry sir, there weren't any Benson And Hedges, so I got you this instead,' and handed him a Wall's pork pie.

Toilet joke backfires

While waiting one day for a client to arrive at the hairdressing salon I manage, myself and one of the girls I worked with were sitting in the staff room, having a conversation about toilet habits. Soon, she went to the toilet and I decided to make coffee. On the way to the kitchen, I passed the toilets, and could not resist making rude noises and shouting, 'I know what you're doing!' Snickering, I walked into the kitchen and, to my horror, there was my colleague making coffee. I screamed, 'I thought you were going to the toilet!' She replied, 'Oh, I was, but your client arrived early and she's in there!' The next hour was the worst of my life.

Unpleasant japery

I used to be the director of a company which built up a relationship with another firm sharing the building. To brighten our days, we would play practical jokes on each other. You know the sort of stuff: weird phone calls, condoms, hidden pornography. But we were being humiliated, so, having identified their best prankster, Bob, we took revenge. He had gone out, leaving his lunch-box helplessly vulnerable to attack. We cut our toenails, spread them into Bob's sarnies and waited for lunch. Not a single word. But we could all sense a case of Humour Systems Failure.

As we were splitting our sides, he marched into our office and crammed his lunch into the fax machine, toenails and all, then stormed back out, calling us a bunch of sick bastards and slamming the door. Bob, rumour has it, now owns a restaurant. I think I'll give it a miss. Just in case.

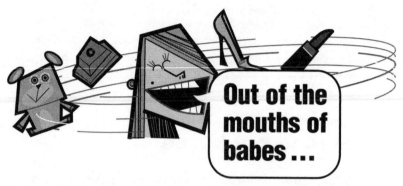

Out of the mouths of babes ...

The other day at the fast-food outlet where I work, one of the girls washed her hands then asked with a puzzled look, "How come these driers never run out of air? Have we received some on delivery?"

Walking with my girlfriend along the seafront the other day, she came over all moody. "When I was a kid, this beach seemed huge," she reminisced. I had to spoil her musings by pointing out that the tide was in.

Taking my wife fishing for the first time, I had no bites at all – so she decided to have a go. Minutes later she was reeling in a 3 1/2lb trout. "Aren't they supposed to be dead when you catch them?" she screamed, then watched horrified as I beat its little head in with a hammer. That was her final angling experience.

Dreadful career move

When I was a student I was employed by a building firm during a summer holiday. Day one, start 7.30am. I was given a pick and shovel and instructed to dig a trench 40 yards long, by two feet wide and three feet deep. This took three days. On the fourth day a surveyor came along and told the foreman that the trench was in the wrong place. I was then told to fill it in and re-dig it ten yards to the left. Four days later, tired, blistered and pissed off, I completed trench two only for another surveyor to come by and say that the first trench was correct after all and that I should fill the second trench in and re-dig the first one. I was not amused to say the least. Four days later both surveyors arrived and concluded that we didn't need any trenches and that I could just fill it in. And if they needed any more trenches dug they promised not to ask me. To this day I have a great aversion to holes.

Toilet blocked

While working as a plumber I was called to a nasty blockage in the ladies toilet of a large office block. I lifted the inspection hatch, and attempted to remove the blockage with my arsenal of pipe cleaners. After 20 futile minutes, I decided there was nothing else for it, and shoved my arm up the main pipe to remove a dam built from shit and tissue. I was almost done when a woman entered the next cubicle. In an attempt not to scare her I lay still, while she laid the smelliest log known to man. When the toilet flushed I realized I was about to get whacked in the face by the giant curler, so I pushed my arm in far enough to completely block the pipe. As her panties disappeared from view, large warm lumps of poo clung to my arm like leeches. She never guessed I was there, but I smelt ripe for the rest of the day.

Tank repulsion

While on exercise in Canada recently the temperature inside our armoured tank used to regularly creep above 100°F. As a consequence of this myself and my crew's intake of water was very high, even though it was usually warm enough to brew up with. During one part of the exercise while filling the internal drinking container from a jerry-can, I noticed a bad smell, which I put down to the heat of the plastic container. At dawn the following day, at the end of a particularly hot exercise, where we had to drink copious amounts of water, I decided we should all wash and clean up. I went first and very refreshing it was to wash and brush my teeth after a hard night of manoeuvres. It was then Ian, my gunner's, turn. He appeared to be having difficulty getting the remaining water from the jerry-can into the washing-up bowl. Then, with a very distinctive plop a pasty, white, hairless and obviously somewhat decayed corpse of a large rat dropped out. After a bout of dry heaving and the appropriate medical checks we then all had to endure weeks of witless Roland Rat jokes for the rest of our posting.

Salesman scammed

Three years ago I was constructing a house for an old couple, who lived next door. One day we were laying bricks when a sales rep called Clive arrived, asking us where the toilet was. Quick as a flash, one of the lads explained that we all used the toilet next door, and Clive immediately scuttled off towards the house. To make matters worse, the labourer told him to put the kettle on, 'And don't worry about the old lady, she's just a cleaner.'

He was gone half an hour, and when he came out he was not a happy bunny. Apparently he had put the kettle on and then wandered down the hall to find the toilet. When the old dear came out, he said, 'Hello love, I'm just going to use the loo,' and the husband appeared and shouted, 'What the bloody hell is going on?' It was at that point Clive realized he had been stitched up, but he opted to blag it, and explained that he was a surveyor, checking for woodworm. Then he shut the toilet door and had a poo. When he emerged, the old man was standing there with a ladder and torch. 'Shall we start upstairs?' he asked, and Clive spent the next half an hour lifting up carpets checking for rotting wood.

Randy fauna

After graduating from college, I spent the summer working in the souvenir shop at my local zoo. At the end of October however I still didn't have a full time job lined up. With the dole queue looking inevitable, I was then fortunately approached by the marketing manager who offered me a job until January – working in Santa's grotto. In an attempt to bolster sales figures they had hit upon the idea of including a live reindeer, and being of a jovial and jolly disposition, I was told I would play the bearded gent. Before the grotto opened we had a press call, and I was chauffeur driven up to the zoo to pose for the local journalists. Despite the enthusiastic reception from the crowd however, Prince the Reindeer was a very reluctant partner and refused to sprint alongside me for the action shots. Every time I began to run, Prince would pull in the opposite direction and knock me off my feet with a quick jerk of his head. The press persuaded me to have one last attempt, and as I pulled his reins, the mighty beast began to follow. As I turned my back to him and shouted 'Ho, ho, ho,' I suddenly felt a hoof on each shoulder. In full view of the cameras and excited children, Prince then tried to shag me. I lost my Santa beard, hat and dignity as I wrestled with the randy mass of antlers, completely unaided by his keeper who was helplessly paralysed with laughter.

Embarrassing thespian error

My friend was playing the character Christopher Wren in The Mousetrap. One Friday night performance the curtain went up and the play started its seemingly perpetual motion of some 34 years. After several unremarkable entrances and bits of routine dialogue – he'd been doing eight shows a week for six months – he came to his favourite scene, the part where he got to sit down on the settee and listen to the rest of the cast discuss the murderous events of the day. Musing on his strenuous partying that week while waiting for his cue he was overcome with a sense of panic at no longer recognizing the lines. Hearing someone going: 'Pssst, pssst', he looked up to the wings where he could see the Stage Manager waving him over. Uncertain whether to move for fear of missing his cue he hung on, only for the dialogue to become even more perplexing. Eventually the Stage Manager's emphatic beckoning and the small crowd of backstage staff gathered round her also signalling time-out convinced him it was time to leave the stage. When she finally hooked him into the wings she told him he'd been asleep for five minutes with the show going on around him, and to compound the felony he should have been in another part of the house providing other cast members with an alibi.

Impromptu karaoke

Two years ago, desperately short of cash, I grudgingly took a job manning the till at a petrol station. Being the new boy, I was immediately assigned the graveyard shift: 11pm to 1am, and apart from the occasional car thief and insomniac the only real company I had was my Walkman. So imagine my delight when half-way through a particularly slow, soul-destroying shift I spotted my first customer in hours, steaming past the pumps towards my booth, perhaps for an urgent pint of semi-skimmed or packet of condoms. However, as the guy got nearer it became obvious that he was not a happy bunny. It turned out that he hadn't appreciated the last 45 minutes of my out-of-tune singalong to Semisonic over the forecourt tannoy, which I'd stupidly left switched on. Neither, it became apparent, were the rest of the nearby estate, nor my new boss, who after receiving umpteen complaints from weary locals gave me the boot.

New year surprise

I am a prison officer and once worked in a segregation unit where any con who breaks prison rules normally ends up. My worst job involved searching human turds. Any inmate who is seen swallowing suspected drugs on a visit is kept in the segregation unit for a process charmingly called 'no slop out'. This means that the con is left in a cell with an adult-sized potty waiting for nature to take its course and the swallowed wrap of drugs to pass through. You would think that in our technically-advanced age there would be a device to search the contents of the pot. There is. It consists of a pair of rubber gloves and a catering-size sieve! It's not the job to do with a hangover. Last New Year's Day, after a night celebrating, it got the better of me and I threw up. I had to search the turds with diced carrot and tomato topping, but it cured the hangover, though.

Army high Jinx

While serving in Tidworth, I heard I was being posted at short notice. As a joke, the bloke across the corridor stole my cold-weather gear and pissed all over the contents of my bergen. I only discovered this when 3,500 miles away, freezing my bollocks off and stinking of piss. Back in Blighty, I went straight out on the piss then returned to the barracks, and noticed that my practical joker pal had left his window open. I climbed in and got busy writing 'WANKER!' in toothpaste on his duvet and pissing in his coffee mug, then throwing the contents onto his posters and family photos. Finally I curled the best aprés-vindaloo turd you ever saw under his bed. The next morning, I was halfway through shaving when the washroom door burst open and a 6ft 7in, 18-stone former Hampshire Schoolboys' lock-forward burst in and barked, 'Who's the fuckin' dead man who's shit under my bed and thrown piss at my parents?' I could barely hold my razor still. My previous neighbour had been posted to a new regiment while I was away. Please don't reveal my name – big, bad Gaz is still on the look-out.

Strange religious vision

A few years ago I worked in an estate agent's office on the corner of a busy high road at the top of a gentle hill. We all parked our company cars on the side street. One Monday morning my car was parked close to the junction, in full view of the office. Someone noticed an old green Fiesta trundling around the corner, with three elderly ladies as passengers, no driver, the driver's door open and another elderly lady running behind the car shouting, dressed in black. She caught up with it just as it crashed into the back of my parked company car. My colleagues and I rushed out with me screaming for an explanation. The elderly lady turned on me, shocked at my bad language, and I saw that the black outfit was actually that of a nun. Her passenger, the Mother Superior, explained that Sister Mary had offered to nip into Boots on the opposite corner, but had forgotten she was driving and just stepped out of the slightly moving car, quickly realizing her mistake. With a wry smile my boss said to the Mother Superior: 'You realize the insurance will never pay up?'

'Why?' asked the horrified nun. 'Act of God,' he mused. The insurance did pay.

School days

I left school last year and started serving my apprenticeship as a plumber. One day the boss and I were called out on a job at my old school to mend a leak in the shower block roof. We dragged ourselves along the roof space to the hole, and once there, the boss decided that I could take care of things by myself. He said he could put up a 'No Entry' sign at the entrance, and then left. I pulled away a ceiling slab for better access and leaned right out to get beneath the hole. It was only when my old teacher – an ageing beast of 47 – wandered in below me that I realized the boss had forgotten the sign. I remained hanging there like a large spider inches above his head, as he spent ten minutes scratching his tiny cock, and guffing.

Candid camera

When I worked for a defence company, I was involved in a missile test. This sounds exciting, but in reality it meant spending a couple of weeks sitting in a concrete bunker waiting for the day to end, and the evening drinking to start. Early one morning, after a particularly heavy night on the ale, I was stuck as normal in my concrete prison – with no chance to get rid of the foul gas my digestive system was producing from the night before. So when someone asked me to go outside to adjust some equipment, I jumped at the chance, and within minutes had let rip with a by now considerable beer fart. After a few minutes spent freezing my arse off, I returned to the bunker, to find everyone gathered around a monitor, killing themselves laughing. I wandered over to take a look and watched as the clearly discernible infrared image of a person came into view, stopped, and bent over. The thermal display from my fart was actually quite impressive, and some clever sod even made it into a screensaver as my leaving present.

Spillage error

Shortly after acquiring a job in a particularly dingy night club, a punter at the bar asked me to mind his beer while he went to the toilet. By the time the bloke returned for his half consumed beverage, I had completely forgotten my lager-minding responsibilities. In haste, I grabbed an unfinished but discarded pint from an uninhabited area of the bar and passed it to the punter. It was a bit warm, but he seemed pleased and said, 'Cheers mate, thought you'd lost it there.' He downed it in one, smiled and wandered off. Come the end of the night, I set about clearing the bar area. My colleague pointed to the end of the bar where I'd found the 'spare' pint and said, 'Don't clear that part of the bar. I always leave it to the cleaner.' He explained, 'It's right under the Gents and they leak. I normally put out a glass to collect the drips, but it's disappeared tonight.'

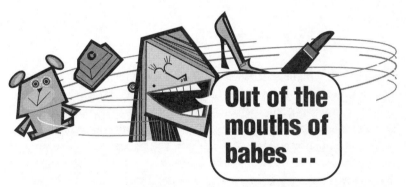

Out of the mouths of babes ...

While I was driving our admittedly filthy motor past a car-wash, my fiancée decided that enough was enough and demanded I put it through the "dishwasher". Then, on realising her mistake, she told me never to send her faux pas "to MFI". No problem.

We were having a barbecue in our friend Cathy's back garden, and the wind was blowing smoke into the kitchen. "Can't you turn the barbie around?" asked Cathy. "Then the smoke would blow the other way."

Career stalled

When I left school in Devon at 16, I began the worst six weeks of my working life. Clocking in at 7am in regulation Wellingtons, hair-net and white overalls, the day started with wedging bagged giblets up still-warm chickens' arses as they sped by on a conveyor belt. After a 15-minute break for breakfast, when all I could stomach was hot chocolate, it was into the freezer to sort the oven-readies into weight categories and a game of 'chicken footie'. After a quick dusting, the 'football' was put back on the conveyor, destined for a supermarket shelf. Watching the other workers at lunch gorging on platefuls of food (sometimes chicken) was almost enough to make me retch. But the biggest treat of the day came in the afternoon when the stench of the coagulated blood and excrement from around 30,000 chickens wafted around the factory floor with the flushing of the drains. I haven't eaten chicken for nine years.

Chompers hidden

One of the few highlights of working on an acute medical ward centred around a sweet old dear who was admitted with severe dementia. It quickly became apparent that she was constipated and would need suppositories to get things going, which she claimed she could do herself. Later that morning, while she was getting washed, an enquiry was made on the whereabouts of her false teeth, to which she replied that she had stuck them up her arse. Finding the suppositories floating in her cornflakes, we decided that she could be right, and whisked her off to X-ray. Sadly, nothing was found. A week later she was still bunged up, so I gave her a mild enema and told her I'd be back in a few minutes. When I returned I was greeted by the sight of granny bending over the bed, with her winking starfish aimed squarely at my face. Then, as I rushed to help her, her arse slowly changed shape, and three front teeth briefly surfaced before being sucked back in. I stood there as her bottom grinned, then frowned at me, until the top set of chompers finally came flying out, followed by a wave of shit. To this day, the bottom set are still missing.

Hot nosh

When I worked on a building site in Brighton, there was a lad there called Beanie. He was a fat, very rude chap, who had absolutely no qualms about wolf-whistling at women, while showing them his bare arse.

One morning in the local café, Beanie had just finished his breakfast when another builder sat down next to him, blocking him in. Beanie asked him to move, but the bloke refused, saying that he was starving and Beanie would just have to wait until he had finished. Not prepared to put up with this, Beanie stood on his stool and proceeded to try and step over the bloke's lap. As he did so, his shorts split open and his bollocks dropped straight out, dragging right through the bloke's mashed potato, leaving a great long spud trench, and a pair of painfully blistered balls.

Foreign language mix-up

It was a Friday afternoon and I had just found out that the department I was expecting to head (I had recruited the staff, obtained the equipment, etc.) had been handed to someone else. Effectively this meant I would be made redundant. So I went to complain to my boss, an Italian. I was about to confront him when two visitors entered. Diplomatically, I told him it could wait until Monday and left. He followed me and demanded to know what was wrong. I bellowed at him 'I'll tell you what's wrong Giuseppe – I'm fucking ANGRY!' He stood silent for a second, looking puzzled before replying 'I 'ave some biscuits in my office if you are 'angry.' I didn't know whether to throw him off the balcony or jump myself.

Princess nightmare

While working as a crew member for an airline, we had to do a short hop from the Bahamas to Trinidad and back. After the passengers had boarded, news soon filtered down to 'chaos class' that Princess Anne and her entourage would be getting on, and that first class was a no-go area for us plebs working in economy. Unfortunately, I had unwisely tried a few of the local 'delicacies' and was subsequently suffering from a bad case of the trots, and the accompanying symptom known locally as 'Caribbean Ring'. Soon after take-off, my bowels decided to evacuate. I couldn't find a free toilet anywhere in the non-cordoned-off area of the plane, so I trespassed into a first class loo, where I unloaded the foulest toxic waste ever known outside Chernobyl. With my business done, I opened the door only to find myself face to face with HRH. After nervously bowing, I sped away, pausing only to glance back and watched her enter that gas chamber. At the very least, I hope I left the seat warm.

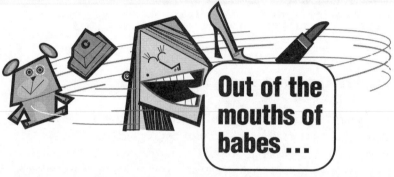

Out of the mouths of babes ...

On Gran Canaria with my girlfriend, I noticed a man doing a spot of paragliding. "I bet he's having a great time up there in the thermals," I said. "Don't be stupid," she replied. "I'm sure they wear wetsuits."

A girl I know was showing me the "Stars & Stripes" bikini she'd bought for her Australian holiday. I said it was a shame she wasn't going to the US. "Don't worry," she told me, "Australia uses the same flag." She qualifies as a doctor in ten months.

Decorating disaster

When I was struggling to earn a crust, and willing to take any work for any price, I once landed a job painting a friend of a friend's parents' house. I went round there on my first day and talked over the colours and details with the owners, then they left me to get on with it. I moved all of the furniture in their living room into the centre of the room, including the big old piano, which I then covered in dust sheets. All seemed to be going well. I did the walls, then began on the woodwork with a lovely deep blue gloss the owners had chosen. Painting the picture rail, I rested the tin of gloss on the piano. After I had finished the first coat, I went to move the tin and noticed with horror that a huge pool of blue paint had leaked through a hole in the dust sheet, and was already half set on the instrument's French-polished surface. I panicked. Instead of carefully trying to clean up my mess, I rubbed it off with sandpaper, ruining the surface forever. I then packed up my things and left, with the room half-painted, the piano a wreck, and a friend of a friend having to be avoided for the rest of my life.

Hotel Horrors

On the first night my girlfriend and I spent in our hotel in the USA, I blocked the toilet and coated the bathroom floor in poo. Later that week, after a heavy seafood and beer session, I started suffering a growling gut that must have woken the place. Giving in to the call of the toilet, I dropped my kecks seconds before the world fell out of my arse. I exited the bathroom swiftly, to avoid being caught by the probable overflow that would follow such a marathon session on the shitter. As I dived into bed, I noticed that it was all hot and sticky: my arse had leaked all of its vile contents during my drunken slumber! I grabbed a nearby bog roll, trying to mop it up. But I'd wrought such anal devastation that my girlfriend's leg was smeared in shit, and she was half-lying in a pool of foul-smelling liquid. When a length of bog roll stuck to her leg and would not come off, I returned, defeated, to the bog, upon which I fell asleep. I awoke to a knock on the bathroom door, and my shit-smeared girlfriend, looking terribly embarrassed, said, 'I'm really sorry, I think I had an accident.' My male survival instincts kicked in, and I slyly countered, 'I know, that's why I had to sleep in here all night.' To this day, although I remain justly proud of the event, I cannot bring myself to tell her the truth.

Lovers' tiff

A few years ago my then girlfriend and I decided to take a romantic break in Paris. The day we set off we both found ourselves very highly strung on the coach journey down to London. It was hot, the coach was crowded, and we began to argue about halfway between Manchester and Victoria. By the time we pulled in at London we were not speaking. My girlfriend stormed off into a café, taking all of our money with her, while I stood outside and stewed. After about ten minutes I was furious. I burst into the café and stood behind my girlfriend ranting for a solid five minutes. I called her a selfish cow and shouted at the top of my voice, 'Now give me a bloody pound so I can buy myself a cup of tea!' At this point a girl I had never seen in my life turned around in tears and told me to please just leave her alone. My girlfriend, in an identical dress, was sitting two seats away laughing her head off.

Nude nightmare

I was hitch-hiking down the Californian coast when I stopped off at a camping resort, full of caravanning American families. It had been a long day on the road, and my only sustenance was some cheese and bottled water, so I decided to get some kip. I promptly fell asleep in my tent in the warm night. At about three in the morning, I awoke to hear a scratching noise, and in the beam of my torch I had the shock of my life to see several rows of gleaming teeth, as the local racoons availed themselves of my hospitality, I jumped, scared shitless, and started to run around my tent, yelling at the top of my voice to scare the buggers away. Unfortunately, the human residents of the campsite were also awoken, so I was illuminated by the lights of various caravans, family faces pressed against windows, as I gradually calmed down to a walking pace encircling my tent. Yes, it was hot. Yes, I was naked. Yes, I left the campsite that morning.

Stile surprise

Last summer I decided to go for a hike around Malham Cove in the Yorkshire Dales. Walking down to the footpath which would lead me to the cove, I could see, behind a stile, an elderly man crouching down, as if trying to catch his breath. Fearing the old soul might be in the grips of a coronary seizure, I increased my pace, thinking I might have to provide some emergency first aid. I sprinted the last hundred yards and vaulted over the stile, only to find that the old man wasn't having a heart attack at all. He was, in fact, having a pee. As I started to turn (to contain both our blushes), the old fellow turned to me with a huge smile. To my shock and amazement I realized he was none other than a prominent peer! I could do nothing but laugh as he offered an apology: 'Excuse me – I was only lubricating the way.'

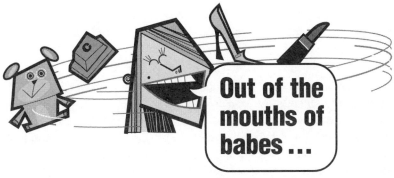

Out of the mouths of babes ...

On the train recently with a female friend, she innocently asked, "How does the train-driver steer? Does he have a wheel, like in car?" Despite seeing my look of utter disbelief, she ploughed on, "How does he change rails?"

My sister-in-law asked what type of bread was most healthy, to which I replied brown. "I don't have any," she said. "Can't I just toast some white bread?"

Listening to a report on the radio about the summer solstice, my girlfriend Lucy asked, "What's the solstice got to do with druids? Aren't they those little robots out of Star Wars?"

Holiday near miss

About three years ago, I was on holiday in Fuerteventura and on my first night there I got predictably drunk. Staggering home I got lost, but vaguely remembered there was a lighthouse near my hotel. Seeing a light in the distance I aimed towards it, and about an hour later I had to climb over a small fence. I was soon relieved to find myself on a tarmac road, and the lighthouse was now quite near. But my relief turned to sheer panic when I heard a huge roar just above me: I'd stumbled onto the runway of the airport, and the 'lighthouse' was in fact the control tower. A jumbo jet with its landing gear down shaved my head by no more than 20 feet, almost shattering my eardrums – and not doing my pants any favours either. When I finally made it home, I looked up the airport on my map. I'd gone about 12 miles off course.

Holiday prank

Heading out on holiday with 12 mates this summer, we expected a few disagreements between us, but didn't account on one individual who became universally hated. After a week of listening to his drivel, we decided to lose him out on the town, then get back early and lock the door, forcing him to climb over the partition from our neighbour's balcony. As we were only on the first floor we loosened the railings, just for good measure. Sure enough, just after two in the morning there was a bump as he fell, and we all ran out to hurl the usual insults. Apparently he landed harder than we expected, and suddenly rolled away down a little path leading to the sea. Springing into action, we all jumped down and chased after him, only for every one of us to run straight off the edge of a cliff. He landed on soft sand; we racked up three broken legs, two dislocated shoulders, two broken arms and serious cuts from a collection of broken glass and rusty cans.

Near death experience

While travelling around India, myself and a group of friends decided to sit on the roof of a bus for our short journey into town. Before too long we found that the previously crowded rooftop only held us four Brits. Where had all those Indians gone? Of course, unlike us, they had known. And – predictable I know – within minutes a low bridge loomed. Being slapped and stung by the overhanging coconut tree leaves had amused us, but a bridge took the piss. One friend peered over the side to seek help. The response? A giggling Indian. Another who was well positioned flew off the tail-end of the bus and held on to the ladder at the back. The rest of us had no chance. Fortunately, by ducking, there was a cool two-inch gap between life and a beheading.

Adult pleasures

A few years ago, five mates and I headed out to Ibiza. Returning from the beach one day, we paused at the shops to get an evening's supply of beer. While two of the boys paid for the crate, the rest of us decided to check out the porn. One centrefold caught my eye – a girl being fisted by her lesbian mate, with two gentlemen giving her a damn good portion. I gave my mate a good elbow in the ribs and said, 'Here, look at this!' A weird silence followed. I looked up, and where I thought I'd flashed the sweat at my grinning chum, I'd just elbowed an elderly Spanish gent, who was now holding his ribcage and gasping for breath, as his wife covered her eyes – comedy style – with both hands. I was so shocked I just handed the mag to the wheezing old boy and walked out the shop.

Cruiser slips

A few years ago during a holiday in Mallorca, myself and six mates went on a booze cruise. After downing gallons of ale as our small vesel pootled round the bay, the boat anchored and my mates proceeded to dance on the deck. However, seeing their antics, the organizer warned everyone to be careful as it was very slippery. My mates duly stopped and sloped off for a swim, leaving me to finish my drink in peace. Soon I decided to join them and walked round the boat towards the steps which led into the sea, only to encounter a buxom lassie coming the other way. As we attempted to pass each other, I decided to make a joke of the situation and, grinning, began dancing like a constipated elephant. Of course, I immediately lost my footing and, as my feet went from beneath me, they connected with the girl's legs, drop-kicking her straight over the side and into the sea. We stuck to dry land from that day on.

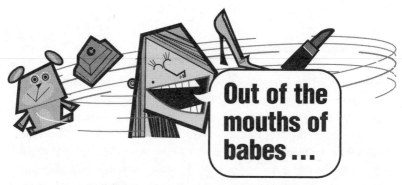

Out of the mouths of babes ...

After constant nagging, I bought my wife a breadmaker. Eyeing the instructions, she turned to me in disappointment and said, "I didn't realise it needed ingredients as well." Silly me – I'd only gone and bought the non-magic version.

Surprised to read that raindrops only fall at 7mph, I wanted to know what my girlfriend would guess. "They come down from quite high..." she mused, "so maybe a few thousand miles per second?"

Supermarket shopping with my beautiful girlfriend, I asked her to grab a pack of medium fresh eggs. With no response I turned to see her staring puzzled at the shelves. "Can't we just get some fully fresh ones?" she asked.

Holiday memento

Last year my fiancée and her friends decided to go to Cyprus for a holiday. As she would be gone a week, I took a Polaroid of myself (naked and sporting a massive stonker) to give her something to remember me by. When she returned I went to meet her at the airport, and before we went back home she decided to change the last of her foreign currency back into pound sterling. We eventually found the Bureau De Change and, without looking, she pushed a large wad of cash under the glass, along with the photograph of my erect knob, and asked, 'How much do I get for that?' Brilliantly, the female teller, who like me was crying with laughter, kept the picture, and gave me a wink when we left.

Crab chased

While on holiday in Ibiza, we decided to liven up our daytime activities with some masks and snorkels, and swimming out to see what we could uncover in San Antonio bay. Tying a large pebble to my underwater camera we would let it drop to the ocean floor, then race down to retrieve it. However, one of my friends became bored of the camera, and tied the rock to his 21st birthday present – a Rolex watch. It fell to the ocean floor without any problems, but just as we started to dive down, a huge crab scuttled over, grabbed it, waved his free claw triumphantly and headed off into deeper waters. My mate chased off after it, a torrent of swear words coming out of his snorkel. Finally, when he was almost out of sight, we heard a muffled, 'Fuck me, he's gone under a rock,' and almost had to be rescued as we were laughing too hard to swim. Needless to say, we bought him crab claws that night.

Card trick

In 1999, I decided to check out Corfu with one of my mates. We booked into a hotel in a town called Sidari, and every night we donned our best clobber and headed out on the piss. On the fourth outing we bumped into an English rep, who was taking a group of holiday-makers on a pub crawl. She didn't mind us joining them, and by 3am, as there was only her and I left, we went back to mine. Our clothes were off as soon as we got through the door. Then she looked me right in the eye and, in a husky voice, said 'Dominate me!' Unsure what to do, I nervously reached over and grabbed one of my adult playing cards. It was an eight of clubs, with a picture of a fat naked lady with her legs spread wide open. Holding it up in front of her, I said, 'See that? That's you!' She was out the door in three seconds flat.

Disaster at 20,000ft

Last Christmas I was on a overnight flight to the Gambia with my girlfriend and her parents who had kindly bought us a two-week break as a present. I was sitting in the aisle seat, with my prospective father-in-law opposite me. To break the ice, we shared a drink or two and it wasn't long before the large quantity I was consuming at altitude made me feel rather light-headed. As the lights in the cabin began to extinguish, there was no option but to adjourn to the little boys' room to relieve my bladder. I had mistimed badly and was leaking slightly as I tried to open the small door. I already had my flies undone and my old fella at the ready. As soon as I swung the door open, I rushed in, closed my eyes and enjoyed the immense pleasure that only such relief can bring. It then came to my attention that, instead of the delightful tinkling noise that I was expecting, there was more of a bass-like thud. It was too dark to see what was happening, so I finished what I had started and returned to my seat. When I next woke up I was dismayed to learn that there was to be no in-flight meal as the trolley which was kept in a room at the back had suffered a mishap.

Hot shot

My holiday in Mexico was going splendidly until an obnoxious American couple moved in next door. Every night they would keep us awake with their sexual marathons; loud slapping noises interjected with the occasional scream, groan and, on one occasion, the encouraging voices of another couple. Despite my complaints to the manager, the noise continued, so I decided to take matters into my own hands. Early one morning I got the wife to engage them in conversation while I dived over the balcony and doused the loud lady's bikini gusset with Mexican white pepper. Then we went to the swimming pool to await the results. Sadly, despite watching them swim for over an hour, nothing happened, and we retreated utterly defeated for another sleepless night. In the early hours of the morning, however, we suddenly heard a Yank voice announce: 'Gee honey, my cock is on fucking fire,' followed by an ear-piercing scream from his wife. Our only conclusion was that the pepper had somehow got inside her, and only made itself known once they had started shagging. We didn't get a peep out of them for the remaining four days.

Cowboy caught

While travelling up the east coast of Australia, I spent a few days in a place called Airlie Beach with a young German girl. Our dorm had six people in it, so one night we left the bar early in an attempt to get some private time before the chaps returned. We had drunk a fair bit, and the result was that I simply couldn't shoot my bolt. Having tried several different positions, I spun her round and took her doggy style, but still no gentleman's gel. Boredom finally got the better of me, and I began to pretend I was a Rodeo cowboy, waving one hand in the air, while pretending to shoot charging Indians with the other. Mid shoot-out I noticed her staring at me in the full-length mirror next to the door, so I gave a sheepish wave, announced I was 'rather tired' and collapsed next to her. She never mentioned the incident.

Traveller's trauma

Just after leaving school, I spent several months travelling around South America. One morning, I boarded a crowded coach for what was to be a seven-hour journey, and took the seat at the back for a few hours' kip. Just before I dozed off, the driver jumped aboard, coughing and wheezing as he settled in for the journey. I must have been more tired than I thought because when I awoke and looked at my watch, six hours had passed. The bus had stopped, but on looking out of the window I saw that we were still in the same spot as when I had nodded off! The other passengers seemed OK about this, but I decided to find out what was going on, so I walked to the front and tapped the driver on the shoulder. To my horror, he pitched forward over the steering wheel. Apparently, his earlier coughing fit had been a heart attack, and he had died while everybody waited for him to start the journey.

Bottle-smashing furore

I was staying on a French campsite with two friends. On our last night we got friendly with a couple of French girls and Dave, who spoke the language fluently. We all got very drunk and, at 5am, there were a million broken beer bottles strewn across the campsite car park, but we just went to the beach to sleep it off. On our return to the scene we were greeted by a trio of irate Frenchmen – the owner of the campsite, the proprietor of a hotel whose guests had been kept awake all night, and a motorcycle cop. It was clear these Gauls were after our balls. Things were looking very merde-like when all of a sudden the cavalry arrived. Dave. He asked what the problem was and went off on the most passionate speech about ... what? We were clueless. When Dave stopped for breath, the Frenchmen looked at us with a sort of nostalgic fondness, smiled weakly, shook each of our hands and left. Apparently, we were grandsons of English war heroes who perished in the D-Day landings, here to celebrate the memories of our relatives in true English fashion – by raising a glass or a thousand, then smashing them all.

Nude photo shame

While travelling around Europe a few years ago, I ended up on the Greek island of Ios. Now Ios has the reputation of being a wild and outrageous resort, so after pitching our tent at the nearest campsite, my mate and I set off to explore. We trawled the bars and clubs and got absolutely leathered. The next morning I was woken by the distant giggle of women and the whirr of camera shutters. As I slowly came to, I realized I was lying on my back in the blazing sun. I tried opening my eyes, squinting at the blinding light, and lifting my medicine ball head to survey my surroundings. After a few minutes it all started coming back to me. I had indeed made it back to the campsite, but hadn't managed to get inside the tent, so after peeling off completely, I'd slept where I'd fallen. To my horror, I found that I'd been sleeping on my back, all morning, in front of the main entrance to the camp, bollock naked and with a hard-on like a blind cobbler's thumb. I've often wondered how many photo albums across the world my morning glory now adorns.

Drug export folly

A couple of years ago I was trekking in the Guyana rainforest with two friends when I chanced upon a particularly distinctive plant with five-fingered leaves. I plucked one of the leaves and pressed it between the pages of my passport. When the time came to leave Guyana, we packed our belongings and headed off to the airport. At passport control, I nonchalantly handed my passport to a very big, ugly Guyanan. As he flicked through it, the marijuana leaf, neatly pressed and dried, slid onto the desk. He looked up at me, and I contemplated a career change from medical student to prison inmate. Time stood still. Then, slowly, a smile began to creep across his face and he let out an almighty bellowing laugh. Catching on, I laughed as well, collected my passport and rejoined my friends. The leaf went into his pocket.

Nautical hygiene worry

Early morning on a cold Saturday about ten years ago, four artists, a printer, a photographer, an account executive and myself sailed five miles out from the Essex coast on a day's mission to catch a whopper. About 6.30 am I went in search of the loo, to be told in a roundabout way that all bodily functions were to be released over the side. At about eight, the skipper came topside with a fag in his mouth and a plastic washing-up bowl in his hands, containing eight cups of a piping hot drink and a plate full of sandwiches. Once finished, he collected the mugs and returned below deck. Within a couple of minutes he was back, yet again clutching the plastic bowl. He moved to the front of the boat and threw the contents of the bowl over the side. Seconds later a huge turd floated past our side of the boat. Bob, David and myself looked at each other in disbelief and burst out laughing. The thing was absolutely huge. Only the three of us had seen what had gone on, and within seconds of going down below the skipper emerged once again from his hole clutching the bowl with yet more food and drinks in it. The three on our side of the boat gave his menu a wide berth for the rest of the trip, while the five on the port side imagined they were getting preferential treatment.

Monkey boy shows off

When I was 14, a few friends and I went camping near the top of a small (only 30 foot or so) cliff. After building a fire, we proceeded to get very drunk. As proof of my courage I drunkenly boasted that I would climb the cliff, overhang and all, without any equipment. At the base of the cliff I slipped and sprained my finger, but I'd had so much to drink it didn't hurt. I could feel my trainers slipping on the rock even at the start but I continued until I conquered the overhang and reached the top. Filled with elation I ran to tell my friends. They didn't believe me. I did it again, but this time with one of them sitting at the top of the cliff. As my head and arms came over the top of the overhang he started crying, saying: 'Don't fall, Huw. Please don't fall.' I couldn't help but laugh. I was holding onto the ledge with my feet dangling over the abyss, while my friend was sobbing drunkenly. I managed to pull myself together and get safely back onto the ledge, but I was badly frightened the next morning when I realized what I'd done.

Amsterdam shocker

Last year a group of us went to Amsterdam for the weekend for a beery break. On the first night we did the usual: got hammered and had a good look at the huge variety of strippers on show. Out of the six of us that were there one of my mates decided he was having too much of a laugh in the transvestite bar, and refused to come back to the hotel with the rest of us. At about five o'clock in the morning we heard him stagger into the hotel, causing a commotion as he banged his way along the corridor. By the time he got to our room we were all awake. He was completely bladdered and could not even talk. Within seconds of hitting the bed he was fast asleep, and it was then that the rest of us decided to wind him up. I spat into a condom, pulled down his pants, and poked the condom up his arse with a pen. Then we pulled his pants back up and left him to sleep. The next morning at breakfast we asked him how he had got on after we'd left, but he refused to talk. He stayed in his room for the whole day, claiming he was too hung-over to come out. That evening he also refused to join us. On the last day of our holiday we finally asked him if he had taken the condom out of his arse. He lost it. He dived across the table and punched me in the face. It took ages before he eventually saw the funny side.

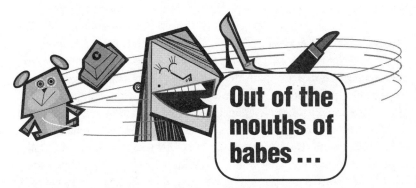

Out of the mouths of babes ...

One night the electricity went off. "It's definitely a power cut," I told the missus, looking out at the street in blackness. "It can't be," she informed me. "All the passing cars still have their lights on."

A news report said how they were going to stop servicing the Hubble Space Telescope after 14 years in orbit. "Does that mean the astronauts on board can finally come home?" asked the girlfriend. She's studying to be a doctor.

Back scratcher

While on holiday in Phuket with my father, we decided to visit the island where the movie The Beach was filmed. For a few pence the locals would take you out over the coral, where you could dive down and feed the fish by hand, giving an amazing view of some big and colourful tropical species. Once in the water, some friends suggested to my dad that he pop a piece of bread between his teeth, and let the fish eat from his mouth. Amazingly, it worked, and we all marvelled at the shoal of little fish that swam bravely up to his chops to have a nibble. Then, suddenly, they all parted as a monster from the deep appeared from nowhere and snatched the entire bun from Dad's gob. The shock forced him to inhale a load of seawater, which promptly made him throw up his breakfast, and his whole body immediately disappeared as every creature on the reef, including crabs, descended on him. We had to leave him down there, floundering underwater, as we were laughing too hard to breathe.

Seaside horror

Several years ago, a group of friends and I set off on our motorbikes for a day in Great Yarmouth. After an uneventful trip, we hit the local hostelries, and six hours later decided to find a place to stay for the night. Unfortunately, as it was high season, most accommodation was fully booked and those places that weren't were unwilling to put up a dozen pissed bikers. Finally, most of us found places to stay, but two mates who were more pissed than the rest of us said they were going to crash out on the local beach. We arranged to meet up in the car park of a café at 9.30 am the next morning.

When we all met up as planned, the two lads who had slept on the beach turned up looking a bit sorry for themselves and stinking like a sewage farm. When asked what had happened, they told us that they had crashed on the beach at high tide, where they had found what they thought was a mound of tarpaulin. But when they woke that morning, they were horrified to discover that what had been keeping them warm all night was, in fact, the bloated carcass of a not-so-recently-deceased seal.

Camp thugs

Back in the summer of 1992, I was participating in a Duke of Edinburgh Silver Award camping trip with several of my school friends. The trip was scheduled to last for three days, and on the first night a group of us decided to go to the village shop to get some beer. The night went well until one lad, who hadn't been invited to our shindig, blabbed to the teachers. We promptly got a bollocking and were threatened with expulsion if we did it again. Later that same night, when the grass was asleep in his bag, we tied belts around his arms and legs and gagged him with an old sock. We then carried him over a couple of fields and dropped him in one of those old wooden cow troughs. The water didn't cover him, so he lay in the few inches of mess at the bottom. We then went back to our tents, planning to pick the mug up a few hours later. At 6am the next morning we were woken by our furious group leaders: the human slug had crawled across the fields inside his bag and turned up at camp. We were excluded from the award and made to buy the bastard a new bag.

Dental disaster

Last year I went on holiday to Mersin in Turkey. Basically, the break was to be an eating and drinking extravaganza. The days blurred into one another and everything was going well on what was turning out to be the holiday of a lifetime, until disaster – I woke up one morning with a toothache which simply wouldn't go away. The agony proved so great that I had to go down to the hotel reception and explain to the bilingual girl behind the counter that I thought I was dying. She very kindly took me to a dental clinic: no moody affair with a rickety chair and a pair of pliers, but a professional-looking place. Anyway, the girl explained my dilemma. The dentist put me in the chair and looked into my mouth, then he injected my gum, making everything numb. Finally, and so quickly that I couldn't believe it had happened, he whipped my tooth out. I was stunned – and even more so when, cleaning out my mouth, he started to laugh. I asked the girl to translate for me and it turned out that, on closer examination, the dentist had realized I simply had a piece of garlic sausage stuck in my gum, and that the tooth hadn't needed to come out at all.

Country violence

Last summer, a friend and I decided to go on a bike ride into the countryside around Nottingham. After several hours of hard riding, we thought we should find a nice country pub and have a few pints to cool off. We walked into a pub full of villagers and local farmers, all of whom started to stare at us as we made our way to the bar. My friend got the drinks in as I nervously looked around the pub, trying to appear relaxed. For some reason, my eyes were drawn to the Guinness pump – the one shaped like a glass of the stuff. Taking anything to be a welcome distraction from the nasty looks I was getting from the other punters, I reached over to the pump and, to my horror, saw my fingers disappear into the head of a genuine pint of Guinness. The huge farmer at the bar whose pint it was didn't even let me finish the first word of an explanation: he smashed me to the floor immediately. Both my friend and I were then physically ejected from the pub without getting a sip of drink.

Traveller welcomed

Two years ago I was on a solo trip around the world, bunking on the floors of relatives and friends whenever I could. While in Jakarta I was quite keen to get in touch with Peter – a friend of my brother – who had offered to put me up during my stay in London. Finally I managed to get through, only to be told by his flatmate that unfortunately Pete had been beaten up. He was in hospital for a few days, and his flatmate, Shane, told me I was welcome to stay in his absence. I had a brilliant week, and on the Friday Peter's mum dropped him off, whereupon I introduced myself as Troy's brother. From behind a busted nose, a confused Pete mumbled 'What? I don't know a Troy.' Somehow I had managed to call the wrong flat that contained another Pete. They kindly let me stay a night, but I left the next day.

Toilet trouble

Last summer a friend and I went on a walking holiday in Snowdonia. As we were using up lots of energy, we ate high fibre foods such as pasta and potatoes, which obviously led to long toilet sessions. One of the campsites had a stand-alone toilet block, complete with showers, and I was sitting there one evening doing my business when I happened to glance up and see a skylight directly above me. In its reflection I could see the tiled floor just outside my cubicle. After wiping, I stepped out and looked up again, and sure enough I could see back inside the bog. Not only that, but I could see down into every other cubicle as well – including the bloke two down, who was still having a dump. Just as I was wondering what sort of pervert had designed such a feature, the bloke looked up, and our eyes locked. Sheepishly, I gave him a little wave, and then legged it back to my tent, from where I watched him stalk around the site for a full hour, looking for me.

Fat pudding

Last summer I went to Florida for a holiday with my wife and parents. While there, we all went to a buffet-style restaurant where you could eat as much as you like. The food wasn't particularly fancy, so we were very surprised when my dad sat down with a huge knickerbocker glory. When we asked where he'd got it from, he said it was from the dessert stand. Our waiter then approached and asked if we were okay. Thirty seconds later he returned with the same question, paying close attention to my father. Then he asked him if he would like to choose another dessert. Dad was almost half-way through the monstrous delight, so he said no. The waiter then patiently explained that the ice-cream was for display purposes only, and was in fact made out of – what we would call in England – lard. Apparently it was several months old, and was put in the freezer every night to keep its shape.

Gift delivered

During an all-boys holiday in Magaluf in 1999 my mate, Keato,
managed to pull a nice-looking girl, and took her back to the apartment.
In the morning we piled into his room for the lowdown on his night of
action. 'Did you get some, then?' I demanded. 'Yep,' he replied, 'and she
clearly loved every minute of it as she's left me a souvenir.' He then
disappeared into the bedroom and returned with a pair of yellow
knickers. 'Smell that, lads, it's the sweet smell of pussy!' he gloated.
And then Dave announced, 'Actually, they're my dirty pants.'

Foreign fiasco

I had been cooped up with seven people on a sailing holiday around the
Greek islands on a 38ft (11.5m) yacht for two weeks. After a long, hot
day at sea, we entered a harbour to moor up and relax for a few days. I
was feeling the urge to splurge, but discovered that nobody had
emptied the bilge tank. As the toilet became unusable for the next two
days, a friend and I trekked off into the town and found a bar with a
toilet. By now, I was facing the biggest evacuation since Towering
Inferno. I opened the door to find a pan in an area big enough to swing
a kitten. There was no light, window or lock. I called to my mate and
asked him to stand guard. By leaving the door open and keeping my
foot against it to make a one-inch gap, I had just enough light to allow
me to place my bare behind on the seat. But when it came time to wipe
up, it wasn't possible to maintain the gap in the door without it
swinging open, so I shut it. I was now in complete darkness. I fumbled
around until I placed my hand on some paper – and pulled. Now, you
must understand that this was my first time in Greece and I didn't
realize that when disposing of used toilet paper, due to their poor
sewage system, they put it into a bin. I was pulling at someone else's
waste! Not unsurprisingly, the closest I ever go to Greece now is a
chicken kebab on a Friday night.

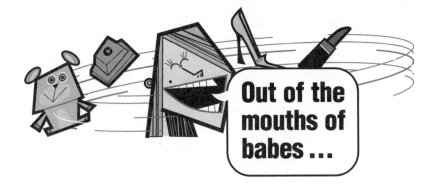

Out of the mouths of babes ...

In Paris, me and the missus went on the Ferris wheel, enabling me to point out the Eiffel Tower. "What's the other tower over there?" asked the wife – pointing at the reflection in a glass building.

Reading "Out Of The Mouths Of Babes" recently, my girlfriend asked, "What's 'WWII' mean?" I told her they were Roman numerals. "Were the Romans involved in World War Two?" she replied.

Desperate measures

I was recently in Kefalonia, where the drainage system is so poor that a single flush of the toilet is woefully inadequate. On the last day we went out to the airport, where I was suddenly hit by serious stomach cramps. I found a secluded toilet just in time, releasing a ferocious explosion that reverberated around the room. The stench was eye-watering, and to make matters worse, the flush was broken. As I strolled out, however, I walked straight into two air stewardesses doing their make-up in the mirror. I was in their rest room, but after their initial shock they saw the funny side, and promised not to tell. Then without warning, one of them walked into the cubicle. There was the briefest of pauses followed by an ear-deafening screech, at which point I sheepishly bolted for the plane, not even slowing down for customs.

Holiday horror

Going on your summer holiday is supposed to be a time of non-stop joviality, drinking and shagging. So, last year I went on holiday with five mates to Tenerife. Naturally, we started our celebrating as soon as the plane left London. We drank all through the flight, and continued chucking it back through our first night on the island. In the morning we were quite shattered and went down to the beach with a few beers to recuperate. After a few cans of lager I fell asleep and woke up some four hours later in great agony. I rushed to the local hospital and was given some cream and told to stay out of the sun for the next few days. Gutted, I returned to my hotel room. And only then did the full horror of my situation hit me. Looking in a mirror for the first time I was shocked to see the word 'WANKER' written on my forehead in sun protection factor 30 by my 'mates' as I slumbered on the sand.

Surprise cuisine

About four years ago I fell in love with a beautiful Lebanese girl, and after a whirlwind romance she took me to Lebanon to meet her family. Sadly, I couldn't help but ogle at the multitude of tanned women strutting around wearing very little, so before long we were having blazing rows and I was sleeping on the sofa. Finally she suggested that we make our peace, and offered to take me for a delicious Arabian lunch. I agreed, and although I took great pains to avoid the raw meats and liver, I couldn't get enough of the sliced potato in lemon sauce she offered me. It was delicious, and I ate three plates of the stuff over the course of two hours. After the feast we went for a stroll along the beach, and it was then that my girlfriend burst out laughing, and mockingly revealed that the potato was in fact sheep's testicles. With two weeks and 28 meals of my stay in Lebanon remaining, I decided not to even glance at another woman.

Filthy tosser

Three mates and I went to Ibiza for two weeks. A few days into the
holiday, three of us were sitting by the hotel pool when some girls
came over and asked if we were in the flat overlooking the main road.
When we said we were, they laughed and said we'd better hang a
towel across the window – which went from floor to ceiling and
appeared frosted from the inside – because it was totally clear from
the café across the road and everybody could see us showering.
Slightly embarrassed, we made our way back to the flat. Later on that
evening our fourth friend, who hadn't heard about the window, went
to have his shower. We thought it would be a laugh not to tell him
about the 'view' and went across to the café, pointing out the
spectacle to fellow holiday-makers. Imagine our horror as our mate
started to have a wank. Worse still, he put the shower head to
unusual and good effect. After all manner of contortions I thought
enough was enough, and knocked on the bathroom door and told him
to stick his head out of the window. When he did he was greeted
with a loud cheer from the crowd below, and he spent the rest of the
holiday refusing to leave the apartment.

Mistaken identity

Many years ago, after being bored rigid by friends' tales of foreign
adventure, my mate Nigel and I went to Australia to see what all the
fuss was about. We ended up in Bondi, and one afternoon we were
walking home when Nigel nudged me and pointed out the British
actor Terence Stamp. I knew it was him, but for no real reason, I said
he looked nothing like Mr Stamp, and teased him all the way home,
pointing at people with moustaches and shouting, 'Look, Burt
Reynolds!' He finally snapped, and marched back to find our great
actor. We found him sitting in the window of a local café, minding
his own business with a coffee and paper. 'See, it is him,' said Nigel
triumphantly, but I just laughed and said Terence had bigger ears.
Terence couldn't help but notice two men pointing at him through
the glass, and he started to look rather irate. Nigel then started
stopping people in the street to get their opinion, even going so far

as to knock loudly on the glass, until Stamp could take no more. He sprinted out the door, and it wasn't until he was within a yard of us that we realized two things: he wanted a fight, and it wasn't Terence Stamp. Suffice to say, Nigel had the shit kicked out of him by Australia's best look-alike.

Ski accident

A few years ago I went on a skiing holiday with friends to a resort in Switzerland. On the first day we caught the cable car, and at the top of the mountain one of the girls in our group decided that she needed to pee. The only available loo was in a terrible condition however, and she convinced herself that she could hold on until she reached the bottom of the slopes. About 300 yards down the hill she realized that she had been wrong, and we waited for her as she promptly skied off into the woods that ran down the left side of the run. Trying to be as quick as possible, she decided against removing her skis, opting instead to simply drop her salopettes, crouch down, and hold onto an overhanging branch. We then heard a loud snap as the branch broke, and could only watch in awe as she came bombing out of the shrubbery, naked from the waist down with her trousers around her ankles, and clutching the remnants of a branch. The lift station was about 50 yards below her, and she crashed into about 500 people standing patiently in the queue. Although they all saw the funny side, she spent the rest of the holiday hiding in the hotel.

Sexual shenanigans

Not long ago, I met a girl in an internet chat-room. We got on well, so she gave me her mobile number and asked me to call. We exchanged a few texts, then a few days later she sent me a really filthy suggestion. I tapped in a suitable reply, searched through my address book for her name, and sent it. Her reply seemed a little strange but I didn't think anything more of it, as we were soon exchanging even more explicit texts. Eventually we decided to meet at a hotel, but when I got there at the appointed time who was there but my cousin. I said 'hi' and was about to ask what she was doing at the hotel, when it hit me; my cousin and the girl I'd originally been chatting to have the same first name, and both their numbers were stored in my phone. I didn't really know what to do, but my cousin's pretty attractive ... so I went through with it with her instead.

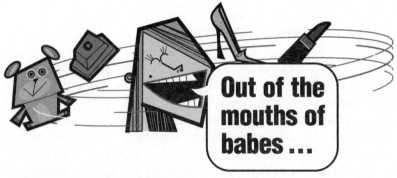

Out of the mouths of babes ...

After a frozen car door incident, my then girlfriend bought me a can of de-icer. A few days later she came round and saw her present in the kitchen. "You should keep it in the glovebox of your car," she suggested. "Then it's always handy."

Me and the missus noticed an old motor in a car park. "It's been there so long, it's sunk into the tarmac!" she said. It had four flat tyres.

My ex saw The Godfather and was halfway through the second one before asking, "Is Michael Corleone something to do with the Mafia?"

Door slammer

Four years ago while attending college in Northern Ireland, myself and my girlfriend decided that we would take a week off college to visit both of our parents. As we settled into our train seats, it suddenly dawned on me that we would have to wait seven long days before having sex again, so I suggested that we nip off to the train toilet for a quick shag.

I thought my woman would say no, but amazingly she agreed, and it wasn't long before we were both half-naked and I was slamming her doggy-style over the little sink. Just as I let rip up her back, I heard a cough behind me, and we turned to discover that, in our haste, we hadn't shut the door properly, giving the entire carriage a free porn show. To make things worse, the train was packed, and we had to stand for two and a half hours with everyone grinning and winking at us.

Private education

In 1997, when I was still in the upper-sixth at school, several French student teachers arrived for teacher training. One night they all turned up in our local pub, and I ended up pulling one of the better-looking ladies of the group. After that, our relationship continued during school hours, every day at 4.10pm in the language lab. After three days of complete success, I decided to arrive a few minutes early to get a head-start on things. To my horror, the next person to arrive was the head of modern languages – an old, chalk-haired duffer who looked stunned to find a naked lad in the darkened room muttering, 'I wanted you so much in class today.' Desperate to keep my girl out of trouble, I chose an excuse that I regret to this very day. I told the old fool that I was confused, and had strange feelings for him. No more was said, but I was dumped two days later for another teacher.

Dirty-talk disaster

I was out with my mates in the local nightclub, when a horny babe came up to me on the dancefloor and started talking really dirty. Astounded by my good fortune, I left my pint and my mates and disappeared outside with her. While searching for a suitable spot to do the dirty deed, I came across a secluded path surrounded by bushes. Perfect. Within seconds we were in the throes of passion, she whispered, 'Put me on the cross, put me on the cross.' Thinking she was moaning to herself, I carried on, but moments later she moaned again, 'Put me on the cross.' Baffled by her rambling, I still carried on regardless. Minutes later, she moaned even louder, 'Put me on the cross.' By now I was beginning to think she knew some sexual position I didn't. Not wanting to appear incompetent, I grabbed her arms, pinned them at right angles to her body, put her legs together so she was in the shape of a crucifix, and kept on pumping. 'What the hell are you doing?' she cried. 'Putting you on the cross,' I said confidently. She replied, 'I said to put me on the grass, these bloody stones are hurting my back.'

Live sex in soho

I had been pursuing a dark beauty from Sierra Leone for several months. Her defences eventually came down and we became a couple. I decided, one weekend, to treat her to a West End show and then a meal in Soho. In the restaurant, we got closer and closer, touching parts of each other that shouldn't really be touched in public ... So, we paid the bill and escaped quickly, scrabbling over the fence into the garden in the middle of Soho Square for a bit of privacy. On a patch of grass, we started to kiss and grope each other. Before we knew it, we were buck naked and humping away. We were loving every minute of it, but, unfortunately our attention was focused on each other and not on the crowd of men from a nearby gay bar who had gathered to watch. Once we realized what was going on, my girlfriend and I really got off on all the attention we were getting. However, we didn't realize that, due to my girlfriend's colour, our audience couldn't see her in the dark. Only my big white butt was visible, as it furiously moved up and down on the grass. Presumably, the various characters from the bar thought I was having sex with a hole in the ground.

Seaside shag

It was to be a romantic weekend away for myself, my girlfriend and another couple. We drove up to Hunstanton on a hot summer's day, parked the car and set off along the beach with our provisions: plenty of drink and some food for cooking on the driftwood fires we planned to build. We set up camp, sipped red wine and ate sausages cooked in cider as the sun went down. The tide drifted out, and the moon rose as the fire slowly died. My mate and his girl went for a walk, while I decided to hit the hay with my new love. We walked back up the beach to a row of beach huts, giggling all the while, and broke into one. We drunkenly fell to the floor and had a great sweaty sex session, before falling into deep slumber. In the morning I woke up and curiously patted the crunchy floor of the cabin with my hands. My girlfriend did the same. As my mate swung the door open and sunlight bathed the room, we were all disgusted to see that we had spent our night of passion on a carpet made up of millions of dead flies.

Christmas lights

When my mother-in-law first bought her flat, my wife and I went to spend a Christmas with her. The sleeping arrangements were tight to say the least, and we found ourselves kipping in a large sleeping-bag on the living room floor. As usual, the missus was feeling horny at the idea of sleeping in a strange place and we spent the night hard at it. In the morning she got up to use the bathroom, when suddenly the hall lights went on, and the door started to open. Attempting to dive back under the covers, the wife stumbled over my outstretched leg, shot along the smooth fabric of the sleeping-bag and, to my complete amazement, tipped head first into the Christmas tree, giving my entering mother-in-law and her 13-year-old nephew a splendid view of her own, personal, decorations.

Caught in the act

One summer I was at a mate's house revising for impending exams. Having spent several hours studying intensively, we were both in need of a break. My mate suggested we reward our hard work by watching one of his brother's porno videos. Within minutes of watching an on-screen orgy, my teenage libido was in overdrive and I needed a wank. Casting an eye across the room, I could see my mate was thinking the same. Not wanting to miss any action, I simply put my hand down the front of my trousers. After ten minutes, my attention was drawn to movement out of the corner of my eye. To my utter horror, my mate's mum had returned home early and was making her way towards the back door. I froze as she looked in through the patio doors, pointing at us with her mouth wide open. 'How many times have I warned you about this,' she bellowed as she entered the lounge. 'I've told you time and time again, you'll get hairs all over the furniture!' I was about to make my excuses when she interrupted. 'Don't let Sandy on the furniture!' she bellowed. Then, with immense relief, the penny dropped. Somehow she had looked straight past the two of us abusing ourselves and had spotted Sandy, the border collie, sitting on a chair at the far end of the room.

Avon calling!

A few years ago, I pulled a 'naughty forty'. She didn't need much persuading to accompany me back to my mother's house, where I was living. During the early stages of foreplay, she left me in no doubt as to what she would like me to do to her ... I can't explain in full, as I'm led to believe it may still be illegal in this country. I left the bedroom and stumbled to the bathroom without turning on the light, so as not to disturb my mother sleeping in the adjacent room, I returned with a pot of the best lubricant I could find and applied it liberally to the appropriate areas. Ten minutes into my routine, I noticed a distinct chafing that I'd never experienced before. But I saw the job through to the end and was soon kipping soundly. Imagine my horror when I awoke in the morning to discover my manhood looking as if it had been dipped in concrete and my mum's Avon face-mask next to the bed.

Washing machine woe

I was once seeing a girl who was renting a room in a house where the washing machine was always breaking down. Whenever her housemate was out, we grabbed the opportunity to make love, and often didn't even make it to the bedroom in our passion. One morning, my girlfriend had agreed to stay in as a man was coming round to fix the washing machine once and for all; we had waited days for an appointment and of course, he hadn't turned up the first time he promised to. We were in the kitchen when we started kissing. After about 30 seconds we were both minus our clothes and using the worktop for our enjoyment. This became a screaming session and most of the screaming came from me. In the (occasional) quiet moments, I could dimly hear voices – I thought it was the TV – and suddenly I saw someone walking through the lounge towards the kitchen. We froze for a moment, then both grabbed what we could and tried to get dressed. But it was going to be too late. Panicking, I walked into the lounge, stark bollock naked, holding a pile of clothes and shouted back into the kitchen without thinking, 'Darling, can you get the rest of the clothes out of the washing machine, they're done.' The plumber looked me up and down in a bemused way and said, 'Has it been fixed? I'll be going then.'

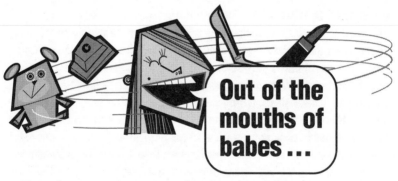

Out of the mouths of babes ...

The pub conversation got round to the subject of anal sex. "I couldn't be doing with that," said my mate's girlfriend. "I'd need more than one bonk a year."

Watching a programme on turtles, my girlfriend became confused. "Are turtles born with shells on their back?" she burbled, "or do they need to find one?"

A colleague of mine looked puzzled the other day. "Who plays Clint Eastwood?" she asked. "Is it Harrison Ford?"

Sex-in-public shame

My girlfriend and I had been out clubbing on a Saturday night and were heading home. On the way, I went to a cashpoint to get some money. It was one of those where the machine is in a foyer inside the bank. While I was completing my transaction, my girlfriend started fondling me from behind. One thing led to another and soon I had her up against the wall and we were going at it like rabbits. After our unexpected passion, we slipped out and thought nothing more of it ... until the Monday morning. The big news in the paper was that there had been a spate of vandalism in the city centre on the Sunday morning. One of the damaged buildings was the very bank that had been the scene of nocturnal passion. According to the report, the bank was planning to run through the security video from the foyer to see if they could find any clues...

A taste of love

After I'd wined and dined my newish girlfriend, we decided on a drink back at my pad, with a side-serving of rumpy-pumpy. Before I could even finish my bottle of beer, we headed for the bedroom and, after a hefty session, fell asleep, exhausted. I woke up with that post-drinking binge 'ashtray' mouth and, seeking to quench my thirst, spotted the unfinished bottle of beer. It was infinitely more appealing than crawling over to the kitchen, so I took a swig. It tasted flat and disgusting, as if someone had put a fag out in it, but I polished it off. Later, I asked my still-dozing girlfriend, 'Did you put something in my beer last night?' She looked at me in sympathy. 'Remember how I said I don't swallow? Well, I had to put it somewhere...'

Wet sheet misjudgment

A few years ago, after a particularly good Friday night session with the lads, I remember getting into a taxi with a young lady just before I fell into an alcohol-induced coma. I awoke some hours later, alone in a double bed in a strange room. I got out of bed to get dressed when I realized my clothes had gone. I went to the bedsit door and called out, but no-one seemed to be in the building. 'Oh shit, I've been rolled,' I thought, and determined to wreak vengeance by pissing over the double bed. I had just begun to do so, when in walked said young lady with my clothes. They were washed and ironed as I'd managed to throw tomato soup all over myself in the cab.

Pulling tricks

A few years ago my wife and I decided to go out for a large night in Paisley, and as such, the missus was kitted out in a very sexy miniskirt and high white boots. As we walked down the street deliberating where to go, my wife stopped to look in the window of an estate agents. Suddenly, out of nowhere, an older man appeared and said quite openly, 'How much?' Still looking at the properties and not paying much attention, my wife replied '£48,000'. The old boy replied in disbelief, 'How much?' Then, just when I thought things couldn't get any funnier, she explained, 'Yes, but that's for a semi.'

Whore's bath

A few years ago I made it my aim in life to pull the gorgeous Irish barmaid in my local, and after several weeks' flirting I finally asked her out. Not only did she say yes, but the rest of the night went so well that she invited me back to her house. After snogging in the taxi, we arrived at hers. As she went to the toilet I was left in a bit of a panic: I hadn't showered that morning. As things were going so well it seemed only a matter of minutes before my old fella would be brought into action, so I crept into the darkened kitchen and gave myself a bit of a clean 'south of the border' with a handy flannel. She soon returned and, sure enough, we got straight down to it, with me lying on the couch while she went down on me. But no sooner had her lips touched my bits than she straightened up. 'What's that?' she asked, pointing to my pubes. On inspection I saw a solitary baked bean nestled among the curly hairs – the 'flannel'

I'd used had, in fact, been a dirty dishcloth. I left red-faced and never saw her again.

Tenting disguised

One Sunday my mate Steve and his fiancée drove to the local garden centre with her parents. During the trip, his good lady started touching him up on the back seat and her fingers soon had the desired effect. Once they arrived at the centre, Steve realized that as the car had no back doors, he would have to take great care exiting the vehicle in order to hide his obvious excitement. When his mother-in-law to be opened the door and pulled the seat down he executed a smooth, half-crouching manoeuvre, before turning swiftly and marching off towards the plants. Relieved that he had escaped a potentially embarrassing situation, he was then stunned to hear a familiar voice on the other side of the conifers exclaim: 'Did you see the size of his hard-on, Frank? I thought he was going to have my bloody eye out.'

Unwelcome surprise

My friend, an airman, had his 21st birthday a few weeks before being posted to Saudi Arabia. His parents asked if he would like a big party to celebrate. He declined the offer, asking instead if he could have a quiet evening at home with his girlfriend, cook her a meal, candles, soft music – and, while his parents were out, a good sex session to keep him going for the four months he'd be away. So, the night came, his parents went out, and a fine meal was prepared. The wine flowed and eventually the pair were rolling around the living room in their favourite position: the 69. While in full swing the phone rang. 'Let's answer it in this position,' my friend suggested, and off they wriggled into the hall. It was his mother on her mobile. 'Your dad thinks he's left his glasses in the kitchen, can you check, please,' she said. Once again, he suggested they stay in the position. 'It'll be a laugh,' he said. Off they wriggled again, laughing all the way. 'Surprise, surprise! Happy birthday!' was their greeting as they opened the door. And, of course, Mum, Dad,

Grandma, aunties, uncles and cousins were all there to congratulate the young man, bless them.

Group-sex cringer

A booze-sodden evening at the nightclub was shaping up very nicely indeed when my cousin Steve and I pulled Sarah and Lindsey, two pert 18-year-olds, and brought them back to my pad. Dispensing with all our clothes, and making the best of a bad deal (I only had one bed), all four of us ended up sharing, and enjoying it loads. In the throes of passion I reached over and started sucking his bird (Lindsey's) nipples. The next day the girls were up and out early on, leaving Steve and me to compare notes on the team acrobatics. We both enjoyed going over my cheeky nuzzling of Lindsey's breasts, but Steve remained strangely quiet when I mentioned that she seemed to have flaky skin on her tits. Then he revealed that he didn't have a condom, so he'd just shot his load over her front and then rubbed it in. My mouth suddenly went very dry as the penny dropped and I realized that her 'dry skin problem' didn't actually involve dry skin.

Rustic lovers

Last summer my girlfriend and I spent a glorious day on the banks of a loch in northern Scotland. Having enjoyed our picnic and a couple of bottles of chilled Chardonnay, we both became very horny. I had the bright idea of setting up the tent early for a bit of afternoon sex, and we crawled inside for a long, drawn-out session. We stayed inside for a couple of hours, running through a variety of positions and thoroughly enjoying ourselves in the fresh Scottish air. Eventually I got dressed and climbed out of the tent for a late afternoon ciggie. On my emergence I saw two fishermen sitting in a rowboat at the shore of the loch. I said hello and they smiled at me, waved, and rowed away. I looked back up at the tent and saw that, due to the setting sun, our tent was totally transparent, and the anglers had obviously had a perfect view of my girlfriend and I going through our contortions.

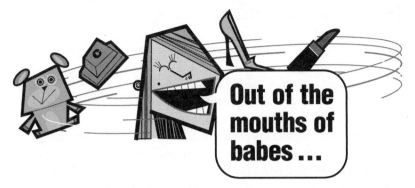

Out of the mouths of babes ...

I caught my missus staring out of the window last week. "Which way is it that clouds go?" she asked. For 21 years, she'd thought clouds moved in the same direction. Help!

When an otter appeared on the TV, my female flatmate said, "Otters are the ones that fly, aren't they?" After we'd stopped laughing, she qualified her statement. "Well, they don't really fly – they glide."

Radio exposure

While at university a few years ago, I was fortunate enough to land a slot on the campus radio. It was a position I turned to my advantage to cultivate an image of hip and coolness – which surprisingly pulled the girls. I would often taken my conquests back to the studio, which I used as a secret shag pad. One evening, I took a girl back there and we started messing about with a bingo game which the station used. We called out the numbers and took our clothes off as a forfeit. Eventually we were both butt-naked as I pulled out a final fake forfeit, which said 'Spread your legs and think of England.' There then ensued a frantic bout of shagging, culminating in the girl shouting, 'House! Bingo!' while in the throes of ecstasy. The following day, we were mortified when walking around campus as fellow students pointed and nudged, with cries of 'Bingo!' It seems I'd inadvertently knocked the broadcast switch on during our high jinks and some community-spirited listener had informed as many people as he could.

Back scratcher

A couple of months ago, while unpacking following a dirty weekend in Amsterdam, my girlfriend came across a large vibrator that we had purchased while we were there. Within minutes the sparks of Holland were flying in our living room, when there was a loud knock at the door. It was her mother, who had popped round to see the holiday snaps, so after a frantic scramble to hide the toy and put some clothes on, we let her in and settled down in front of the television. Then, right in the middle of Blind Date, her mum whips out the vibrator from behind a cushion, looks at it closely and announces, 'Ooh, your sister's got one of these.' Apparently, the crafty cow had claimed that the plastic purple monster was a totally innocent back massager, and I sat there utterly speechless while the old crone sighed with obvious pleasure and started rubbing her neck with the very same electrical appliance that had only recently been right up her daughter's jacksie.

Post-shag cock-up

Last summer, I caught up with an old flame and ended up having a totally unexpected night of passion. Alas, the only suitable venue was the lounge floor of her parents' house. In the morning, despite having had no sleep, I had my wits about me and, being a decent chap, I secreted the now full (but tightly knotted) condom on my person, rather than have her mother find the dried version some months later behind her sideboard. Being stranded some miles from my house in the bright morning glare and with about £2 left from the night before, I selected public transport as the best route home. With thoughts now centred on a very long sleep, I joined the queue at the train station to purchase my ticket. Imagine the look of horror on the face of the woman behind the window when I innocently delved into my pocket and brought out not only the correct change but a thoroughly well-used condom. She advised me to buy my ticket on the train.

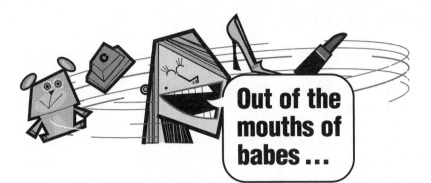

Out of the mouths of babes ...

Discussing fake IDs, a mate said you could get a good one via the black market. "What day's that on?" asked my girl.

After visiting the London Dungeons I told my girlfriend the story of Jack The Ripper. "Did they ever catch him?" she asked. I explained that they hadn't, but there had been many suspects. "Then he could still be wandering the streets of London today!" she gasped.

Eating in bed

Stone me if I wasn't sitting at a table for two with a babe! Not wanting to seem the gannet by ordering a 12oz steak, I settled for the lighter option of a tuna and sweetcorn pasta plus a couple of glasses of house red. A few bottles later and we're talking about this, that ... and the other. She soon invited me back to her place for the other. Game on! We moved from position to position, until we got to number 69 when a distinct rumble from my stomach informed me of an imminent bum eruption. Clenching my buttocks but at the point of no return, I climaxed and passed wind simultaneously. To my horror, out popped a single knob of corn, smiling up at me from the black silk sheets. My mother always told me to chew my food. I'm just grateful I didn't have the fruit cocktail.

Office sex

Recently I decided to start seeing a work colleague. Bearing in mind that I work in an office with over 20 females and only two males, my years of office celibacy were highly commendable – or stupid! So one Sunday, said colleague and I were working hard, when she challenged me to a bout of shagging round the office! Always up for a challenge, I duly obliged. After 45 minutes' worth of some of the best nookie I've ever had, it was time to cover our tracks. We had, however, left a 'wet patch' on one desk and, agonizingly, there was not a jot of toilet paper in the whole damn office. Using our initiative, we grabbed a tea towel, wiped up and made tracks home! Imagine my horror the next day when, with clients arriving at 9.15am, a secretary was wiping the cups with the same towel we'd used not 12 hours earlier. My guilt was further increased when the client noted a peculiar taste on the rim of his cup! The towel, which had an oddly musky smell, was identified as the culprit. No-one could identify this odour; the offending item was sent for a wash and the client given a clean cup.

Bathroom shocker

When I was a student I lived in a 'mixed' household, which thankfully meant that the boys and the girls all lived together. My girlfriend at the time was a lively lass, and liked to experiment sexually. With this in mind she arranged for us to have a sexy bath together one evening when all the other students were out 'studying'. We lit the draughty old bathroom with candles which we rested on the window sill, filled the bath to the brim with bubbles, and slipped into the water for some serious cleansing. Suddenly, just as I was soaping some interesting body parts, and having some of mine vigorously rubbed clean, there was a thundering crash at the door, followed by loud shouting. Two security guards were battering down the door with fire extinguishers. After a few seconds of stunned silence from both sides they started to piss themselves with laughter. It seems they had been patrolling the grounds near our house and had seen a 'massive fire' in one of our windows. Our flickering candles, through the frosted glass, had led them to storm in on our sexy bubble-bath. After they had left we couldn't quite recreate the atmosphere, so the whole night was a write-off.

Video exposure

Years ago, I worked in a hotel during my summer holidays. The place only had one till, and this was shared between the bar and the restaurant. There was a lot of pilfering. As it was used by so many members of staff, it was very hard for the management to find out who had the sticky fingers, so they decided to install a security camera to catch the culprits. At the end of the first session with the new equipment we were all called into the office to watch as our boss fast-forwarded through the tape. This boring task produced no evidence at all, and we were all just about to fall asleep when, on the screen, one of the waitresses, clearly getting a bit carried away with the task of kissing one of the barmen goodnight, dropped to her knees and gave him a very expert blow job – much to our amusement. The video tape still survives to this day, and works perfectly well as a training video for new staff members.

Lodger knocked up

My girlfriend and I first started having sex when she lived with her father. We didn't hear him come in one night, and he embarrassed us the next morning with a stern lecture on the subject of manners and not having sex under his roof. We left things for a while, but tried again after a night on the piss, only to be met in the morning with the words, 'This is the last time I'll tell you, boy.' Finally, after my company's Christmas party I decided not to risk it and slept in the spare room. During the night the cat tried to get in, and commenced a rhythmic scratching at the door. This lasted a few minutes, until a furious voice bellowed out: 'Stop fucking my daughter!'

First date horror

I was working in Edinburgh as a nightclub manager a few years ago, and one evening a gorgeous girl came up to me and asked me if I would like to go out with her the following night. I couldn't believe my luck and shared my good news with two of the club's bouncers, Steve and Tom. The following night I was changing in the club and getting excited about my big date. Suddenly Tom and Steve came in, held me down and poured green food colouring all over my bollocks. As I was only minutes away from my date, I let the stuff dry, got dressed and went to meet Jackie. We had a great evening: a meal with some wine, some dancing with plenty of drinks, and she invited me back to her place. We got down to some drunken shagging and I fell asleep a very contented man. I was woken at 7 am by Jackie screaming. She was standing in front of the mirror: her face was green, her tits were green, her hands were green and her thighs were green. She had to take the day off work and never spoke to me again.

Trainee fireman

A few years ago I was seeing a young girl who still lived with her parents. Every Thursday evening I would go round to her house and disappear upstairs with her to 'play on her PC'. This particular evening she had some perfumed candles littered around the place, and we got straight down to things. I kept the groans to a minimum so that her parents wouldn't become suspicious, and after we had finished I slipped off the condom, dropped it in the bin, and snuggled back up with my girl. It was then that I noticed the smell of burning and realized that one of the candles had set fire to the bin's contents – basically a load of tissues and a used rubber johnny. As I leapt out of bed, I accidentally kicked the contents across the room, and we suddenly had a serious fire on our hands. So naked as the day I was born, I heroically grabbed the nearest thing – a 10-inch (25-cm) rubber dildo that we used for foreplay – and began beating the carpet furiously. And then her father burst through the door shouting, 'What's all the noise about up here?' Needless to say, I took advantage of his few moments of shocked disbelief, grabbed my trousers and legged it, pausing only once to throw a blackened plastic cock into their hedge.

Chubby chaser

A while ago, after more than a few delicious beverages at my local I pulled a rather large woman, and persuaded her to let me go back to her house when the pub shut. We soon got down to business, and despite the room being pitch black, it wasn't hard to locate her massive boobies, so I started sucking greedily on a hardened nipple. And then, rather surprisingly, I got a gob full of warm milk. Being the perfect gentleman, I immediately asked her if she had recently given birth, but she rather testily claimed that she hadn't. So I carried on regardless and had a thoroughly enjoyable night of blubber-bashing with the chubby goer. When I woke in the morning I looked down at the beached whale and was rather horrified to see, about half an inch from her nipple, the shrivelled remains of a monstrous boil which I had clearly sucked dry during our night of passion.

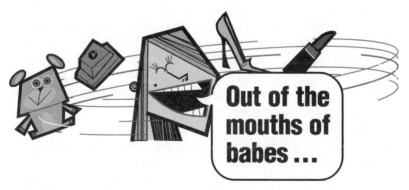

Out of the mouths of babes ...

Told by a casualty nurse that they'd had to remove a bottle from a guy's back passage, my naive mother-in-law asked, "How did he swallow that then?"

Visiting Ireland recently, a friend took the wife and I on a coastal tour. "They call this U-Boat Rock," he told us. "It looks more like a submarine," replied the wife, quick as a flash.

Art appreciation

Last summer I rented a villa on the Canary Islands with my girlfriend and her parents. It was situated right on the beach front and, one hot evening, the lovely romantic setting had us feeling a little saucy, so the love of my life led me down to the sand for some sexual activity. Things were going great, but as I took her doggy style she looked over her shoulder and grumpily shouted, 'Do me harder, you ginger tosser!' Devastated, I stopped, and headed back to the house to sleep alone on the sofa. Things got much worse at breakfast however, when her mother haughtily told us that during their evening stroll, a young girl was heard to shout, 'Do me harder, you ginger tosser.' Then suddenly they noticed my bright red barnet. We got back to Blighty, and I was well and truly dumped.

Mother-in-law mix-up

After spending a long week on a course, I drove to my mother-in-law's house, where my wife was staying for the weekend. I had a huge pile of work to get through before Monday, so I figured if I could get most of it cracked that night, I could spend the rest of my weekend with my gorgeous wife. She and my mother-in-law headed off to bed at 1am, while I knuckled down to some hard graft. I finished at around 2.30am and proceeded to get a shower, hoping to find my wife in bed in a state of semi-consciousness and ready for a spot of romance (a good hard shag) after a week apart. In nothing but my birthday suit, my mind and body raring to go and a semi lob-on rearing its perky head, I made my way into the main bedroom. Pulling back the quilt and whispering sweet nothings, I got the fright of my life when, to my horror, my mother-in-law screamed out loud. No-one had told me the room plans for that night. Needless to say, breakfast the next morning wasn't a pleasant experience.

Furniture frolics

One night my girlfriend and I decided to christen my mum's new sofa, while she was out on the town with a few friends. After the session I dropped the now full Durex into the nearest thing available – a used tea mug – and we settled down in front of the television.

Mum came home with a couple of her friends, and they sat in the kitchen to have a cup of tea and a chat. Needing some more cups, mum popped into the lounge and rounded up the few on the table, including the one that contained our little 'present', while we sat oblivious on the couch, engrossed in what was on the box. Exactly one boiled kettle later, we heard screaming from the kitchen, and what sounded remarkably like someone being sick.

Drunken disaster

Last summer, I moved into a house with five mates: three blokes and two girls, one of whom I had a slight 'thing' for. My first night there, I got arseholed, hit the jackpot and retired with my extremely fit flatmate to her room. Nothing major happened, until I woke up to the sound of laughter. Noticing my mates, in stitches, at the door – and realizing the girl in bed had now risen – I deliriously asked what their problem was. Then I really woke up as I realized that my pants were around my ankles and I was squatting over the girl's laundry basket. As I caught the unpleasant smell, it dawned on me what I had done. Gutted, I looked at the girl and realized I'd never pull her again. I had been infamous for sleep-walking, but never for sleep-shitting. I hoped it was all a bad dream, until I looked in the basket to find the messy legacy on the girl's clothes.

Gaming session

One afternoon my girlfriend suggested that we play nude hide and seek in her bedroom. Her parents were somewhere in the house, but as I had only been seeing her for a couple of weeks I decided to chance it, stripped off, and counted to ten while she went and hid. Her bedroom was a small loft conversion and it didn't take a genius to figure that she was hiding behind the bed, but in my haste to reach her I jumped across the floor, forgot that the floorboards didn't quite stretch all the way across the eaves, and went straight through the living-room ceiling. Not only did my hairy arse interrupt her mum and dad's television viewing that afternoon, but they were also blessed with an unrivalled view of my swinging todger. I'm still with Claire, but they haven't spoken to me since.

Mistake with pants

After a busy evening clubbing, I found myself being taken home by a young divorcee for a night of passion. We paid off her baby-sitter and settled down to the evening's entertainment. Having to work the next day – and wanting to escape – I awoke early and left my conquest asleep. I noticed a pair of ski pants lying in a tangled mess with a pair of knickers inside them. I immediately retrieved the underwear as a trophy and stuffed them in my trouser pocket. I went straight to work and during my mid-morning tea break, I entertained my colleagues with tales of my previous night's exploits. I spared no detail and played to the crowd, building up to the finale: the unveiling of my lady friend's underwear. At the appropriate point, I whipped out the aforementioned smalls and proudly held them aloft. It was only when I saw my workmate's shocked faces that I lowered my arms to find not the scanty women's knickers I was expecting, but a tiny pair of slightly soiled cotton briefs. Last owner: my sexual partner's four-year-old daughter!

Disastrous leak

Believe me, safe sex can get messy. On the final leg of an infamous pub crawl I spotted a gorgeous redhead. Egged on by my mates, I decided to go over and chat her up. We got on great and the conversation and drinks flowed until closing time. By the time we left the pub, we couldn't keep our hands off each other. However, as Debbie lived with her parents and I lived with mine, we decided there was only one thing for it – we would have to have sex under the stars. So, I found myself on my back in a field, with Debbie riding me senseless. After the deed was done I had an urgent need to empty my, by now bursting, bladder. I staggered over to some trees and promptly began to relieve myself. I felt the customary warm sensation but realized that I couldn't hear the familiar sound of pee. I looked down and, in the moonlight, noticed I'd forgotten to remove the condom, which by now was inflated like a balloon with my piss. Before I could react, the weight of fluid pulled the condom off my cock, drenching my trousers and shoes in the process. Debbie, who had witnessed all this, was so impressed that she left me to stagger home on my own and completely avoided me in the future.

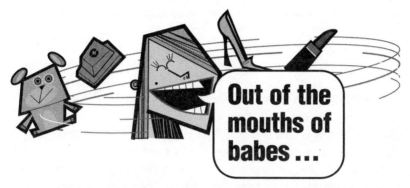

Out of the mouths of babes ...

My father couldn't decide whether to sell his personalised numberplate or transfer it from his car onto his motorcycle. "Won't it stick out on either side?" chipped in my sister.

On holiday, during dinner, a girl at my table pointed out that it felt like we were moving. We were on a cruise.

Horror with pants

While on a business trip to France, I was invited to a party in a bar. Soon I got talking to a stunning girl, Francine. A shag seemed an absolute certainty, so I got fairly pissed. Suddenly I felt the need to have a crap, so I told Francine I'd be back. Spotting a sign saying 'Hommes', I made a mad dash and found myself in a dark alley behind the café with a door at the end. Inside was a typical French bog: two footplates and a septic hole in the ground. I dropped my kecks and laid cable, which proved to be pretty nasty. Then I realized that there was no paper. A sock just wasn't going to do the trick, so I decided to use my boxer shorts. Removing them required a real balancing act: I always had to keep one shoe on and not fall into the mire below. I couldn't leave the soiled boxers in the trap so I went out into the alley to find a bin. Just then, the far door opened, and Francine appeared. So I panicked and lobbed the boxers onto the roof of the khazi. She walked slowly towards me. I lit a cigarette. She came up, I leaned down to kiss her – and suddenly there was a rolling noise, then a splat next to my left shoe, as if a wet packet of sand had just fallen. It was my 'turd-ridden' boxers, which I had thrown onto a sloping roof. I spent the night alone.

Props poorly chosen

Back in the Sixties, the cult television show for us kids was The Lone Ranger. One of the lads, Barry, received the full outfit for his ninth birthday, and we were all immediately dispatched to find suitable props so that we could join his Lone Ranger gang. Mum had gone to the shops, so I searched through the house until I found some suitable material, and cut two holes in it to make a brilliant mask. Then we galloped off behind Lone Ranger to Dead-Man's Gulch (back of the Co-Op). As we passed through the throngs of shoppers however, I was suddenly whisked off my feet by my furious mother, who spanked me all the way home. Apparently, seeing her five-year-old son charging through the local shopping centre with her sanitary towel tied around his head had played a little on her nerves.

Vitamin allowance

Shortly after the wife and I were married, she suggested that we try something new during our bedroom activities. Happy to oblige, I soon discovered that she enjoyed masturbating with various vegetables. One fine evening, after several drinks, we headed upstairs armed with a cucumber and embarked on a marathon session, during which the used cucumber ended up being discarded on the floor. When I awoke the next morning however, I let my eyes drift to where I had dropped the oblong vegetable and let out a loud scream. Sitting bolt upright, the wife followed my gaze and promptly followed suit. On the floor sat our two-year-old son, munching his way happily through the cucumber. Needless to say, that kind of sexual antic has only been repeated under the tightest of security.

Pet torture

Visiting my parents for the weekend, I went into the lounge expecting to be pounced upon by my parents' dog, an adorable Yorkshire terrier named Crosby. But the dog remained prostrate on a blanket on the sofa, looking extremely sorry for himself. 'What's up with the dog?' I asked. My father burst out laughing and my mother put down the newspaper she was reading and stormed off, muttering, 'Oh don't start again, Harold!' Dad continued laughing hysterically, then explained: 'At breakfast, your mum decided to spray Crosby with flea spray. She got hold of him, laid him belly up and gave him a good old spray. But, as she was knelt in front of the gas fire, the flea spray ignited like in Live And Let Die and set the dog's balls aflame! Crosby sprang up and ran around with his balls on fire! I chased him around the lounge for 40 seconds before I managed to stop him and slap his balls to put the flames out!'

Brotherly love

During his teenage years, my friend Pete did his fair share of wanking. Not wanting his mother to become suspicious about the rapidly diminishing supplies of toilet roll, he searched for alternative methods of 'absorption'. After dabbling with various materials – including a karate suit – he settled on an old pair of track suit bottoms, which he stored at the base of his wardrobe. The trackie bottoms served him well, until eventually he left for university, leaving them – and his past life – behind. But on returning for the Christmas holiday, Pete was met at the door by his 13-year-old sister, who appeared to be wearing a hauntingly familiar – not to mention rather rigid-looking – pair of track suit bottoms. Upon questioning, the innocent youngster replied: 'Mum's just given them to me.' Aghast that his little sister was unwittingly wearing his semen, Pete felt compelled to sneak into her room as she slept, steal back the track suit and wash clean the spunk-stained relic of his misspent youth.

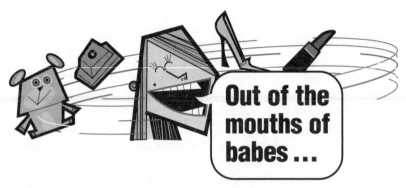

Out of the mouths of babes ...

Driving into town I had to stop at a railway crossing. As the barrier closed, my girlfriend's mate asked why there was a bell ringing. "So blind drivers know when to stop," replied my lovely girlfriend.

Surfing the internet, I asked my girlfriend to go to the FHM website. She paused before asking, "How do you spell FHM?" Oh, and she's studying for a degree!

Unfortunately mocked

While shopping in our local supermarket with my five-year-old son, Jordan, I noticed a young 'differently abled' girl walking through the fresh fruit section with the aid of a pair of tripod crutches. Jordan began staring, so I picked him up and we quickly disappeared off into the aisles. Having bought half the store, I paid for our groceries, then we joined the back of a large queue for lottery tickets. As we waited, the same girl walked past with her entire family in tow – prompting the ever-curious Jordan to tug at my trousers, point at her walking aids and demand, 'What are they for, dad?' Feeling myself going a deep shade of crimson, I gave the girl an embarrassed smile before saying to my lad, 'They're to help the girl walk better, son.' To my horror the 'girl' looked me straight in the eye and bellowed, 'I'm not a girl, I'm a boy!' before storming out. Slowly. Needless to say, I didn't get to play the lottery that weekend.

Unprincipled seaman

A couple of years ago, while on home leave from the Navy in my home town of Cockermouth, I was asked to take my little brother to the local Donkey Derby. On arrival we saw helium balloons floating in the breeze, and realized there was some sort of competition going on. We wandered off to find the relevant stand, and discovered that for 50p you could buy a ticket, leave your name and address, and attach half the ticket to the balloon. After a certain amount of time the ticket which had been sent back from the most distant place from the fair won a top-of-the-range mountain bike. I duly bought a balloon, filled in my details and let it go. My brother, however, simply wanted something to play around with, so I bought another one for 50p, pocketed the ticket stub and gave him the balloon. We enjoyed the rest of the day, and I thought no more about the incident until I went back to my ship in Portsmouth. On looking in my wallet, I found I still had the ticket from my brother's balloon. Our next port of call was the Canary Islands: I duly posted back the ticket and my brother received a nice new mountain bike, all courtesy of his dishonest older brother. To make matters worse, when next back home I sold the bike and went out on the piss for a couple of days on the proceeds.

Cabling interrupted

The other Saturday morning the doorbell rang, and before I could stop him, my four-year-old son raced up and opened the door. 'Hello, young man, is your daddy home?' enquired the visiting lady. After a short pause for thought, my son nodded, took two steps back and opened the door to the downstairs toilet, where I was sitting on the bog. Fortunately, the door screened me from view of our visitor, but my son had perfect vision of the pair of us. Ignoring my wild, silent, imploring gestures to shut the door, he grandly announced that there was a lady at the door. I just remained silent, trying to maintain the pretence that I wasn't there and was simply a figment of his imagination. So, after staring at me for a good ten seconds, my darling boy turned back to the woman and duly informed her that, 'Daddy is having a poo.' Fortunately, this prompted the woman to mutter something about coming back later, before fleeing down the driveway. We never did discover her identity.

Training trauma

After a pretty horrendous training weekend with the Royal Marines Reserves, I came home and fell asleep on the sofa – only to wake up to a tingling sensation in my feet. My young daughter had taken my shoes and socks off. I went back to my well-deserved kip. The next morning, I found out what my daughter had done, but by then it was too late to do anything about it. I just made a mental note to deal with her later. At the camp, five minutes into a run with the lads and our instructor, I twisted my ankle in a pothole and was carried off to sickbay. All gathered round to see if it was a juicy injury (sick bastards, these marine types). Then the doc took off my sock. To my – and everyone else's – horror, my toe nails were painted with pink Barbie doll nail varnish! And did they believe my story? Did they fuck!

Pet cemetery

My gran and grandad have kept the same tortoises since I was a child. Because they are now fairly valuable, the duo are locked in a small hutch every night and brought out again the following morning. My gran used to do this, but last year she was in hospital for six months, leaving the job to grandad. One afternoon I popped over for a beer, and while the pair of us lounged in the garden, I asked after his pets. He said they were fine, although 'Timmy' was so old now he didn't walk about much. Bending down to stroke its head, I discovered that

Timmy's shell was nothing but a festering mulch of green rotting meat, infested with maggots. The old fool had been putting his deceased chum in and out of the hutch for months.

Adult education

A few months ago my girlfriend had to babysit her young cousin. She was told by the very conservative aunt that I was not allowed into the house other than to pick her up at the end of the night. Needless to say, as soon as they had gone I was round there – and with the little chap in bed, was soon receiving outstanding oral sex on the sofa. I was in heaven, until I noticed her little cousin standing about a metre away, staring intently at my girlfriend's bobbing action. Leaping up, we fobbed him off with a story of 'that's what adults do'. All was fine until the following weekend, when my girlfriend got a call from her incensed aunt, who demanded to know why her six-year-old son kept trying to give himself a blow-job at the kitchen table.

Damp feline

Some years ago I went to my cousin's engagement party in Greenwich, where the toilet was an outhouse in the back yard. When I needed to relieve myself, there was a long queue, so I decided to do it in the fish pond. In my haste I didn't realize that my aunt's cat was sitting at the water's edge, and the poor thing got covered. Shortly afterwards my aunt entered the garden and picked up the cat. While stroking it she said: 'The cat's all wet!' 'Oh,' I said, 'she must have fallen in the pond.'

Thoughtless prank

When I was at school, we used to play a game in our dinner break which involved locking some unsuspecting young lad in one of the lockers. The idea was that we'd roll the locker onto its side, kick it for a bit, then let the poor bugger out, who would usually stumble around dazed for a few minutes. One dinner break we locked someone in, rolled the locker over and gave it our customary kick, then couldn't unlock it. At first our prisoner thought we were joking, only realizing things were a little more serious when he heard the key snap in the lock. Dinner break ended and we still couldn't force open the locker, so I promised I'd return after school to let him out. But we had PE in the afternoon and I sprained my ankle playing football. Such was the pain, I caught the school bus straight home. It wasn't until later that evening that I remembered the locker, when my mum came off the phone saying, 'I've got Mrs Thompson on in a bit of a state, wondering if you've seen her boy, as he didn't come home from school.' I daren't own up at the time, but did get to school very early in the morning, only to be confronted by the police, the caretaker – with crow-bar – and the gasping boy.

Dumb childhood antic

When I was a child, friends and I would play on the railway line just outside our town. We would wave to drivers and passengers and occasionally place an ear on the line to see if we could hear a train approaching. One day I decided to listen, and squatted down, took hold of the track and put my ear against it. There was a loud bang, a bright flash and I landed, rather stunned, in a bush ten feet away. I'd forgotten that there were three lines with one carrying the electric current. Presumably my rubber-soled plimsolls and both hands making simultaneous contact had saved my life. The short-term effects were some faint burns down the inside of my arms and legs. Longer term was the mixture of awe and derision with which I was treated by my peers. And of course I never told my mother – she would have killed me.

Appalling child

When I was seven, my parents divorced and my sister and I went to live with my mother and her new husband. My step-father ran the house like a POW camp. According to him we were constantly 'disobedient' and as punishment had to endure his incessant temper-tantrums, criticisms and bullying. In reality we were average children and he was a complete tyrant. My sister and I became increasingly resentful of him and spent hours plotting his grisly death. One day he returned home from work early with a 'mystery' illness and stayed in bed for two days. Of course, he was unaware that we had smothered his Y-fronts with Deep Heat. He never did have any more kids.

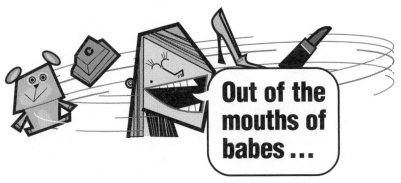

Out of the mouths of babes ...

Watching Who Wants To Be A Millionaire, the question, "Which Biblical character was famed for his enormous strength?" came up. "Popeye!" exclaimed the missus.

Watching football on the telly, a player was taking a throw-in. "What's that thing on his back?" asked my girlfriend. "Is it a backwards 'E'?" It was, of course, the number three. She's currently at the University of Newcastle, studying mathematics.

Dead rabbit confusion

We have a golden retriever who has a habit of digging up prized miniature rose bushes and making off with neighbouring dogs' bowls of food. Last weekend, he came in carrying the corpse of a very limp and dirty white rabbit in his jaws. One of our neighbours has pet white rabbits, so I freaked and called my wife to look at the damage. Fortunately there was no blood on the animal, so we decided to make it took like a natural death. We washed it and my wife blow-dried its white coat and brushed the fur. That night we placed the rabbit on Barry's lawn and sneaked back home for a fitful night's steep. Later in the week, I met my neighbour, who said: 'You know, a really weird thing happened to us last week. One of our pet rabbits died of old age, and we gave it a proper burial in the back yard. You won't believe this, but the next morning when we got up we found it on the back lawn all clean and white and bright!'

Show-off bounced

When I was eight years old I had a girlfriend called Antoinette. I thought we would last forever, until I saw her snogging a boy called Ross in the playground after school. I was gutted, but decided to try and win her back. My plan was to impress her with my football skills, so one afternoon I stood outside her house and began a lengthy session of 'keepy-ups'. Eventually she came to the window to watch, so I started getting a little cockier, and eventually lost control of the ball. She smiled, I waved, turned to get the ball, and got run over by a white Ford Sierra. All I remember is her scream as I bounced off the bonnet and somersaulted off down the street. I spent the entire Easter holiday in traction, and never spoke to her again.

Wild beast

Not so long ago, I agreed to help my girlfriend babysit her nine-year-old niece at her sister's house, knowing a decent shag would be my reward. Before long – with the brat safely tucked away – the couch became my jungle of love as I unveiled my surprise – a novelty elephant posing-pouch. With my glistening little chap fitting the trunk, and my sweaty balls swinging sweetly in its cheeks, I danced my arse off like a horny Zulu, all to the desired effect: the sopping jizz-filled pouch was finally abandoned and we embarked on a humping safari. In the morning, long after we had departed, my lover's sister gasped in horror as her daughter shook her awake and proudly said: 'Mummy, Look at my new mask.'

Feline surprise

Last Christmas Eve, after a heavy week on the beers, I found myself in the company of a very attractive girl. Somehow I managed to convince her to invite me home, and despite our drunken state we found a condom and got down to business, before eventually nodding off. Sometime later I was woken by the sound of her alarm clock, and as she made no attempt to get up and turn it off, I jumped out of bed, and staggered around in the darkness until I found it. I then felt her cat jump up between my legs, and as the girl had woken up, I asked her to turn the lamp on. Glancing down, I then noticed that the condom I had been wearing was still attached to my knob. Worse, I had inadvertently managed to piss myself during the night, and the whole bulbous mass was swaying wildly between my legs. Then, as the pair of us stared in horror, the cat made a final leap and speared the balloon with its razor-sharp talons, covering the room in cold sperm and urine. I left so quickly, I never even found out her name.

Bolshy brothers

When young, it was not uncommon for my brother and I to engage in a bit of sibling fighting. One particular balmy night, we were too feisty to sleep. As my parents relaxed downstairs in front of the TV, I crept from my bedroom and into my brother's, where I set about knocking eight bells out of him with a pillow. The commotion led to shouts from downstairs for us to cease our rowdy fighting and get back to bed. However, a few minutes later, I was on the receiving end of an attack. This time my father bounded in, warning us that if he heard so much as another whisper, there would be trouble. He was a man who commanded respect, and we meekly returned to our beds. But there must have been mischief in the air that night, because I soon found myself creeping into my brother's room for one last belt – but he had scattered drawing pins across the threshold to his room! As I stole into the darkness, I miraculously avoided the many tacks that lay across my path, and set about pummelling the startled youth. His cries alerted my furious parents, and as my father's footsteps pounded the stairs I scurried out the room – incredibly missing the tacks again – just in time to witness dad's bare feet sinking into the drawing pins. You can imagine the rest.

Unhappy discovery

When I was a young lad of eight or nine, my friends and I would use the recreation ground near where we lived as a shortcut to school. One morning my friend Dave and I climbed the fence and jumped down on the other side. As we got to our feet, Dave proudly held up a balloon which had been thrown away in the grass and proceeded to try to blow the thing up ready for school – a great talking point for nine-year-olds in any playground. As we walked through the rec, Dave struggled with the balloon, and he finally managed to get the thing going. It was then that I noticed a load of liquid in the expanding globe. As Dave attempted to get the balloon to full inflation, the liquid sloshed back into his mouth, where he swallowed it. He chucked the balloon down and said with disgust that the liquid had tasted 'salty'. It was only a few years later, when we were practising our new-found safe sex techniques with the local easy girls, that we realized Dave must have swallowed a mouthful of Harry Monk out of a used condom!

Royal shame

It was 1981, and the country was gripped with Royal Wedding fever as Prince Charles and Lady Di got set to tie the knot. My parents, being staunch supporters of the royal family, decided to drag my younger brother and I down to Buckingham Palace so we could see the happy couple out on the balcony. Naturally, the nation's capital was heaving, and the throng around Buck House was awesome. Being an inquisitive ten-year-old, I wormed my way through the grown-ups' legs right to the very front of the crowd and stuck my head through the Palace railings – where it remained firmly wedged when I tried to pull it out. The next thing I knew I had a policeman on one leg, my dad on the other and my mum smearing margarine, kindly donated by a fat man from a hamburger stand, all over my ears. Nothing worked. Eventually a huge section of the crowd had to move out of the way so that a fire engine could get up to the fence. They had to cut a section out of the fence (which I wasn't allowed to keep as a souvenir) to free me, and the whole story made the papers. I not only ruined the day for my parents and a large section of the crowd, I was also responsible for an act of vandalism on the home of our great Queen. I apologize.

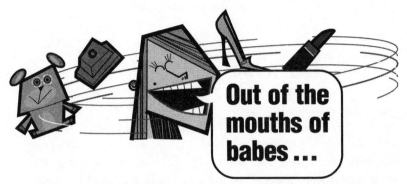

Out of the mouths of babes ...

Watching TV, the film Event Horizon was coming up. My girlfriend asked what it was about. I explained it was set in the future, when some professor goes mental aboard a spaceship and kills people. "Is it a true story?" she said.

Out walking on a hot summer's day with my girlfriend, we saw some bin-men lugging dripping bags of rubbish across the road. "I don't fancy their job..." I commented. "Yeah, but they only work one day a week," she replied.

Sporting snacks

When I was 10 years old I went on a primary school skiing trip to Austria. At the time I was a very fat and very short little boy, and my mum had elected to dress me in tight white polo neck jumpers, and emerald green, arse-hugging ski pants, which only served to emphasis my porcine features. Towards the end of an afternoon on the slopes, my mate Mark and I snuck off to a café, popped our skis on the rack, and headed inside. Mark asked me to get him a king-size chocolate bar while he went to the loo. I bought the food, but when Mark had failed to return after five minutes, I began to eye his share of the grub hungrily. Eventually I succumbed to temptation but just as I began to nibble at the top of the choccy feast, a group of Englishmen strolled in and stopped to stare at me. I can only assume they thought I was a local and couldn't speak English, as one nudged his mate and said, 'I bet that fat twat is going to eat the lot.' And I did.

Kamikaze fowl

Having just moved into a three-bedroom bungalow, my wife and I thought that it would be nice to buy our two small children a budgie. The kids loved the idea, and chose a nice cage and toys, as well as a chirpy little bird. Once back home, I hung the cage in the lounge and while they stood underneath it, pointing and squealing, I helped the wife with dinner. Eventually my son ran in, screaming that the budgie had escaped. True enough, we found it flapping round the curtains, and in the following excitement, it took refuge in the kitchen. Everyone then had a hilarious ten minutes as the feathery sod thwarted all my efforts to snare him with a tea towel. But the laughter came to an abrupt halt when, for no real reason, the bird soared to maximum altitude, tucked up its wings, and dive-bombed straight into the deep-pan chip fryer. Yes, it did sizzle, yes the kids still have nightmares, and yes, for weeks afterwards our mates would phone us, order Kentucky Fried Budgie, then burst out laughing and hang up.

Choking dog fiasco

After six months of being blanked, I finally managed to secure a date with the girl of my dreams. We went first to see a film, then headed on to a top-notch restaurant for a meal. Things went much better than expected as Lucy became more and more amorous as the evening went on. I drove her home and she invited me in for coffee, but warned me that there would be no messing about, as her parents were in. Anyway, I sat down with her mum and dad and we all got along very well. So well, in fact, that I accepted her father's offer of a large whisky or two, which put me over the limit to drive. Even this wasn't a problem on my night of nights, as Lucy's old man kindly offered me the sofa to sleep on. Lucy and her folks went up to bed and I settled down, only to be nudged awake half an hour later by a giggling and slightly tipsy Lucy, who proceeded to treat me to the best shag of my life. When we were both exhausted but happy, Lucy snuck back up to bed and I fell asleep.In the morning, we all had a lovely breakfast and I reflected on my good fortune with Lucy's parents, who obviously had a lot of time for a pleasant, responsible chap such as me. Then, just as I was about to leave, their pet terrier came running in from the living room, choking and obviously in great distress. So, seizing the opportunity to win more brownie points with Lucy's folks, I picked up the mutt and performed a mini Heimlich manoeuvre. Lucy and I then watched in horror as a used condom shot from the dog's mouth and landed with a splat on the kitchen table, destroying my good work and banishing me from the house forever.

Canine treats

The mutual dislike between myself and my girlfriend's mother stems from the fact that she hates animals, and her daughter has just moved in with me and my large black Labrador, Zac. In an attempt to improve the relationship between us, my girlfriend persuaded her to come round for dinner on the understanding that Zac would be locked outside. But somehow the bugger managed to find a way back in, and made his way straight for the daft bat, plonking his head on her lap in hope of some scraps. She reacted by frantically pushing his head away, which was followed by an audible 'phut' as she inadvertently popped a large abscess under his chin. A considerable amount of foul-smelling, slightly bloody pus shot out onto her expensive dress, leaving a great stain. She looked up at me, then opened her mouth and vomited all over the table, with Zac heartily lapping up whatever ran onto the floor.

Hangover horror

After getting violently pissed to celebrate my friend's birthday, he and I staggered back to his parents' house to crash out. I was directed to a room which was full of ladders and without lights, so getting to the bathroom was going to be difficult. As the room started spinning I decided that it would be best to puke on the floor and clean it up in the morning. According to plan, I awoke early but then reality reared its ugly head. A great spray of puke had gone over his mother's clothes and had liberally covered the bed. Have you ever tried removing dried vomit from the channels in corduroys? Keeping a cool head I scraped all the spew into a pillow case with a birthday card, deposited it in the neighbour's garden and put the sheets and clothes back in the washing machine. Later, while having breakfast with the family, an eerie scratching came from the door. It swung open to reveal their dog with a multicoloured pungent pillow case swinging from its mouth.

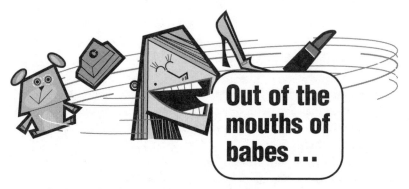

Out of the mouths of babes ...

In The Sum Of All Fears, there's a scene where one plane refuels another, mid-flight. "Is it towing the other one?" asked my girlfriend. "Has it broken down?"

Watching Lord Of The Rings with the family, my 17-year-old sister asked, "When were all the creatures from Middle Earth around? Was it before or after the dinosaurs?"

Ball games

When I was 14, I would secretly masturbate in as many weird places as possible, and in secondary school it was not uncommon for me to tease one out during double history or a particularly dull maths class. Yet perhaps the strangest place of all was on the sports field during a games lesson. I was playing rugby on a cold November afternoon, and, becoming increasingly bored stuck out on the wing, I slipped my hands down my shorts to keep them warm. It was then that I decided to have a furtive jostle and proceeded to go at it hammer and tongs – climaxing in that inevitable warm feeling rising up my shaft. Suddenly someone shouted my name, and I looked up to see a high ball hurtling towards me. By now I had reached the point of no return, and, as the ball landed beside me and both teams stared, I gave an idiotic, buck-toothed grin ... and ejaculated into my shorts. I was never picked for rugby again.

Weird love triangle

One night, feeling amorous, I convinced my girlfriend to don a figure-hugging basque and black fishnet stockings. She duly obliged and we soon got down to business. To get the best view of her perfectly-formed mesh-covered legs, I suggested we do it 'doggy fashion' over her favourite armchair. We were indulging in some frantic sex when I realized my right leg was too close to her two-bar electric fire. But I was too near the point of no return to change position, so instead I began to yelp involuntarily, which my girlfriend took as a signal of my increasing ecstasy. She started moaning and yelping in a similar fashion, and the sideways jerks I made to distance myself from the heat only made her more enthusiastic. Then I had an even stranger sensation. Just as I was about to come, her labrador stuck its cold, wet nose right up my arse.

My body spasmed in every direction – with shock and pain – while my girlfriend was in ecstasy. I never told her about our third party!

Holiday fiasco

I was on holiday in Paris a couple of years ago, and was fortunate enough to have the loan of a friend's flat while he was away on business. The only thing he wanted in return for the flat was that I looked after his cat for the two weeks, which I agreed to do. Anyway, two days before my mate was due back, I decided to go out and celebrate my final 48 hours in Paris. I went on a bender with some friends, leaving a good supply of catfood and water for little Napoleon. When I came in from my epic binge, I could barely stand up. All I wanted to do was sleep, so I went straight to the bedroom and crashed out on the bed. Early the next morning, I woke up to the sound of a key in the lock, and looked up at my friend, who was looking at me in abject horror. The poor cat, having had twice as much as usual to eat, and nowhere to go for a crap as he hadn't been let out, had used the bed as a toilet, and I had spent an alcoholic night tossing and turning in his shit. It took a lot of explaining, laundry and several glasses of wine before my mate saw the funny side of things and believed I wasn't a shit fetishist.

Ballistic shell

Many years ago, my mother decided to buy two baby tortoises. As they were young, they didn't hibernate, and during the winter they were kept inside in a large plastic container, which contained some cabbage leaves and an electrically heated imitation rock. One Saturday morning, I popped round to visit, only to be told that one of the tortoises had died. After a brief inspection, however, I suspected that it could just be sleeping, and I managed to persuade the old dear to place it on the heated rock in the container and crank the power up in order to disturb it from its slumber. Five minutes of serious heat later, the tortoise gave a little shake, started emitting a strange hissing sound, and then exploded, covering us all in hot flesh and jagged shell.

Links high jinks

I'm a keen golfer, and recently played a quick 18 holes one sunny afternoon. I was hitting the ball cleanly, and hard. At the fifth tee I selected my new driver with a 9.5 degree loft and larruped the ball down the fairway. It went low and hard and, to my horror, struck a passing kestrel, taking its wing clean off. It really was an horrific sight. The poor bird flapped around on the ground in a small circle, obviously in great pain. In an almost instinctive action I took a seven iron from my bag and put the raptor out of its misery. It was a quick, clean, humane kill, and I chucked the bird into the rough and continued my round – shooting a 75, which was below my handicap. But back at the clubhouse I was shocked to be hauled aside by two uniformed RSPCA inspectors. They had been told I'd been clubbing birds to death, and only when I explained that I had injured the bird first did they let me off – with a warning.

Tights consumed

While walking the dog one afternoon, my mum noticed that our mutt seemed to be having a little difficulty passing a strange-looking stool. On closer inspection, we both decided that it was in actual fact a small length of one of my mother's tights, and in a fit of generosity, she placed a firm foot on the piece of material that was dragging along the ground. My task was to then walk the dog along the road, thus pulling the offending article out of its arse. Neither of us realized that I would have to walk the dog for a good ten metres however, and when it finally popped out, the second leg headed back towards mum like a rocket, smacking her square in the mouth and giving her an impressive streak of shit right across her face.

Coin swallower

Fifteen years ago, as a wee seven-year-old, I decided it was time to find out what a ten pence piece would taste like. In full view of my parents, I stuck the coin in my mouth. My father yelled at me to spit it out at once. 'I can't,' I replied. 'I've swallowed it.' After my mother had got over her histrionics and rung round every doctor she could, she was finally assured that the best course of action was to leave the coin to pass naturally through my body. I was told that I had to shit in a bucket until the two shillings passed out of my arse. My poor parents had to wade through dozens of buckets of shit, morning, noon and night, searching for the elusive piece of silver. This went on for just over a week. I never had the heart to tell them that I hadn't really swallowed the coin, and planted it in the bucket when the joke began to wear thin.

Student politics

While I was a student, I became mixed up in left-wing politics. Part of my initiation was to demonstrate my dedication to the protection of a group of animals which were being cruelly practised upon in the labs of the local university biology department. Some of the beasts really were being appallingly treated: skin was shaved from little puppies so that after shave could be tested; mice were force-fed with drugs; and rabbits were jacked up with steroids – all in the name of research. One night a gang of like-minded mini-revolutionaries and I decided to set free the rabbits – which happened to be the most accessible animals, as they were kept in hutches which backed onto the fields at the edge of town. We donned our balaclavas and black donkey jackets and crept down to the labs. Nobody was about, so we bolt-cropped the locks and opened the hatch doors onto the fields, and freedom. Naturally, we didn't stick around to watch the results of our handiwork. The following day at lectures we heard we had been successful: the rabbits had all got out. Unfortunately, we hadn't considered their steroidal history. It turns out that 35 rabbits made a grab for freedom – animals that weighed, on average, just over 25lb each. Tragically, the rabbits had all been unnaturally thirsty due to steroid dehydration, and the first source of water they had come across was the cess-pipe of the local cereal factory. The poor bunnies had lapped at the fetid water until dead, and the local newspaper described the eerie scene the following morning as a 'floating, fluffy armada of death'.

Retriever exercised

Last year, after a heavy lunchtime drinking session, my girlfriend and I became proud owners of an 11-inch purple latex dildo which eventually ended up at the bottom of our wardrobe. This summer we went for a last minute holiday, and her dad kindly agreed to look after our one-year-old Labrador, Ralph, for the two weeks we were away. Everything went well, and we returned to find that the pair had become inseparable. Nothing was too much for the dog as far as Dad was concerned, and I felt jealous at the obvious bond that had grown between the two. You can only imagine my delight therefore, when on returning the dog one afternoon, the old boy nipped out to get Ralph's favourite toy. Yes, the silly twat had been round every park in the county with an amazing Dildo Retrieving Labrador, and was still none the wiser. Sadly, this triggered an outbreak of hostilities between my beloved and myself, as she's convinced that I put the toy in the basket on purpose. As I still have hopes of a reconciliation I would like this story to be attributed to someone with a different name from a different country.

Bath-tub accident

When I was a lot younger – just nine years old, to be exact – the Sunday evening rituals always included a weekly bath. My younger brother, Nigel, and I used to enjoy sharing a tub, and our mother would counsel us on the damage small objects could cause. Even though we had been warned, it didn't stop us sneaking model soldiers, bricks of Lego and countless other small objects into the bathroom to play with in the steaming water.

One of our favourite bath-time toys was a large, purple, clear glass marble. One Sunday evening my brother and I were playing our soapy games, as usual, when a terrible accident occurred. My younger brother, having stood up to 'dive bomb' some of the floating plastic soldiers with pieces of Lego, sat down with a splash, having successfully taken out three men.

Nigel also sat down with a high-pitched scream, which drove me to have a fit of hysterical laughter, not knowing why he was causing such a fuss. The large purple marble, lurking unseen like a mine at the bottom of the soapy water, had been forced up my poor brother's brown star.

Consequently, poor Nigel spent a long, drawn-out evening face down on the kitchen table, having the glass marble removed with the aid of the ends of two teaspoons and a liberal amount of olive oil.

Cruel dad

When I was nine years old, as I was walking home from school one afternoon I had the misfortune to tread in a huge pile of dog shit. Engrossed at the time with ruffling through my collection of Topps Trading Cards, I failed to notice anything wrong at the time, and went on to walk the shit all through the hall, into the front room and out into the kitchen, leaving a trail of prints all over the house. My mum was really pissed off and scolded me harshly. But later on that evening I explained to my dad what had happened and he told me not to worry, because it was considered 'very good luck' to tread in dog shit. This cheered me up a lot.

So following my father's advice, the following day I trod in every pile of dog muck I could find. By the time I got to school I was covered in the stuff. Both my shoes were caked in shit, as were the bottoms of my trousers. I left a trail of faeces on the floor as I made my way happily into class – at which point my teacher went insane and sent me home to a battering from my mum. I obviously hadn't found any lucky excrement.

Helpful brochure

During my penultimate year of school, pupils were required to attend a careers seminar to help fashion a plan for our futures. Being an active chap, I decided to attend the lecture on the sports industry. Our speaker was a local entrepreneur who had formed a successful sports agency and, having been issued a copy of the company prospectus, I noticed that on the second page there was a picture of him with Colin Montgomerie, the rather rotund, red-faced Scottish golfer. Such a lucrative client must have proven invaluable to the company and, keen to make an impression, I saw it as an ideal point to bring up at the question and answer session. Right on cue, at the end of a somewhat tedious speech, I thrust my hand in the air and made my point to the speaker, who simply stared at me, totally bemused. 'See,' I began, holding the prospectus in the air for all to see. 'Colin Montgomerie.' Looking closely at the page, the entrepreneur made eye-contact and said, 'That, young man, is my wife and I.' Needless to say, my summer job at the company never materialized.

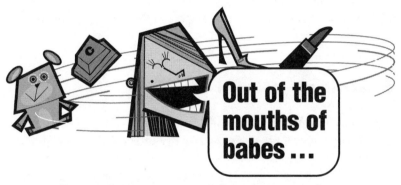

Out of the mouths of babes ...

On Walking With Dinosaurs, one of the creatures was dying on a beach, looking as if it was in extreme pain. "Can't the camera crew do anything to help?" my girlfriend piped up.

A female friend of mine was shown a blow-up sex doll at a party. Noticing the rounded, cavernous mouth, she blurted out: "Eeew! That wouldn't be very nice to kiss."

Parrot exercised

When I was aged about ten my dad used to breed parrots. Not just ordinary parrots, but expensive and exotic ones he'd managed to get his hands on from somewhere overseas. Anyway, his job required him to be away a lot, and mum and I would took after the birds while he was gone. One time when he was away and mum was at the shops, I decided to be helpful and take his best bird for a walk – I figured it didn't get much exercise in the aviary. And I also thought I'd look pretty cool walking a giant parrot. I made a leash out of some string and tied it to the bird's foot, put it in a box and took it to the park. All during the journey it went crazy, flapping like mad, squawking and bashing into the lid, so when I got there I held the string tightly and immediately set the bird free. It flew straight up to the full extent of its leash, about three metres overhead – but didn't, as I had expected, stop and circle contentedly. In fact it scrammed so fast that the string tore its foot clean off, and it flew away screeching. All I was left with was a pathetic foot on a string. I looked for ages, but I couldn't find the bird. When dad got home I copped a clip over the ear and a month's grounding.

Flatulent camel

On holiday in Egypt, my mates and I realized that after a week hanging around the bars of Cairo, we should do the decent thing and visit the pyramids – and have a monkey about on the camels. We had a root around the ruins before paying one of the camel handlers a few pence and clambering aboard a bundle of bored-looking beasts. Almost immediately, my camel started farting – much to the amusement of my mates, and also a young American couple, whose porky little toddler found it especially hilarious. Predictably, the Egyptian camel owner went to town with the gag, pointing at me every time the mangy animal let rip, and sharing a smile with the Americans, who he was obviously tapping up for his next trip. For five long minutes, my mates and I were led around like idiots, the camel parping merrily away all the time. Just as I was getting off the beast, the American couple swaggered over and started haggling with the owner, when the camel opened its voluminous bowels straight onto the head of their over-fed child, spattering him with hard, lumpy shit. Suddenly, without warning, the kid's father lunged at me and gave me a hard thump on the arm, as if I was responsible, before joining his fretting wife, busy clearing poo from the mewling brat's face. Outraged but confused, all I could think of doing was picking up a turd and flinging it at the trio, which I did – before running off into a big crowd of tourists.

Child's clean-up

A few years ago I was invited to my girlfriend's house for a first-time meeting with her young son. As luck would have it, the child turned out to be a likeable wee boy of four, who immediately decided that he wanted to be my friend. It wasn't long before his mum left to start preparing a meal. 'I'm Batman,' the little chap announced, eyeing up my denim jacket. 'But I haven't got a cape.' Determined to get into his good books, I whipped my jacket off and tied it around the little scamp's shoulders. Everything went well until, on his second circuit of the room, a condom fell out of the pocket. 'What's this?' squealed the nipper, excitedly. Panicking, I searched for an innocent – yet plausible – explanation. 'It's one of those tissues from the chicken and chip boxes,' I announced ... then watched in disbelief as he exclaimed 'Just what I need!' and ripped it open. Unfortunately, as I made a lunge to grab the johnny, I caught the edge of the carpet with my biker boots and hit the deck with a massive thud. Concerned, my girlfriend popped her head around the door – just in time to see me spread-eagled across the floor while her precious son stood over me, frantically wiping his face with a strawberry-flavoured ribbed condom. I'm now banned from all house visits.

Surfing horror

The Christmas before last I was in a pub being drunk and obnoxious, and was thrown out. Leaving the pub, I saw a huge tanker lorry driving very slowly up the narrow street, and thought I would have some fun. I jogged up behind the lorry and jumped onto the small ladder on the back, then got on the roof and tried a bit of 'urban surfing'. All was going well until the lorry suddenly sped up, and before I knew it I was lying on the roof as the thing pulled onto a dual carriageway. I went to the back of the lorry and climbed down the ladder, but the road was moving past very, very fast. Panicking, I decided I could jump off and simply manage to run along the road really quickly. The next few hours are a blur. Apparently a car ran over my foot, which was broken in six places, and I got a blood clot on my big toe. Besides this, I suffered bruising and contusions. Sadly, my toe went black and scummy. Three months later, when pulling on my jeans, I snagged the manky toe, and the whole bloody thing fell off. Thankfully, I can now walk again, but I don't do urban surfing anymore.

Patient monitored

Following a bad motorcycle accident last year, I awoke to find myself wired up in a bed in hospital, with, among other injuries, a broken right ankle. I had to suffer more than a week of bed baths and pissing into a tube before I was given use of a commode chair – a sort of potty on wheels I could use to move from my bed to the loo. For my first moment of privacy in ten days, I decided to check that no damage had been done to my little soldier, so I wheeled myself down to the toilets for a spot of well-deserved self-abuse. All was going well until, approaching the Grand Finale, I stood up on my good leg and balanced myself against the basin.

The chair then shot out from under me and slammed against the door, swinging it open and allowing the chair, me and my rapidly deflating manhood to fall with a crash into the bright lights of Ward 16. To cover my embarrassment I told the nurses I'd fainted – so they kept me in for another four days 'just in case'.

Flour fiasco

As any professional cook will tell you, long hours spent in front of the stoves can result in the condition we call Chef's Arse – where your ring becomes red-raw and sitting down is difficult, to say the least. The best remedy is a good handful of cornflour, up and around the offending area. I was halfway through a double-shift when Chef's Arse last struck. The chafing was unbearable, so, unable to locate the cornflour, I took a packet of plain flour into the loo, gratefully slathered it over my hairy arse, and finished my shift, pain-free. Next morning, I launched into my usual routine: black coffee, ciggy, followed by turd time – so I entered the loo, dropped my trousers and went for the big squeeze. My scream woke the entire house. My arsespiders had meshed with the flour and sweat to create a near-impenetrable, hairy net over my crack, through which I'd attempted to crimp off a length.

Dangerous rumpty

Out clubbing one night I noticed a girl smiling at me from across the bar. So I bought her a drink and ended up taking her outside for a quick knee-trembler. I was pounding away, with her spreadeagled over a parked mini, when all of a sudden the banjo string under my helmet snapped, and blood went everywhere, bringing a sudden end to the evening's entertainment. Sadly, five days later I was running out of excuses as to why I didn't want to have sex with my regular girlfriend, so I decided to blame her. With the lights off and teeth clenched, I slammed into her, and my knob nearly snapped in half. Blood gushed out, but amazingly she asked if I was alright, cleaned me up, and after a month of guilty cups of tea, and no sex, I'm back on the job again.

Sparkler gobbled

A few weekends ago, my mates and I had congregated for our usual Saturday afternoon piss-up when a girl we all knew arrived at the pub to show off her new £800 engagement ring. My friend Les asked for a better look, and as she proudly handed him the sparkler he tossed it into the air, deftly caught it in his mouth and 'hilariously' pretended to swallow it. Unfortunately, seconds later Les started to turn blue, followed by an enormous belch and the words, 'It's gone...' The poor lass then burst into tears and fled. It was three days and five craps before Les's wife was able to present the girl with her diamond ring, sparkling and as good as new. It was some small consolation that its passage had ripped a three-inch hole in his rectum, hospitalizing him for two days.

Holidaymakers relax

After finishing our exams, my mate and I took a well-earned holiday in
Spain. After our first night out, we decided that the best way to cure
our hangovers would be a long session in the hotel sauna. It was nice
enough, with coals in the centre of the room and long, wide-slatted
benches circling the wails. We were in there for about half-an-hour, and
in his completely relaxed state, my mate's left testicle managed to fall
down through the gap in the bench without him noticing. I eventually
stood up to leave, and was halfway to the door when my eardrums
were pierced with the most blood-curdling screams I have ever heard.
My friend was lying on the floor with blood pumping out of his sack,
and things didn't get any better at the hospital; I was left nursing a lone
testicle in a surgical bowl, while the paramedics did their best to stop
the bleeding.

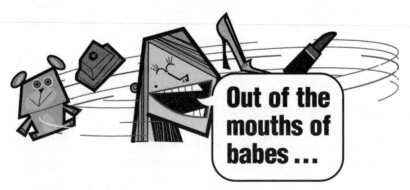

Out of the mouths of babes ...

*I recently overheard one of our three secretaries asking, "How many
kilos in a kilogram?" What's worse is that the other two didn't know
either.*

*While taking the last of her three daily inhalers, my girlfriend
exclaimed, "I seem to spend half my life just breathing in!"*

Vacation incident

Last summer my mate and I went to Ibiza for our holidays, and one
night, while having a game of pool, two amazing looking older ladies
joined us and asked for a game of doubles. We played a few games, and
then one leaned over and seductively whispered that she would like to
give me a blow job that 'I would never forget'. I didn't need asking
twice, and we headed straight upstairs while my mate took the other
one away down the beach. Once in my room, she told me to lie down
and strip and, true to her word, proceeded to give me some of the best
oral sex I have ever had. As I approached the vinegar strokes I slipped
my hands under the bedboard and moaned in ecstasy. Then, for some
unknown reason, she slammed not one, but two fingers straight up my
starfish. I sat up so quickly that I lifted the headboard clean out of its
mounting, straight over my head and directly down onto her bobbing
bonce. Not only did it knock her out, it also caused her to bite right
into my bell end and leave a false nail up my arse.

Hole puncher

While working in a large furniture showroom, I was asked by the
manager to lift a remarkably heavy worktop. Seeing me struggle, a
workmate who shall remain nameless, and was working nearby drilling
holes into doors – rushed over to help. Needing to use both hands, he
popped the cordless drill into the waistband of his jeans, and leaned
down to get a decent grip. As he did so, his belt pulled on the trigger,
and the drill spun into action, promptly wrapping his scrotum round the
3-inch drill bit. We thought he was screaming loudly at that point, but
when we were then forced to switch the thing into reverse to unwrap
his squashed goolies, he very nearly burst our eardrums. When he
finally returned to work, he had three stitches and a comedy John
Wayne walk.

Snagged knackers

Several years ago a friend of mine held her 19th birthday party at a local hockey club. A group of us decided to travel down from university in order to conduct a full weekend of drinking, which included imbibing several pints while watching the rugby on TV in the afternoon. We were all in high spirits before we headed off for the do, looking forward to a night of merriment. Plenty of drinks were had at the party and everyone had a good time. That is, until I went outside to clear my head. Once in the fresh air I was drawn to the hockey team's clubhouse, and in particular to the flagpole that stood next to it. I climbed onto the roof of the clubhouse and, when the party emptied out, leapt across to the pole and slid down, to grand applause. However, I had failed to notice a small cleat on the pole, which ripped a hole not only in my trousers but also in my scrotum – a wound that required 14 stitches at West Middlesex University Hospital.

Sofa sex shock

My girlfriend and I had been together for four months when we decided, at last, to consummate our relationship. I'm not afraid to admit that I was nervous – I wanted our first time together to be special. In short, I wanted to prove that I was an insatiable sex god. We had the house to ourselves and began to get closer in the living room. Heavy petting, panting and foreplay ensued, and I pushed forward. But instead of getting that joyous, warm sensation, my willy was hit by a rough jolt which caused immense pain. On top of that, I was getting a strange feeling which can only be compared to a cocktail stick wiggling about in a bucket. After five minutes of very little pleasure and occasional agonizing stabs, I gave up and looked down, expecting to see my willy in tatters. Fortunately, I was still intact, but I found I had been shagging the gap between the cushions on the sofa. Instead of hitting her G-spot, I hit a metal spring and a copy of Reader's Digest.

Reveller's reward

It was Hogmanay and I was out with my friends with one goal in mind: to get absolutely melted. We went from pub to club and became steadily more drunk. Next, after closing, we headed to a party where we drank vast amounts of Jack Daniels and vodka. We were thoroughly shit-faced. The next thing I knew, I woke up in hospital, in a bed and with a great urge to go to the bathroom. But I could hardly move. After several moments of investigation, I discovered that this was due to me being coated in tin foil. Having struggled, eventually, out of the turkey wrapping and staggered to the toilet, I returned to my bed to find a doctor waiting for me, ready to lecture me on the dangers of drinking. I'd been found by an ambulance crew at 4.45am, two miles from the town centre, lying in a bank of snow. Apparently, I was lucky to be alive. The funny thing was, I found far more money in my trousers than I'd gone out with. I'd either robbed a charity box or been given change by people who had taken me for a homeless guy.

Bloody sex

I was once having a relationship with a girl who decided to get her bellybutton pierced. I was all for this, and was even more up for it when I saw how sexy it made her stomach look. I was so turned on, in fact, that we got down to some heavy petting, which was going along swimmingly until she decided to pull my jeans down for some more hardcore action. Somehow, in the heat of the moment, the button on my jeans got caught up in her bellybutton ring. And as she tugged my jeans she ripped down hard on the ring. Blood squirted from her stomach and she let out a howl. I quickly held a towel to the wound, hoping it was just a slight scratch. But when we pulled back the bloodsoaked towel we were horrified to find my girl's bellybutton, complete with ring, hanging at the end of a strip of skin. Instead of spending the summer with a beautifully exposed midriff my girlfriend ended up covering up a stitched wound, which turned into a hideous scar.

Sandwich horror

My girlfriend and I had been going out together for a couple of months when we decided we should go on holiday together. We thought a long weekend near one of the Scottish lochs would be romantic, so we set off in the car early one morning. A couple of hours into the journey, my girlfriend reached into her bag and got out a French stick sandwich she had prepared for the journey. As I was driving, I had no hands free, so she held it to my mouth for me to take a bite. I bit into the sandwich, which was ham, but felt something slightly hard between my teeth, so clamped down a little harder to get through the piece of 'gristle'. Only when I saw the look on my girlfriend's pale, shocked face, and looked at the blood dripping onto my lap, did I realize that I had bitten clean through to the bone in her finger. She later forgave me for the incident, but was scarred forever.

Drama down under

Some years ago my tank squadron was engaged in training exercises in the northern outback of Australia. We covered huge expanses of hot and hostile territory with a driver nicknamed Horse. After one very long drive, he stopped our truck, complaining that his face was burnt and he needed a break. Remembering a choice purchase during our last visit to town, I offered him a bowl filled with something that looked like Germolene to soothe his burn. Horse smeared it liberally all over his face. Within minutes, the poor bloke's head had ballooned up to twice its size, sending him careering off into the outback, followed by a swarm of red flying ants that were smitten by the smell of the freshly applied cream. Everybody stood with their mouths open as I admitted that Horse was running around like an idiot with 'Sammy Stay Hard' erection cream all over his face. He hasn't retaliated yet, but after-sun on my cock wouldn't seem nearly as bad.

Toilet predicament

Twenty-six years ago, I fractured my femur and ended up in the North Staffs Royal Infirmary. After six weeks of bed-pans I was finally ready to take my first trip to the bog, for which I was to travel on a converted wheelchair with a hole that went conveniently over the loo. The nurse said, 'Press the button when you've finished,' and left me to perform. Unfortunately the button was behind me and, as I went to press it, the wheelchair tipped; I ended up arse over tit between wall and toilet. Try as I might, I couldn't get anywhere near that frigging button, so I lay shouting for help with my lungs fit to burst. Only after about 20 minutes did the nurse come to release me from my predicament. A few days later I shat the bed, and to this day I can't decide which was the most embarrassing incident of the two.

Skate rink love tragedy

As a hospital porter I was in lust with a nurse who bore a striking resemblance to Ali McGraw in Love Story. Fancying myself as a bit of a Ryan O'Neal, I reckoned the way to tempt her into my trousers was to recreate the film's ice rink scene. On the rink I murmured casually, 'Watch me go backwards'. Next thing I knew, I was lying in the hospital we worked at with two broken wrists. Urgent questions began to present themselves. How was I going to pull my trousers down? How could I piss? The answer arrived with Ali McGraw tangling with my trunks, though not quite how I'd intended!

Glasgow kiss

When he was 18, my friend Simon was still a virgin, so as a favour I arranged for my girlfriend's best friend to come out on a double date. Before the event, he was very nervous, and full of questions about who should make the first move, and so on. However, his date was bowled over by him and the evening was a great success – or it was until he tried to kiss her good night outside her house. You see, Simon had a problem with his eyes, which meant he couldn't judge depths properly (his dire performances on the football field proved this). As she puckered up, he leaned in for the kill, thinking she was about six inches further away than she actually was... and bang! He was travelling at a fair rate of knots when he head-butted her on the bridge of her nose, so she reeled back, stepped onto the rockery, lost her balance and travelled uncontrollably into her father's car. End result? One heavily bleeding nose, one broken wing mirror, and one short-sighted man still in possession of his cherry.

Painful urination mistake

While touring the Lake District my friend drew my attention to the temperature gauge on my Fiesta, which was struggling to cope with the mountainous terrain. We pulled into the nearest lay-by and found the cooling system bone-dry. My friend began abusing and insulting the vehicle while I began searching for an appropriate receptacle in which to collect some water from a nearby brook. Realizing nothing was at hand, we decided to urinate into the expansion tank. I went first and the deed was completed without trauma. However, as my friend lined up his equipment with the filler cap a sudden surge of back pressure sent a hissing torrent of steam and boiling piss spewing from the orifice. My friend suffered no permanent damage, but to this day winces whenever he sees a Fiesta Popular.

Welsh accident

During my early teenage years, a bunch of mates and I would bike several miles to a river near Llangollen in north Wales. Here we had constructed a rope swing fairly high up on the bank, tied to the branch of a tree. We would swing out over the river and drop into the dark, still waters below – at times we must have reached a height of a good 20ft before letting go of the rope. Anyway, the years rolled by, and in May this year we went back to the area for a few beers near our old haunt. The day was hot and dusty, so we decided to nip down to the rope for a dip. We staggered along the riverbank, and before long one of my mates spotted an old rope swinging in the breeze. He tore off his clothes and ran at the rope, getting a great swing out over the river, and let go a good 25ft above the surface. To our horror, my mate splashed into just three feet of water and let out an horrific scream. It was the wrong place. He ended up with two broken ankles.

Nightmare at festival

Like many people, I attended my first big music festival in my late teens. I was hoping to take shed loads of drugs and have as much sex as possible for three whole days. And I wasn't disappointed. The long weekend of debauchery was everything I could possibly have hoped for. I danced, drank and smoked myself into a frenzy, frolicked in the fields with topless hippie chicks and shared a sleeping bag with several of them. Basically, I managed to have the best time of my life. On the final Sunday I realized the one traditional bit of festival fun I'd not had yet was the mud bath. The weather had been too good, but I saw a way round this. Cunningly, I directed the water from a standpipe tap onto a path, and turned it into a perfect mudslide. People were cheering as I stood at the top of the path and prepared for my run-up. They clapped as I dived belly-first into the quagmire. But they were soon dumbstruck as I screamed like a pig halfway through my slide. Embedded in the track, and unseen to me, was a large piece of broken beer bottle. As I slid, it sliced into my stomach, leaving a seven-inch gash. I was rushed to hospital and had 16 stitches. I've never been to another festival since.

Pylon shocker

A lad I know works on the oil rigs, on a two-weeks-on, two-weeks-off rota, and whenever he's home he always calls in on his old Dad to see if any jobs need doing. On this one occasion, his Dad had asked him to weed the end of the garden, so, spade in hand, he set about the task. After a short while, he became aware of a small stone in his boot, which he struggled to dislodge. This proved more and more difficult as the stone worked its way further into his boot, so he leant on the leg of a nearby electricity pylon to try to shake it out. At this point, his Dad, who was washing up, glanced out of the kitchen window to see his son 'stuck' to the pylon, shaking his leg like crazy. Thinking the worst, the old man ran out of the house, picked up a spade and twatted his son with all his might in an attempt to break the 'current'. Instead, all he succeeded in breaking was his poor son's arm.

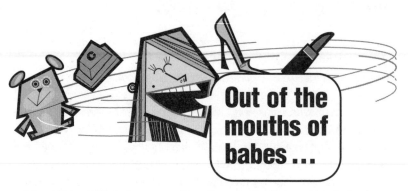

Out of the mouths of babes ...

My girlfriend Christine was telling her mates about a friend of mine who was on the England karate team, only for one of them to ask, "What song does he sing?"

Arriving at Heathrow, my sister squealed with excitement on seeing the air traffic control tower. "Oooh!" she exclaimed. "I've never seen a lighthouse before!" She's studying law at university.

Styling horror

While preparing for a lads' night out last year with five of my mates, I discovered one of them preening himself in the bathroom of my flat. Not wanting to get his hair sticky with gel or wax, my friend decided to use some of my girlfriend's hairspray. We took the piss out of him for a while, but after many beers forgot all about it. Later that night, my mate asked a girl to join him in drinking some flaming sambucas. However, due to the fact that he was less than coordinated after nine pints, he managed to spill the flaming liquid on his face. The mixture of fire and hairspray was disastrous, as his curly locks shot up. In the confusion the bloke next to him at the bar emptied a pint over his head; he succeeded in putting the flames out, but also covered a passing skinhead, who proceeded to punch the bloke and start a brawl. The only saving grace for my friend was that the blood he spilled covered up the burns on his face.

Unsafe sex

When I was a lad I joined a Youth Training Scheme, and one week we were taken on an Outward Bound course in the Brecon Beacons. Once there we found, to our dismay, that the girls were split from the lads for our sleeping arrangements. Naturally, the next week was spent sneaking to and fro, and generally getting together at night was the prime concern of us all. But my mate Paul was very inexperienced with girls, and one evening he asked me about condoms. I told him to make sure he covered it all up because he didn't want the horror of crabs. Anyway, this one night we were all in the girls' dorm, quietly trying to have our shags, when a terrible piercing scream came from one of the beds. Out jumped Paul, who had a look of excruciating pain on his face: the stupid idiot had pulled the condom open and snapped it over not just his penis but also his scrotum. The tightened johnny not only caused awful pain in his nuts but also scooped a healthy bunch of pubic hair, causing agony to my naive friend.

Fella caught

One Easter holiday, back at home from university, I decided to go down to my local gym. I'd been using the Uni gym for a while, so thought it would be great to use the luxurious, private gym near my house. I picked up my mate, Richard, and we went down to begin our session. The first exercise we did was a shoulder and back work-out, which involved holding a 30kg dumbbell in each hand. Then we'd shrug our shoulders back, holding the weights slightly apart and straight in front of us. Finally, we'd relax our shoulders and bring the weights back together in front of us. The first time we did this I nearly caught the front of my tracksuit bottoms, and thought, 'That was close.' Not as close as the second rep though: this time the momentum of the action caused the weights to clang together, catching my penis between the two metal ends of the dumbbell bars. The pain was, quite frankly, awesome. I dropped the weights, let out a high-pitched scream and fell over. Pulling down my trackies and skids, I saw a bloody pulp where my glans used to be.

Freak injury

When I was studying in Ireland, I took up rugby. As my first season wore on, the lads and I were eventually scheduled to play a team which had quite a reputation for violent play. Considering that we weren't the most talented outfit to have ever taken the field, we decided to accept the challenge with a 'do or die' attitude, hoping things would eventually swing our way. They didn't, and to make matters worse our star player, Alan, dislocated his hip after a particularly ferocious tackle. He was clearly in a lot of pain, so we all stood back to watch the medic who, in one swift movement, managed to slot the hip back into its socket. Then Alan began a long, blood-curdling scream. To our horror, we realized that one of his testicles had also been jammed into the socket, and was now firmly held in place by the hip. Incidentally, Alan managed to rip a vocal chord with his screaming.

Cosmetics inserted

A few weeks ago, in preparation for a romantic restaurant meal, my girlfriend decided to manicure her nails, even going to the extent of adding a few false ones. The meal was a success, and afterwards we headed home for some serious bedroom activity. In a frenzy of drunken foreplay I decided to stick an adventurous couple of fingers up her arse, and she immediately returned the favour. This lasted for a few minutes until her arm started to feel a little tired, so we knocked the fingering on the head and got down to business. Everything was fine until the following morning, when, during my morning visit to the toilet, I experienced a feeling of some discomfort. Assuming that my girlfriend had probably stretched my rectum with her enthusiastic finger-thrusting, I didn't panic; but after a few agonizing days I finally came to the conclusion that there was some serious damage up there, and reluctantly booked a trip to the doctor. It was then that I had the worst shit of my life – it felt like a herd of hedgehogs were passing through me. Afterwards, to my amazement, there was a bright red fingernail sitting in the bowl. Still, it saved me an expensive removal operation.

Chopping horror

A few years ago I was working on a YTS engineering course and I had a nasty accident, chopping the end off my right index finger with a milling machine. I was rushed to hospital where, luckily, they managed to sew my severed finger back on again. After several weeks, my bandages were removed and I was horrified to find the finger hadn't healed properly, and was still very scabby. It was a nasty sight, but the nurse assured me this was quite normal, and all would be well within a few weeks. Anyway, two weeks later I was indulging in some vigorous 'finger sex' with my girlfriend after the annual Judo Club Disco. When I'd finished pleasuring the lucky girl I was horrified to find that the end of my finger was missing! After a vigorous body search we eventually found the offending stub, and I'm happy to say my fingers are now all in one piece.

Plums impaled

When I was about 16, a mate and I were up to no good in one of our local parks on a Sunday afternoon. As it was getting a bit late, we decided to jog through the park and catch the bus home, pausing only to play a game of 'leapfrog' over some rusty metal fenceposts. My mate found the going hard as he was only 5ft 3in, and he eventually gave up in order to watch me hurl my 6ft frame over the posts. Sadly, as I gained momentum and attempted to hurdle the seventh – and last – post, my foot twisted in a divot. Unable to stop, I soared through the air, impaling my bollocks on the razor-sharp rusty tip and coming to an immediate halt with my feet hanging approximately six inches off the ground. Climbing off in agony, I discovered an inch-wide gash in my sack, with what looked like a white ball protruding from it. When my mother saw the damage, however, she just laughed, cleaned my wound and told me it would heal within few weeks. To cap it all, my pubic hairs grew into the cut as it healed, forcing me to split the new flesh as I pulled the little buggers out of my pustulous 'nad.

Inmate examined

While working as a medical student one hungover Monday morning, the consultant asked me to examine a patient. All would have been well, had the patient not been a huge prisoner with a severe case of rectal bleeding. To ensure he didn't escape, he was attached to a guard via a six-foot chain that went under the door. I donned the glove, and inserted my finger up to the knuckle. I then twisted my digit to examine the prostate gland, but in my still-drunken state gave it too much welly, and my fingernail ripped through the glove and sliced into his tender fudge pipe. Screaming with rage he leapt forward – ripping his arse more – followed by a thump and another scream as the guard was pulled off his seat and into the door.

Ironing board mishap

One afternoon, a friend had a few problems that required discussion over a few pints in the local pub. One thing led to another and before I realized the time, my friend and I had sunk one too many and staggered home. I was living in student accommodation at the time so the house was in a right state – shite everywhere – including the ironing board and iron just outside my room. Expecting my girlfriend to pick me up in an hour or so, I headed off to iron a shirt, but a tremendous fatigue entered my body and I thought, 'Well OK, just a quick lie down'. Six hours later I was woken by the telephone ringing. I crashed out of my room, knowing I was horribly late, at exactly the same time as one of my house mates picked up the phone and shouted to me that it was my girlfriend. To this day, I cannot explain or comprehend why I did what I did, but, on hearing my mate, I grabbed the iron thinking it was the telephone and felt it sizzle my cheek as I held it up to my ear. It had been on for six hours and by this stage it compared to the heat generated at the core of the earth. I looked in the mirror and saw V shaped indentations burnt onto my cheek. You could even see the holes where the steam comes out. The public humiliation lasted almost as long as the scar.

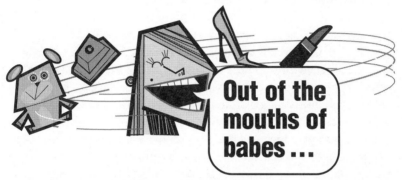

Out of the mouths of babes ...

Out shopping with my girlfriend, we bought a copy of the Big Issue. The vendor told us it was his last one. "You can go home now," my girl informed him, helpfully.

When a TV trail for Dr Zhivago came on, my wife said how sweet it was that they'd made a series about the man who started all those children's homes. She had a confused look when I explained about that nice Dr Barnardo.

Sticky wicket

While serving in the Royal Marines in Norway, my company was stationed in an isolated hotel, 60 miles from the nearest town. For entertainment, Saturday night usually consisted of a meal and lots of beer, followed by a an excursion into the cold air to have a piss. On one such night, one of the lads staggered out, had a slash, gave his little fella a shake, and turned to head back to the hotel. Unluckily, he walked straight into a metal dustbin before he had zipped up, and naturally his dick stuck fast to the minus 20 degrees metal. Ten minutes passed before we realized he hadn't returned and we dashed outside to find him walking backwards, pulling the bin along as if it was his lost friend. He thawed out at the hospital and returned two days later with a big bandage round his todger.

Brother aids recovery

A couple of days ago my brother was rushed to hospital with appendicitis, and underwent an emergency operation. Feeling slightly guilty that I hadn't realized the seriousness of the situation when he first complained of a sore abdomen, I walked to the hospital determined to cheer him up. When I got there he seemed rather depressed – he'd only been out of theatre for a few hours – so to raise a smile I leant over and gave his foot a brotherly tickle. He jumped, and gave a contented chuckle, and then blood started streaming through his robe. The movement had ripped out all the stitches, causing his stomach to split open and pump its contents onto the bed. Naturally, I didn't speak to him again until he was safely out of hospital.

Wipe last straw

A few years ago, while playing in an office five-aside game, I took a heavy knock which threw me against the goal post, damaging my right shoulder. The pain was unbearable, but although I whimpered off the park, I couldn't bring myself to cancel a dinner date with my girlfriend and her parents, who I was meeting for the first time. Dosed up on heavy duty painkillers, I went round to eat. Dinner went very well, and despite the occasional grimace, nobody seemed to notice my agony. After dessert, and some well-received double whiskeys, I stopped off at the toilet before heading home. As I reached round to wipe my arse however, I heard a sickening crack as my shoulder completely dislocated itself from the socket, leaving my trembling arm locked in full wipe position. Which is exactly how my girlfriend found me after I passed out, mid-scream.

Batteries included

One Christmas, about seven years ago, I was lying in bed in my parents' house watching TV. When I tried to change channel, I discovered that the remote wasn't working, and despite whacking it on the bedside table, it refused to come to life. It was bloody cold, so I took the batteries out and popped them under the pillow to warm some life into them. Five minutes later, still nothing, so I put them in the warmest place I knew – right between my buttocks. Then I realized that the batteries were leaking – the pain was incredible, and I ran to the bathroom. Keeping one leg on the floor, I lifted the other up into the sink, and furiously splashed water onto my burning starfish. It was then I realized I wasn't alone. My father had been woken by my groans, and was standing behind me with an extremely stern expression. Eventually he accepted my explanation, but he rarely lets me near the remote when I'm at home now.

Morning shaving incident

One morning, after staggering bleary-eyed from the shower, a glance in the mirror confirmed I needed a shave. As I had little faith in my hand-to-eye coordination so early on in the day, a wet shave was out of the question. I grabbed the electric shaver and switched it on. I don't remember which thoughts had crept into my semi-conscious mind, but they certainly had nothing to do with the job in hand. I stood looking at the razor, feeling its vibrations in my hand and listening to the hypnotic hum. Then I inexplicably brought it slowly towards my face and licked it. I stood motionless, transfixed by pain and mesmerized by my sheer stupidity, watching droplets of deep red blood rapidly appear and spread from the tiny grazes across the tip of my tongue. The bathroom mirror misted up once more. I was late for work.

Wheezing ignored

When I was at boarding school we slept in dorms. One night, I awoke to the sound of ferocious movement of sheets and heavy panting to my right. Knowing that the lad in that bed was an asthmatic, I went over to check that he was okay – only to find him secreted with a torch under his sheets, having the tug of his life. When he heard me chuckling, he emerged from his tent of sin and said that he would kick the crap out of me if I were to ever mention the incident. He was a big fella so I kept my mouth shut, and when I heard the same sounds a couple of nights later I turned over and tried to go back to sleep. Five minutes later, there was a thud, and I was greeted by the sight of the big man rolling on the ground, turning purple. He ended up in the medical centre, while I had a great night's kip.

Thick fog

Working as a care assistant, I was recently 'volunteered' to supervise a group of unruly kids on a canal barge trip. I soon understood why my work colleagues were so keen to stay in the office: four hours of navigating around dead dogs and shopping trolleys while attempting to control a load of screaming, hyperactive children. But suddenly, near the halfway mark, we hit a stretch of the canal blanketed by thick, odd, yellowish fog, apparently emanating from a house on the bank. There was nothing else for it: inspired by boredom and exasperation, I grabbed the set of bongos I kept below deck and sat cross-legged on the bow. As the barge drifted into the sepia gloom, I began to strike a tribal beat – and, grinning wildly, the kids began to dance. It was like something out of Apocalypse Now. We were still chuckling, in fact, when we got home. And then we were told there'd been a fire at a local chemical refinery, and one of the tanks had leaked toxic, sulphurous fumes across the area. With the noise of the engine, we hadn't heard local radio reports cautioning people to stay indoors. Three of the children had to spend the night in casualty before getting the all-clear, and I was promptly fired.

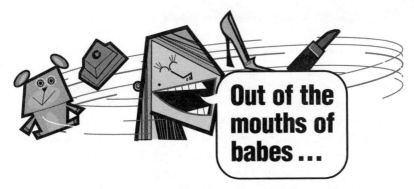

Out of the mouths of babes ...

Sitting round the breakfast table, my sister stared at the bottle of milk before asking how farmers could tell the difference between semi-skimmed and full-cream cows.

My mother-in-law was struggling with a celebrity crossword. "It's Sam somebody..." she said. I reeled off all the Sams I knew, to no avail. Then she said, "I've got it! Sam Anthamumba!"

Cock beheaded

Two weeks ago I was sitting watching TV with my girlfriend, when I decided the afternoon could be better spent performing lewd sexual acts. Leaning across to kiss her, I moved my hands down to her trousers and undid the first button, only to be stopped dead in my tracks and sweetly told that this was one of her 'special' days in the month. Determined to extract some gratification from the moment and noticing that her tight trousers were made of Spandex, I decided some mutual rubbing may be in order, and placed my penis between her legs. The subsequent frottage quickly reached a frantic pace, but as I embarked on my vinegar strokes there was a very quiet 'ping', followed by an agonizing rip. Looking down, I was confronted by horror. My foreskin had been ripped off entirely, exposing a huge blue vein that was spraying blood everywhere. On arrival at the local hospital, a nurse gingerly held my pecker for examination – and I immediately grew another stonker, requiring a further two agonizing stitches. I'm now fully prepared to become a monk.

Copper caught short

I'm a police officer, and a few years ago I was out on night patrol with my shift partner, Dave. The sarge radioed us and explained that there had been a death at a nearby top-floor flat, and that he would meet us there. When we arrived we found an old dear, completely dead, with her head resting on the toilet seat – tragically, she had passed away while attempting to vomit. I went into the living room and began filling out the forms, when the sarge suddenly got another call, and shot off, taking Dave with him. Ten minutes later I had finished the forms, and now had a more pressing problem – I was desperate for a pee, and couldn't use her sink as it was full of washing. I lasted about an hour-and-a-half before I could take no more. Straddling the old woman, I let rip; using all my skill to keep the golden stream about three inches from her wrinkled face. At that moment the sarge walked in, followed by Dave, two undertakers and the woman's middle-aged daughter. To round things off, I zipped up so quickly that the daughter saw me splash warm piss dribble all over her dead mother's head.

Roundabout drop-off

Some time back, on returning from a trip to America, I collected my BMW from the car park, and started the drive back home. In an attempt to avoid the motorway traffic, I decided to stick to the back roads. Then, as I pulled up at a mini roundabout, I was stunned to see a man lying in the middle of it, bleeding profusely and unable to speak. I called an ambulance, but five minutes later, a car came screeching to a halt next to us. A bloke leapt out and said, 'Oh thank God, there he is.' Apparently, the victim had also arrived on a flight, but had cleared customs so drunk he could hardly walk. In an attempt to get him home without puking, his mate had put him on the back seat, where he'd chosen to sit with his head hanging out the window to get a bit of air. As they hit the roundabout, the door had swung open, sending the fool flying into the road. The driver had gone on for five minutes before he had realized what had happened. Amazingly, the drunk recovered during this story, decided to headbutt his friend and a fight started in the lay-by. They didn't even notice me leave.

Student scorched

During my final year at university I lived in a student house with a
Scouser and other assorted drunken yobs, where we had a tradition:
whoever lasted longest on the piss would set off the smoke alarm on
their return home. So it came as no surprise at 3am one morning to be
woken by an alarm. Placing a pillow over my head, I waited for the
triumphant drinker to reset the alarm and head off for bed. However,
after ten minutes it became obvious that something was different, as a
girl's screams penetrated the electronic wail. I tumbled out of my pit
and followed the screams to the Scouser's room, where I was greeted by
the sight of his bird jumping up and down on the bed, half naked,
waving a sheet at the smoke alarm – while the Scally ran about with his
dressing gown on fire. It turned out that when his girlfriend had
spurned his offer of a night of lurve, he'd waited till she was asleep
then, bored, started lighting his own farts – until he produced such a
ripper that he set his nightwear on fire. After extinguishing the flames,
we of course called him Ring of Fire for the rest of his university life – a
fact I shall remind him of when I attend his wedding this summer.

Gent's confusion

It was my stag night and I was out with a bunch of mates. We
followed our old pub crawl route and were about halfway down the
card when, several pints and a gallon of Nelson's blood later, the call
of the porcelain was sounded. The pub we were in had been
refurbished so I made enquiries and staggered, head down, in the
direction of the bog. It took forever to fight my way through the
crowd but, finally, I reached the white door I had been seeking. My
back teeth were floating, so I cared little for decorum. Therefore, I
unzipped as I opened the door, and had myself in hand ready for
immediate release. Pissed and bladder driven, I crashed through the
white door to find myself faced by another. I blundered through this
second door and, in my head-down position, marvelled at the extent
of the refurbishment. There was carpet, loud music, flashing lights ...
and atmosphere. I raised my head to locate the shiny white bowl, only
to find myself, dick in hand, confronted by a roomful of gaping

revellers frozen by the shock of what they saw. Not to mention two large bouncers heading in my direction. Mustering all the dignity I could, I glanced round the room, shouting back through the door, 'No, he's not in here!' I retreated and vacated the pub, gathering the lads as I went. We bundled out of the boozer, giggling and farting as we went, with me pissing at the same time – and with the angry shouts of the bouncers ringing in my ears. At this point, my prospective father-in-law – having been stupid enough to accompany me in the first place – made his excuses and went home, after leaving me in no doubt as to what would happen if I failed to make it to the wedding ceremony on time. Fortunately, I did.

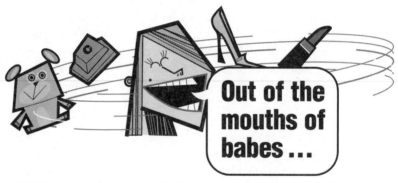

Out of the mouths of babes ...

Walking past the Greenwich Observatory, my sister helpfully pointed out, "That was where time was invented."

Watching the news with my wife, it was announced that, sadly, Richard Harris had died. "What will happen to Orville?" my beloved wailed.

Karate cock-up

In the middle of an all-day drinking binge with a friend of mine – who happened to be a karate instructor – we decided to pay a visit to a house where several of our friends lived, to stretch the day's fun as far as possible. Then all of us went into town to a pub, where, with the usual brash bravado, play-fights started to develop. My friend, who was very much the worse for wear, then decided to challenge everyone to a karate battle. Naturally, everybody declined, which led to the drunken martial arts instructor becoming more and more agitated. He loudly proclaimed that he could whip anyone with just his little finger, which was met with howls of derision. He next shouted that he could beat everyone with his ear, his eye and, finally, with his cock. When this final bullshit claim produced no takers, he unzipped his jeans, pulled out his flaccid johnson and began waving it in the air shouting, 'I could have you with this!' What he hadn't noticed was that the window – which made up one side of the pub – had filled with dozens of curious on-lookers, all of whom were loudly applauding his humiliating performance. To this day, he's still known in town as 'Maggot'.

Lavatorial mêlée

A few months ago a friend and I went on a real bender. Nothing extraordinary about that, you might think, except that we live in a part of London with less nightlife than a Norfolk village, and it was already 10.30pm. However, we decided to try an illicit drinking den in our manor which was, reportedly, open all night. Amazingly, we got in, and proceeded to neck premium-strength imported lager at speed. After a few hours a bloke sat in my chair as I was buying a round. I asked him to move, but he ignored me and when my mate went to the bog I simply sat in his vacant chair. A few seconds later the ignorant man got up and followed my friend to the toilet, so I followed to check nothing untoward was happening. As I swung open the bog door I saw my mate holding his nose, and sprinted to get the huge bouncer on the door. He steamed into the toilet, dragged the man out and kicked the living shit out of him, before turfing him out into the night. Only later did my friend tell me that all he was doing was blowing his nose, while the poor chap who took a leathering calmly had a slash.

Filthy cocktail

At a college party several months ago, I found myself in the kitchen, drunk, and messing about with a knife. My friend and I were taking turns spinning the knife in the air and trying to catch it by its handle as it came down. Naturally, after several drunken attempts I missed the handle and grabbed the knife by the blade, causing a really deep gash in my finger. In our pissed state, my friend and I deemed the wound not serious enough for a trip to the hospital, and decided to drain my blood into a glass before attending to the wound. We did this successfully, managing to get about a third of a glassful of blood, which we topped up with vodka, Worcestershire Sauce and a few drops of Tabasco. We gave the drink a swirl, and decided to present it to the next person to walk into the kitchen. I would just like to take this opportunity to say to my mate Laney: that's the most authentic Bloody Mary you'll ever have.

Manmade cocktail

Having been recently dumped by my girlfriend, my mates decided that I needed cheering up and dragged me down the local nightclub. I was having a brilliant time, when the ex suddenly walked in with her new boyfriend in tow. Spotting me, the pair performed a victory snog right in front of me, before heading for the bar. Determined to dish out a suitable punishment, I nipped to the toilet where, with the help of several revellers, I filled a pint glass with warm pee, and headed out to the bar where they were standing. My plan was to launch the pint over my shoulder catching them square in the face with piss, but as my arm shot up, I noticed that they were watching my every move. Panicking, I tried to stop my arm, but succeeded only in pouring the frothy liquid straight over my head and down my back. They laughed so much, one of the bouncers brought over some chairs, shortly before throwing me out.

Drunken high jinks

Walking home after an evening of heavy drinking several years ago, a couple of friends and I decided, irresponsibly and in typical sad 15-year-old style, to do a spot of vandalism to liven up our dull journey through the rain. On the first quiet street we walked down we pulled up several 'For Sale' signs, and used them for spot of improvized 'street jousting'. This was followed on the next street by 'hedge diving', and in the third street we played 'steal the bike saddle'. On the fourth street we came to we were pleased to see that a row of traffic cones had been lined up around a workman's hole, obviously positioned there for three drunk gits to kick into the street for a game of football. We walked along, taking turns to thwack the cones as far as we could. At the last cone, I decided to really go for glory, and took a long run up before aiming a vicious Lorimer of a kick at a Ford Escort that was parked right in front of me. Tragically, the workmen had obviously planned ahead. They'd placed the last cone over a concrete bollard, and I subsequently spent six weeks in plaster with three broken bones in my foot.

Barfing blunder

My girlfriend and I arrived late at her boss's house party so, to make up for lost drinking time, I started to gulp down the free-flowing wine. Suddenly, I felt very ill and rushed to the bathroom. On arrival, I couldn't find the light. As I was in a desperate hurry, instead of feeling for the loo, I headed for a chink of light which turned out to be the window, and just managed to get my head out in time. When my eyes cleared, I realized that below me was the glass roof of the conservatory where the party was going on. I went cold when I saw the puke sliding slowly down the roof and the sea of appalled faces – including my girlfriend's boss – staring up at me through the glass.

Bursting bladder

Arriving late for a party after a few drinks in the pub I charged upstairs to the toilet, only to find it engaged. Luckily it was one of those houses in which the bath was in one room and the loo in another. Desperate and bursting, I figured I would simply piss in the tub, so I lunged for the bathroom. After 30 seconds spent fishing unsuccessfully for the string light-pull, I shuffled into the near blackness, bumped into the bath and gratefully let rip. One hour later, the hostess mentioned to me that the dozen mini-trifles, two jellies and the gateau we'd just eaten had spent the earlier part of the evening defrosting – in the bath.

Fatal attraction

Unwanted attention is frustrating at the best of times, but during the three years of your life when you're supposed to be nobbing yourself lame, it's positively infuriating. At university I was unlucky enough to attract the attention of the most irritating girl on campus. She was fat, noisy, always stuck her nose in where it didn't belong, and followed me around with a look of puppy dog adoration on her face no matter how often I told her to go away. After several months of this style cramping I'd had enough, and I told anyone who cared to listen that I was sick of her and I was going to put a stop to her evil ways. One night in the bar I was drunkenly ranting to some friends about what a cow she was when, unseen to me, she sat down just behind me. I had become highly animated by this point and told everyone that I would like to knock her out. I illustrated this by swinging a giant haymaker. Unfortunately, I swung right round and lamped the girl in the face, knocking her clean out of her seat, and splattering her face with blood. Everybody assumed I'd done it deliberately and for months I was labelled as a woman-beater, while she became very popular as the innocent victim.

Public oration

During the summer of 2000, I had the good fortune to be invited to a friend's wedding in the north-west of England. The best man has always been known to like a drink, but we were somewhat surprised at how quickly he succeeded in getting pissed on the day itself. The reason, he explained in a drunken slur, was that he had forgotten his speech, and was suffering a sudden bout of nerves. But he seemed to have pulled himself together by the time the reception started, and when the groom's polite thanks came to a close, everyone was ready for a few entertaining stories from the best man. Standing up, he slowly unzipped his trousers, pulled out his manhood, and announced to the stunned crowd, which naturally included several elderly relatives, 'I have a massive cock.' Then he sat down and clapped like a rabid baboon. Incidentally, he has never been seen since.

Reveller repulsed

During the Christmas party season in London, every late-night tube home is packed with drunks – which is how I found myself opposite a smartly dressed middle-aged woman who must have had one too many and fallen asleep. Sitting beside her was a scruffy old wino who was drifting in and out of consciousness and swaying all over the place, finally slumping with his head inches above the woman's arm. A stream of green, lumpy mucus then began to stream out of the old lush's mouth, falling into a neat pile on the woman's arm, until the train bumped into a station and the old man slumped in the other direction. The woman jerked awake, and as her eyes opened she caught sight of the green slime on her sleeve. Before my astonished eyes, assuming it was her own, she greedily gobbled up the old man's mucus.

Sad toilet episode

I was standing in the lavatory during a rugby international at Twickenham, when in lurched a smartly dressed but obviously drunk middle-aged chap. On reaching the latrine, he unzipped his fly and pulled out what he thought was his penis and began to pee. Unfortunately it was his testicle he had in his hand and consequently a large stain appeared down his leg along with a growing pool of urine around his shoe. Oblivious to everything, he finished, shook off his testicle, zipped up his fly and wandered out.

Hi-fi incontinence error

I was sharing a house with three friends and we had decided to throw the customary house warming party. The usual preparations were made – turning the TV to face the wall, putting up little direction signs to the toilet, filling the fridge with thirty quid's worth of lager etc. However, a party would not be much of a party without music, and so my flatmate Justine's Panasonic ME 109 turbo bastard midi-system was brought out into the living room.

As parties went, this was a bloody good one. At about 3am, my eyelids grew heavy with lager and I nodded off on the settee. Sometime the next morning, I was rudely awoken by Justine, who was very pissed off, and subjected me to a barrage of foul-mouthed insults. What the hell had I done? Justine pointed to her pride and joy, the Panasonic. 'Lift up the lid,' she demanded. I did as I was told, then immediately wished I hadn't. There, lying curled around the centre pin of the record turntable was a huge and perfectly formed turd! Oh no! I had 'given birth to an otter' on top of six hundred quid's worth of Japanese technology. A dim memory of getting up for a crap in the night came back to me. I decided to lie. I denied everything and blamed it on one of the guests. Amazingly, she believed me. But Justine, if you should ever read this, I am very, very sorry, but it was me who shat on your stereo...

Nightmare on 16th green

Needing a crap on the way home from a day-time drinking session with some college friends, I managed to persuade my boozing buddies to take a short-cut across the golf course so I could have a dump on their private, well-manicured lawns. However, much to the amusement of my mates, I decided to squat over the hole on the 16th green and let a perfect turd slip into the cup. We then retired to the safety of the trees as a group of players appeared on the horizon. They played up to the green, and met with our polite applause as they neared the hole and their final putts. Finally, the star player, with much posturing, sank his putt, and strutted over to the hole to smugly retrieve his winning ball. Then everything seemed to go into slow motion as he knelt down, still grinning at the crowd, lowered his hand into the hole and slowly withdrew his ball. As he looked down, his face became confused, then contorted, as he realized that his hand, and his ball, were speckled with smudges of shit. He didn't even have the decency to yell 'Fore!' as he threw caution to the wind and launched the brown-stained projectile at the cackling drunks who were by now legging it through the rough.

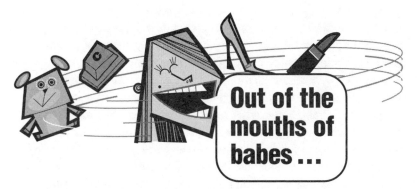

Out of the mouths of babes ...

In the pub, I asked my girlfriend's friend if she could tell me the cricket score, as my view of the TV was obscured. "Seventeen-nil!" she proudly exclaimed.

Organising the Royal Naval Air Station Yeovilton International Air Day, I took a phone call from a lady asking if it was to be an indoor event. The Red Arrows were due to appear!

Piss-up goes awry

My father used to meet up with his two brothers every year for the
Rugby League Challenge Cup final at Wembley. One year, after
watching the match, they went to a pub for a few bevvies. During the
course of the evening, my uncle came back from the toilets in a panic.
He told my dad and other uncle they had to drink up and leave at
once. They did this, and while looking for another pub, my dad
demanded an explanation. My uncle talked of that moment when your
eyes get accustomed to the dark and things become clearer. Well, he'd
just been to the toilet and it was dark there, so he pissed against the
wall, knowing the urinals had to be there somewhere. As his eyes
became accustomed to the dark, however, he noticed a TV in the
corner of the room, then a dressing table appeared, then a bed, then,
finally, the stark realization that he was pissing against the wall of the
landlord's bedroom.

Golden showers

One hot day last year I went to an all-day music festival with a bunch
of mates. Because of the enormous crowd it took ages to fight our
way to the front for the best view. Unfortunately, because we had
spent the entire morning drinking, by the time we were in pole
position we were all desperate for a pee. Unwilling to lose our hard-
won vantage point we were resigned to spending the next few hours
in agony, until one bright spark realized that we could piss into our
now empty plastic beer glasses and then drop them over the other
side of the crowd barrier. Bladders now emptied, we relaxed to enjoy
the bands. Unluckily for us, as the sun grew hotter the security guards
began to work their way along the barrier, throwing pints of water
onto the parched crowd. Far too late for us to escape we realized that
this water was also in plastic pint glasses, placed strategically behind
the crowd barrier. We stood helpless and unable to move as the
bouncers got to where we were and threw seven pints of warm, fresh
piss all over us.

Night bus incident

A few months ago, having been out for a few drinks with some friends, I decided to catch the bus home. As I strolled to the bus stop I saw the bus coming – there's only one an hour at that time of night – and dashed to catch it. Luckily the driver waited for me and I boarded the bus. I sat down in a seat next to a group of fairly drunk girls, and before long I was desperate for a pee. There was no way I was getting off and waiting another hour for a bus, so I tried to think of other things. The girls got talking to me and I found myself in the odd position of having to control my bladder while I was being chatted up. Every bump, corner and sudden stop was a nightmare as I strained to control my bladder. Finally, I had a bright idea. I pulled out my fags and made my way to the top deck. Luck! Nobody was up there, so had a long, joyous pee, taking care to put my jacket over the driver's spy-mirror. I zipped up and went downstairs, only to be sworn at, pushed and hit by the previously friendly girls. What I didn't know was that there were drains on the top deck, and my pee had gone down one and back in the sliding window – all over the girls.

Shower refuge

While out on a session, a mate and I pulled two nice looking ladies, and went back to their house for what promised to be a great night. I ended up in the kitchen getting the best blow job of my life, when there was a knock at the door. My girl looked up at me in complete horror – it was her boyfriend, so my mate and I were dispatched to the bathroom to wait for him to leave. We stood there for half-an-hour – me holding a bottle of shampoo as a defensive weapon, and my pal clutching a soap-on-a-rope – until we heard grunting from downstairs. We crept down to be greeted by the sight of a man-mountain giving my bird the best shag of her life. The guy could clearly hurt us, so we scuttled back to the bathroom. Ten minutes passed, and we heard footsteps on the stairs. The door burst open, and in walked the man, naked. Failing to notice us, he started having a piss. Knowing that as soon as he finished he would turn and see us, we looked at each other, nodded, and charged him. I twatted him around the head with the shampoo and my mate slapped him around the arse with the soap. We charged down the stairs and out the door, pausing only to look back at a redbottomed man, staring at us in utter disbelief.

Frothy pint

While in Gibraltar with the navy, some friends and I decided to go out on a sightseeing trip. We were joined by an old steward – all tattoos and no teeth – who had invited himself along. While we were having a few beers in a café, our sweaty guest suddenly nipped off to the bar and returned with some cheese and onion crisps. He didn't eat them however, and it was only when one of the lads went for a pee that their purpose became apparent. Having opened the pack, he beckoned over the owner's poodle. Then, while the dog happily munched away, the dirty sod reached down and started to toss it off. With a little whimper the dog finally shot his puppy paste, which the steward promptly scooped into our man's pint. Having been ordered not to say a word, we could only stare in disbelief when our pal returned and downed his poodle-top beer in one. To this day I finish my pint before going to the toilet.

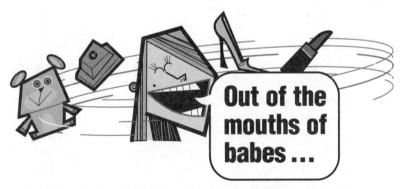

Out of the mouths of babes ...

At a party, we were playing "Six Degrees Of Kevin Bacon" – connecting any movie to the eponymous film star through six actors or less. My girlfriend set me a tough one: Footloose. Starring, er, Kevin Bacon.

Watching Executive Decision with my girlfriend, we came to the part where the two planes were hooked together. After popping out to answer a call of nature, I asked her what had happened in my absence. "The pilot ejaculated," she answered innocently.

Water-gun pranks

On Christmas Day in 1995, I was lucky enough to find myself on the other side of the world, in Sydney, Australia. Twenty-five or so close friends and I were enjoying a marvellous barbecue in the sweltering weather, complete with cold beers and plenty of party games. One girl, Liz, who had drunk enough Castlemaine XXXX to stun the Wallabies, amused herself for several hours by running around with a high-powered water rifle, and took great delight in shooting powerful jets of water at unsuspecting friends. This was quite funny for an hour or two, but pretty soon people began to get a bit tired of having their beer and backs watered down every five minutes. Eventually I snatched the watergun off her, leaving her to find some other form of amusement. I then took the rifle into the khazi and filled it with piss. Back at the barbie, I set about finding the original shooter, who, when I tracked her down, proved to be a good sport. Instead of running away she simply lay down on the grass, laughing. She urged me to 'fill her up' and opened her mouth. Needless to say, I complied, and directed a hot, high-powered jet of pee straight into her wide open mouth. Revenge has perhaps never been sweeter, although Liz left the following day for Tasmania.

Toe trouble

Back in the mid-Nineties I was asked to go camping by mates, sharing a tent with my girlfriend. We happy campers had a great first night, drinking copiously around the fire in a field in the middle of nowhere. Once we'd retired to my tent, my girlfriend got the horn, and after drunkenly undressing we were soon at it like rabbits, before dropping off into a booze-fuelled sleep. Naturally, I awoke a few hours later dying for a piss, so wandered out into the darkness to take a leak. On my return I found my girl awake and ready to go again – and as that ginger sponger Fergie was all over the papers at the time, she treated me to five minutes of toe-sucking. Next morning we awoke to a dreadful smell, prompting my girlfriend to quit the tent in search of breakfast. I then peeled back the sleeping bag-to find both my feet encrusted in dried cow-shit from my small-hours ramble. Except, of course, the one big toe my missus had lovingly caressed the night before.

Pub lunacy

About ten years ago I worked as a barman in one of Bolton's roughest pubs. There was nothing the regulars wouldn't do for a drink, and during my time there I saw men drink their own piss and scoff horse shit. The worst moment came when one of the locals bet another that he wouldn't eat a handful of maggots for a pint. The chap agreed, and after a quick trip round to the fishing tackle shop, an ashtray of maggots was produced. The cheers went up, the maggots went down, and the pint was won. But it didn't end there. The next day the maggot eater came bursting out of the toilet and demanded we went and had a look. Amazingly, some of the little buggers had made it right through his system alive, and were wriggling round in the water. 'I bet you wouldn't eat them now,' one of the lads jokingly said to the man. He did.

Romeo's urination blunder

In my first month at college I started going out with a girl and, after a while, the time came to meet Mum and Dad. A few pints were needed to help me pluck up the courage just to knock on the front door. A while later, brimming with beer and tea, I went to the bathroom, but could find neither a switch nor a cord to turn on the light. In the dark, I found the sink, into which I relieved myself, rather than wasting any more trouser-threatening seconds, then briefly ran the tap and merrily skipped downstairs. I soon noticed a distinct cooling of relations between me and this family. Glances were exchanged. No-one talked. My girlfriend, no longer holding my hand, sat at the far end of the settee. Having eventually said my goodbyes, I was hurried to the front door by my girlfriend, who said, 'Did you piss in the sink?' Then I realised – the plug! It must have still been in the plughole! That was the end of our relationship.

Lucrative sickie

A couple of years ago me and my flatmate worked for a large company organizing staff incentives, to which we invariably managed to invite ourselves. One such freebie involved taking 30 wage-slaves to a restaurant in London's Chinatown one Friday night. Due to the amount of alcohol I'd previously consumed I couldn't face any Chinese food, but nevertheless carried on drinking until I could hardly walk. The rest of the weekend consisted of hair of the dog, while my mate put his sickness and diarrhoea down to too much wine – but come Monday he was still doubled up in pain. I phoned work on his behalf, when my boss told me that 24 of the people who'd been out that evening had also called in with food poisoning, so naturally I jumped on the bandwagon and, hungover, claimed a couple of sick days myself. I left the company a year later, but three months ago I received a letter from my old employers stating that the Chinese restaurant had admitted responsibility for the food poisoning, and due to the distress were enclosing a cheque for £1,027.50. Now, every time I look at my new dining table and chairs, I happily recall the most profitable hangover I've ever had.

Drunken horror

Several years ago, I was flicking through a listings magazine when I saw an advert for a club in Soho which was having a party to celebrate the release of the film Return Of The Living Dead, telling people to come dressed as zombies with the best zombie outfits getting in for free. Well, getting in the mood with a bottle of whisky and a bottle of port, a mate and I, with the help of my girlfriend, made ourselves up. For some reason I decided I would wear a skirt and blouse, and after covering ourselves in mud and flour and suitably ripping up our clothes, we staggered out into the night. Sadly, on arrival at the club, we found the party had been cancelled. Undeterred, we decided to get a few more bottles and do a tour of Soho. This went well, save for occasional bemused looks from passers-by. Later, at some hazy point, my mate chucked me onto a night bus. I fell asleep in the luggage compartment and woke up at half past eight the next morning in a shop doorway, with Saturday morning shoppers looking on in horror at the white-faced transvestite zombie with port-coloured puke all over 'herself'. I have to say I walked home in shame, some brave soul having robbed my pockets of my cab fare. Isn't it amazing how many of your neighbours clean their cars on a Saturday morning?

Hooker chunders

Several years ago my rugby team went on its annual coach tour of France. Our hooker at the time was notorious for his excessive booze intake, and by the time we reached Dover, he was ready to burst – which he promptly did, puking up his ring into an empty burger bag. Drunk and weak, he then shoved it up into the skylight and went to sleep. Mercifully, we travelled 120km across France without further incident. When the coach arrived at our town, a small Renault cut us up at the lights, causing the bus driver to slam on the brakes. At that moment our hooker was walking back up the bus and was suddenly catapulted headlong down the aisle. The putrid, freezing carton of sick shot out of its resting place and twatted him straight in the face, exploding on impact. To cap things off, the stench caused another nine hardened players to puke into their laps.

Work skiver

Bunking off work one fine summer's day several years ago, I put my free time to good use by going on the piss with a couple of friends. We went into town nice and early, and got stuck into some serious drinking. As we staggered from pub to pub we got caught up with another gang of merry-makers, and they joined us in our drinking session. During the course of the afternoon I vaguely remember marching down the high street with a big gang of lads, laughing and shouting and generally having fun. I finally got home some time in the small hours, horribly drunk, but happy. At work the next day I used my hangover as cover, saying I'd had a 24-hour bug which left me bed-ridden. The smiles which greeted me left me suspicious, but it was only when I saw the front page of the local newspaper that I clicked that my drinking bender had been rumbled. There I was on the front page, a huge smile across my face, with a can of beer in one hand, arms slung around another couple of fellows, underneath the headline 'Gay rights march takes over city centre'.

Exit error

The Saturday before Wales played England in the first Six Nations Rugby championships, my wife and I decided to go on a bender in our local pub. After a heavy afternoon's drinking we had decided to head home, when it came to my attention that the England International, Garath Archer, had been leaning against my wife, inebriated. Being a passionate Welshman, and fired up by the forthcoming match, I spun around as we reached the exit, raised a triumphant arm and hollered 'Wales!' at the top of my voice.
Mortified by the sudden silence that ensued, my wife bundled me through the door, and it was then that we realized the extent of our mistake. Instead of the car park, we were, rather worryingly, standing in the gents toilets. When we emerged they were all waiting for us, and what felt like a hundred silent smirking faces watched our departure as we sheepishly shuffled through the crowd to the exit. Incidentally, England stuffed us a week later.

Light bulb craze

A few weeks ago, after a mind-melting Saturday night on the town, my mates and I headed home for a few vodka nightcaps. After sinking the best part of a bottle, one of the chaps suddenly informed us that if you force a light bulb into your mouth, its particular size and shape apparently forces your jaw to lock. Obviously one of us had to put this theory to the test, and sure enough, within 20 minutes, the four of us were in a taxi on our way to hospital to have a light bulb removed from a locked jaw. After queuing for several hours, we were finally seen by a sympathetic doctor who unscrewed the metal part of the bulb, inserted a small cloth and carefully smashed the glass. Fortunately, other than a sore mouth, my mate wasn't injured, so we headed for home. Just as we were leaving however, a sheepish-looking man walked in with a light bulb wedged in his mouth. It was none other than the same taxi driver who had driven us to the hospital four hours earlier.

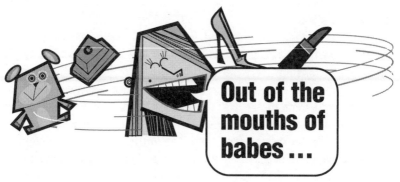

Out of the mouths of babes ...

My father bought an antique wireless radio. Showing it to my girlfriend of the time, he explained that it needed to warm up, before tuning it in to Radio One. "Oh my God!" exclaimed my woman, bewitched. "It plays modern music!"

Watching a TV ad for Durex where men dressed up as sperm followed a bloke around, one of my female friends piped up: "What have spring onions got to do with condoms?"

Spewing mishap

The bastard bolted out of nowhere and hammered into my jaw with the top of his skull, smashing it up and sending me straight to hospital. But there is a fine tradition in our rugby club. Even when sent to hospital, you're still expected to attend the post-match drinkfest – body-cast, crutches and all, if need be. My jaw was wired shut. It didn't hurt so much; my doctor knows some wonderful drugs. Despite the tangle of teflon wires, I could still part my lips enough to stick a straw into my mouth. I could drink! Four or five pints later, my mates had left me leaning against a wall, facing the dancefloor, when a strangely familiar taste began to creep into my mouth. Mere seconds passed before my stomach went into overdrive. I retched. Hard. But my clenched jaws refused to open. So, instead of blowing big chunks harmlessly to the floor, the pressure of the retching caused me to spray a fine mist of puke through my teeth, and giving it quite a distance. The hapless dancers in front of me soon realized what was happening and fled in all directions. It was like watching the victims of Pompeii in a vain attempt to escape the vile drizzle. When, at last, it seemed as if the rain of digestive juices and warm beer had ceased, the chunks that had lodged against the back of my teeth began to slither down my throat, causing me to barf anew. Any stragglers that had stayed behind were spewed again with fresh vomit. There was no more dancing after that.

Fire fighter

In the summer of 1993, my friend – whom I'll refer to only as Corky – was considering applying to join the fire service. I was in the pub one night with Corky when a girl ran in shouting that there was a burning car outside. Corky, by now in a drunken stupor, seized his chance of gaining firefighting credentials and ran out to assess the situation. Through the plumes of smoke, Corky could just make out a figure slumped against the steering wheel. Ignoring the advice of boozed-up onlookers, he ran to the blazing car, opened the door and attempted to extract the driver. Suddenly, a fire engine arrived: two real firemen jumped out and struggled to remove my choking friend from the wreck. Corky was treated for smoke inhalation and second-degree burns, and was whisked off, unconscious, to the local hospital. Two hours later, he came round, expecting a hero's reception – only to discover that the 'body' was the driver's seat slumped forward, with a furry seat cover hanging from the 'head'.

Academy regurgitation

A few years back, I decided to attend a police training course for my local constabulary. About 50 of us hopefuls were sent to a country retreat for a week; after tests during the day, we all went out and partied in the evening. One night, just before the course finished, I returned to my room, incredibly pissed, and crashed out on the floor. Next morning, rather worse for wear, the contractions started in my stomach and I knew I was about to honk, but as I didn't have time to make it to the toilet and I didn't want to mess up the room, I chucked up out of my fifth-floor window, then went to breakfast. As I entered the canteen, I spotted the chief instructor and ten recruits peering out of the window of the quadrangle at a commotion that was going on outside. Shitting myself, I looked out over the shoulders of the huddle, where I saw a swarm of flapping seagulls fighting over the choice cuts from my spew. Not only that, but there was a trail of sick over the outside ledge of the windowto my room. Strangely, I never made it as a copper.

Rollercoaster hurling worry

It was my birthday and I had a stinking hangover from a heavy night's drinking, so I tried the traditional cure – a full English breakfast, washed down with a ceremonious pint of lager. Later, some friends were treating me to a free day at the infamous Liverpool show in Wavertree. We headed straight for the beer tent, sunk three pints and moved on to the rides. 'The Enterprise' was the first, a rollercoaster featuring a daring swoop from 30ft, with a finale of death rolls. I was loving it, until the death rolls, when my breakfast and beer decided to part company with my stomach. It was like a scene from Hellraiser II or The Exorcist, I was a 360° human vomit spraying machine. I got off the ride slightly dazed, and staggered to the toilet to splash my face, where I saw a distinctly beefy man swearing and cursing by the wash basin. He shouted, 'Some bastard threw up over my new jacket.' He then noticed that I had vomit all over me, and his eyes narrowed in anger. Somehow able to think straight, I quickly said, 'Oh yeah? Me too!'

Drinker unloads

Many years ago I attended a friend's stag party in London. All the usual shenanigans took place, but although there was many a tale of woe to be told the next morning, I somehow managed to avoid embarrassing myself. Rather pleased, I headed home, but trying to steer down the motorway made me realize that I was in no fit state to be in charge of a car, and by the time I reached Brighton I desperately needed to vomit. Pulling over on a quiet street, I hurriedly wound down the window and leaned out. Sadly, a pair of nice old pensioners, out enjoying a morning stroll, decided that I must be stopping to ask for directions, and approached the car with big smiles. They came right up, and in a frail, quivering voice, one asked 'Yes, dear?' And then, with a mighty roar, I disposed of a gutload of beer and carrots straight onto their feet. Desperate to get away from the hapless duo, I looked straight ahead, wound the window up, and drove off, pausing only to look in the rear-view mirror, where a pair of vomit-soaked old biddies stood side by side, waving angry fists.

Football error

I was watching the recent England vs Tunisia game with the lads in the pub, but after a couple of drinks we decided to switch venues, as the boozer we were in was getting more and more crowded. We left at half-time with England winning one-nil. After several failed attempts at finding a gaff with a bit of space and a TV, we finally stumbled upon a pub with the game on and a group of five or six people quietly drinking in the corner. Result! We went in, ordered our drinks and began watching. After ten minutes or so, full of beer and national pride, we started to get annoyed with the other group – they didn't seem bothered about our lads, even when we went two-nil up. We began shouting at them, including a relentless chant of 'Traitors! Traitors!' They simply ignored us, fuelling more and more vitriolic abuse. Finally, the barman came over and barred us! It seems we had somewhat upset a family mourning the death of a grandparent.

Trainee drinker's error

A few years ago, my main goal in life was to improve my drinking capacity. One evening, I had perhaps taken a little too much alcohol on board, and I was frankly paralytic. Bedtime that night at my girlfriend's place was a frosty affair. During the night nature called and I went to the bathroom, an achievement in itself. I kept the light off in the bedroom and carefully felt the bed to avoid crushing my girlfriend as I got back in. Barely had I made myself comfortable than the bedroom door opened and a shaft of light fell across the bed from the hallway. I looked up to see my girlfriend standing in the doorway with a look of total horror on her face. Not half as horrified as her 16-year-old brother did, though, crushed up against the wall after I had inadvertently staggered into the wrong bedroom and climbed into his bed! Needless to say, the relationship did not last long after that little gem.

Balls-up in boozer

A few months ago, several friends and I were on a pub crawl. On entering one pub, we noticed a huge dog turd on the doormat and all walked over it – apart from my mate, Gumbo, who stepped into the stool and trod it into the pub carpet. About 15 minutes later four huge skinheads came into the boozer, and the largest of them seemed to be trying to wipe shit from his boots, much to the amusement of his three mates. Without thinking, Gumbo suddenly got off his stool and walked over to the gang of thugs. 'Oi, mate,' he said to the lead skinhead, 'I've just done that!' And he pointed at the shit on the skinhead's boot. The skinhead, obviously thinking Gumbo had shat on the pub doorstep, proceeded to twat him, breaking his nose.

Mother hears too much

During a particularly heavy drinking session, I managed to pull an equally smashed young lady, through the simple technique of rubbing my crotch against her bottom. When the pub shut I walked her to the taxi rank, and while we had a little kiss, my mate punched her number into his phone. Then she jumped in a cab, and we walked home. On the way, we went into great detail as to what I would do to her the next time we met, and as my mate already knew her, he filled me in on what I could expect. A few days later I nervously called her, and found that things hadn't exactly gone to plan. After punching the number in, my mate had then accidentally pressed the dial button. Her mother was woken by a ringing phone, and answered to a couple of drunken louts describing the hard shagging her daughter was soon to receive, including various props, and perhaps the aid of unspecified fruit. Worse still, the daughter got home before us, and they put us on the speaker phone. Amazingly however, she was still very keen to meet up for another drink.

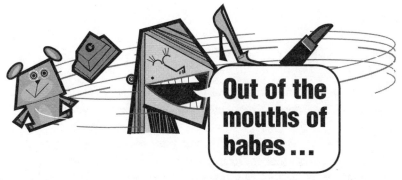

Out of the mouths of babes ...

During a dispute with my mate about who was taller, my girlfriend made us stand back-to-back. When she declared that my mate was taller, I protested. "Come and have a look for yourself," she told me, calmly.

Watching that great British zombie flick 28 Days Later, my beautiful young lady got agitated at the point in the film where we see a wind farm. "If there ain't any electricity," she piped up, "how come those wind turbines are going around?"

Underground fiasco

A few months ago I was in Soho on a Saturday-night bar crawl with my best mate. Passing a 'specialist literature' shop, my friend persuaded me to buy a publication that catered to both our sordid tastes. We then returned to the night's mission: drinking. After chucking-out time, we found ourselves in the Tube station racing each other down parallel escalators. Within seconds, we were travelling at 80mph, taking 14 steps at a time and completely unable to stop. Reaching the bottom, my legs gave out and my mate also tripped – we both ended up in a heap on the ground. Everybody looked up. Meanwhile, a group of young girls seemed amused at finding that my jazz mag had flown out of my pocket during the tumble so that loads of naked women performing various lewd acts were splayed all over the platform. As the girls passed us, they smirked and started screaming, 'Happy wanking, boys!' as they headed up the escalator. Not a pulling stunt I'd particularly recommend...

Photo blunder

Following a fairly heavy night on the booze, my friend Alex and I made our way to the station to catch our train home. Feeling pissed and merry, we decided to kill the 15 minutes' wait for our train by mucking about in the passport photo booth. We stuck our two quid in the machine, struck a variety of hilarious poses, then fell out and waited for the results of our work. Unfortunately, while we were waiting, my female boss came up and started a conversation. She was getting the same train as us, and stood chatting as the photo booth made ominous rumblings. Then our photos dropped out. She has never mentioned the episode at work, but I often wonder what she thought of the four pictures of me and Alex waving our todgers at the camera lens, and I still get the odd grin from other female members of staff.

Fancy-dress fiasco

I had been trying to pull this bird for several weeks when I was invited to her fancy-dress party. Having long hair, I went for the easy option: grow a goatee, don a loin cloth and go as Jesus Christ. While breaking in my costume with a drink at the local, I was invited to a friend's house to 'assimilate' a 24-can pack of golden throat charmer. By now, I was convinced that I could walk on water and impress this girl with my divine powers. Clutching my cross (a nicked 'For Sale' sign), I rapped on the door and was greeted by the young lady. Shocked, she explained that her parents were ultra-devout Catholics, and the sight of me dressed as the Messiah could end the party. She advised me to play down the religious angle, but my mind was too bent by now to grasp this. So off I stumbled, into the throng. Later I approached a fellow prankster – some bloke in full drag with a massive pair of fake tits – and laid my hands on the knockers, commenting, 'Nice set, mate!' My joy turned to dismay: 'he' was a 'she', and my paws were squeezing a complete stranger's breasts. And no ordinary stranger. Suddenly her husband, the host, appeared. Sensing that my chances of a bunk-up with the now-enraged daughter were not too good, I said to the gentleman dressed as Yosemite Sam, 'Sorry, I thought she was a bloke.' Upon which the hostess became hysterical and I was asked, in no uncertain terms, to leave or pick a window.

Stag night crucifixion

A few years ago I was best man at my mate's wedding. At the stag party, 20 or so close friends downed pints and chasers, then triple spirits with pint chasers. We were pretty far gone. After the pub closed, myself, the groom and two friends decided that a walk through the graveyard would be fun! Having been sick over one gravestone, the groom stumbled over to the door of the church and passed out. So we stripped him of all his clothes, lifted him up and tied him, stark naked, to a large stone cross. The next day, our antics gradually came back to me and I rushed to the church, where I found him still fast asleep, tied to the cross. I managed to untie him and get him dressed before he woke up. He thanked me for not embarrassing him the previous night – although he was puzzled as to why he woke up in a graveyard. The week after the wedding, an article appeared in the local paper about a young man having been seen naked in the graveyard that night. Word got round as to his identity – for which I received a black eye and a broken nose!

Telephone error

Like many a feckless student, I recently spent most of my grant cheque in a single night's drinking at the Student Union. Not being a complete idiot I managed to stagger back to my room for some well-earned sleep in the early hours of the morning. I drank a pint of water and lay down on the bed. Naturally the whole room started swimming, so I stood up to try to work out how to kill some time to get rid of the dizziness. I decided to give my girlfriend a call. This was no simple matter as she was on her year out in India, I had no money, and my phone only took incoming calls. Remembering that my parents had said I could use their chargecard for emergency calls, I decided to put it to use. After several unsuccessful attempts I actually managed to get through and proceeded to have a drunken argument with my highly annoyed girlfriend, who quite rightly pointed out what a wanker and a bore I was. At this I terminated the call, staggered back to bed and crashed out. In the afternoon I woke up and saw the phone was off the hook. By sheer chance both my girlfriend and I had failed to hang up properly, resulting in a staggering 11-hour call between Newcastle and India. I haven't seen the bill yet.

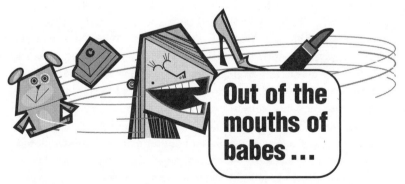

Out of the mouths of babes ...

One cold morning in the office, I exclaimed, "It's like Greenland in here!" A female colleague looked up in confusion and said, "Isn't that where Elvis lived?"

My current girlfriend's sister had a summer job in a department store. I asked if that meant she got a discount. "No," my girl replied, "although she does only pay three-quarters of the price."

Take-away prank

A couple of years ago, a group of us embarked on a stag night pub crawl in the Wavertree area of Liverpool. After getting the groom absolutely paralytic, we decided to go to an Indian restaurant to complete the night's events. But not long after the food arrived, Gordon, the groom, disappeared into the toilet – and failed to return. Eventually, my brother went in to see if he was alright; he returned with Gordon slung over his shoulder, so we put his curry in a doggie-bag and caught a taxi home. Ten minutes into the journey, Gordon announced that he was going to be sick, and – not wanting to face the wrath of an irate taxi driver – I decided it was best to sacrifice the dinner and gave him the bag, which he promptly filled. Our other friend, Robbie, had fallen asleep during the ride and missed the whole incident, so when we arrived at his front door and woke him up, I couldn't resist handing him the carrier bag, telling him that Gordon couldn't face it and that one of the containers had split, but that otherwise the food was okay. He took the bag and a few days later thanked me for the meal, proudly stating that he had polished the lot off and found it delicious, if a little mushy.

Disco shame

It started out as the usual Friday night: beers, chatting and eventually a club. The week in question me and a few mates went to a club which had just opened. We were fairly drunk but by no means bladdered, but we did decide to have a game of 'spoof' – a variation on the paper/rock/scissors game – with the loser having to do the forfeit of his mates' choice. After I lost a round I was instructed to go onto the half-filled dancefloor and dance like, for want of a better word, a spaz. I duly went down in front of the speakers and jerked around, dragging my leg behind me in terrible taste. After several minutes I felt a vicious punch to my cheek, and turned around to fight the bastard who'd hit me. We exchanged hard blows for a solid minute, then the bouncers came over and dragged me out. A minute or so later my friends came out to find me black and blue, sitting dejectedly on the kerb, our fun evening over. It was then that my mates pointed out the lad I'd fought sported an orthopaedic shoe.

Toilet trauma

Following our graduation ceremony at Newcastle University, a group of friends and I went out to celebrate. Considerably the worse for wear, my friend Paresh and I zigzagged our way to the gents. Paresh, now out of his student gear and wearing some Cerruti slacks and Gucci cufflinks, went into the cubicle to avoid getting splashback on his expensive attire. What he didn't realize was that a huge Geordie bloke had followed us into the toilets and was standing next to me at the urinal. I finished my slash and went to wash my hands, while the Geordie, much to everyone's surprise, squeezed out a huge anal fanfare. 'You smelly fucker!' shouted Paresh from his cubicle, thinking I was the only one there. He then must have balanced himself on the rim of the bowl, because a jet of hot urine shot over the partition and all over our Geordie pal. I chose this moment to leave, just as the enraged bloke began to kick down the door of the cubicle. I returned to the toilets ten minutes later to find Paresh half-conscious in a pool of blood.

Uncomfortable pudding event

A few years ago, I was with my girlfriend at my best friend's sleep-over party. The vodka trifles I had made went down very well, and eventually everyone crashed out. I was woken by an excited friend dragging me towards the stairs telling me that there was a commotion going on outside. The house was on the side of a hill and the front door was upstairs. As I left the house I could see a circle of my friends peering through a window. As we got closer I could make out the master bedroom and a naked male arse atop a blonde girl. I was jeering and cheering along with the other voyeurs until I recognized the girl as being my girlfriend, the bloke as my best friend and my vodka trifle being licked off her bare breasts.

Flatulence faux-pas

When I was at college, I had it bad for a gorgeous Dutch girl. I spent many lectures gazing longingly at the blonde, leggy Annika, but she never even gave me a passing glance. I was living in halls at the time, in a small box of a room. One night, as finals were approaching, I was holed up in my bunker studying like crazy. With the door and window shut, I was enjoying a good old farting session, ridding my body of the day's built-up wind. Several violent emissions later, the room was shimmering in a haze of noxious gas. Then suddenly there was a knock on the door and, before I could leap up, the lovely Annika popped her head in and smiled invitingly: 'Hi, are you busy?' I could do nothing but get her away as quickly as possible. I shouted, 'Get out! How dare you barge in here without knocking!' A look of horror struck her, and she turned and fled. Needless to say, she went back to treating me with disdain.

Thatch snipped

About five years ago, I was sitting half naked in front of the TV, when I discovered a large tangled knot in my pubes. I reached for some scissors and snipped around the offending clump. Once done, I realized I needed something to put the hairs into, so I grabbed a piece of paper, and neatly folded the little bush away before putting it into my pocket and staggering off to bed. A few days later I was in a restaurant having lunch with three important clients. We discussed another client, and I asked one of my contacts for his phone number, fumbling around for a piece of paper to write it down on. Closely watched by my bemused colleagues, I then meticulously unfolded my A4 sheet to reveal a neatly pressed pubic topiary display, which then blew straight into my colleague's chicken supreme.

Sour grapes

Several years ago I found myself between flats, and a very close friend of the family agreed to put me up for a week or two while I sorted out a place to live. Everything went smoothly and I eventually found a new flat, and decided to buy a present for my kind host by way of a thank you. Knowing he was a bit of a wine buff I went down to the local off-licence to choose a decent bottle of wine. Too proud to ask advice from the man behind the counter, I eventually selected a bottle of red, thinking that the '£7.99' sticker on the shelf put it in the 'pretty good' range. I took the bottle up to the counter and the man seemed most impressed by my choice. He asked me if I had tasted it before, and I said yes. I lied that only a week before I had bought a bottle, and found it superb. He smiled and said that they didn't sell many because of the price, and I nodded knowingly, and said that it was worth every single penny. Then the man rang the till: '£47.99'. The '4' sticker had obviously fallen off the shelf. I was too embarrassed to backtrack though, so my friend ended up with the best leaving present ever.

Bicycle bungle

I cycled into town for a 9am appointment with fear – well, my dentist actually. When all the fillings were done, after about an hour, I rode to the shops, bought two cans of Whiskas for the cat and a bottle of Lucozade, and set off home to nurse my aching mouth. Two hundred yards from my door, I swerved to avoid a pothole and crashed into the kerb. I lay in the gutter, clothes torn, knees bleeding, with tins of Whiskas rolling down the street and a smashed bottle of Lucozade all over the pavement. I looked up to see an old woman peering over me. 'Are you okay, son?' she enquired. I nodded, staggered to my feet and opened my mouth to respond. All that came out was an incoherent 'zsa zsa zsa' as my mouth was still frozen from the dentist. Her concern evaporated into a cold look of disgust. 'It's a disgrace! Someone so drunk at 10 o'clock in the morning! You ought to be ashamed of yourself, young man. Serves you right!' I haven't been to see the dentist since.

'Phone sex' faux pas

One night, having consumed too much alcohol and a greasy kebab, my mates and I retired to a friend's house to watch an 'adult' video. Struggling out of bed the next day, I decided to give one of the crew a ring. When he answered the phone, I began to repeat some of the dialogue from the film. 'Oooh, come on. Johnny, fuck me ... I want that big cock inside me ... that's it! Harder ... HARDER! You're so big!' The next thing I heard was the sound of a phone being slammed down; but, mysteriously, I could still hear my friend on the line, blathering away in a blind panic. His mother, a woman so strait-laced that she'd make Mother Teresa took like Tabatha Cash, had picked up the phone at the same time downstairs. So Mrs M, if you come across this piece, it was me who made the obscene phone call, and I'm sorry if you've spent years in torment about the sexual activities of your favourite son.

Boarding school blunder

As a young man at a mixed boarding school, I, like many others, turned to drinking to cheer up the mind-numbing dullness of the routine. Naturally, storage of the illicit sauce was a problem, as privacy is not one of the benefits of a private education. Then one day I hit upon a novel hiding place: the inside of my stereo speaker-case. To combat the clinking of bottles, I packed out the spare space with empty plastic bags and toilet paper. I could even play music as the teachers searched for the booze. One day just such a hunt occurred, and I casually flicked through the tracks on my CD as the teacher looked through the dorm. He found nothing, and we both left, me to go to chapel for two hours and he to continue his search. Returning to my dorm after chapel, I could smell smoke as I walked upstairs. Looking across the room as I entered, I saw the gin-filled speaker explode like a Molotov cocktail. Then the curtains caught fire and the room filled up with thick smoke. It seems a short circuit had ignited my padding and sent the whole lot up. Needless to say, I was well and truly rumbled.

Celebrity trouser torment

A few years ago I worked for a menswear shop which specialized in hiring out dress suits for weddings. The Solent athletic team all came in to get fitted one afternoon. While I started measuring one tall black guy, he mumbled something about having big thighs and said he would need extra size trousers. I ignored him, knowing most men don't know their true sizes. I gave him 32-inch trousers and he disappeared into the changing room. After a minute, he reappeared with his trousers at half mast, clearly unable to pull them up over the most muscular thighs I have ever seen. He ended up with 38-inch trousers, which had to be held up with braces, making him look like Coco the Clown. He was very annoyed by now, and when I took his name, I wrote it down as 'Kriss Akapussy'. 'No, Aka-BUSI,' he shouted. I could hear my colleague giggling behind me. Needless to say, I never did watch much athletics on TV.

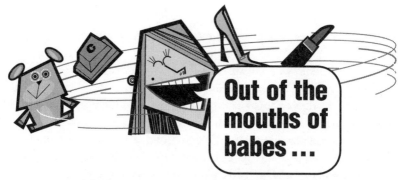

Out of the mouths of babes ...

A female friend of mine recently moved into a house where the fridge didn't work, so her dad bought her some dried milk. "How do I use this with cornflakes?" she asked me. "Do I sprinkle it on?" Brilliant.

My Scottish mate had just become a dad, and joked that his little boy would probably end up with his huge conk and flat feet. "Will he inherit your accent, or will he speak English like your wife?" queried my girlfriend, in all seriousness.

Car repair backfires

When I was 17, my dad bought me my first car: a Mini 1000. Already 15 years old, it looked knackered, but for £150 it was a great deal. As part of my present I had the car sprayed British Racing Green, which made it look better, but its rusty wheels and old fashioned hubcaps let it down. Unable to afford alloy sports wheels, I decided to spray the existing crappy wheels silver and get rid of the hubcaps. I dismantled the wheels and got to work with a can of silver spray, noticing in the process that each wheel-nut had a straight side and a rounded side. The rounded side, I thought, was far sportier, so I sprayed the wheels silver with the rounded sides on show. Later, after half an hour or so on the road, I heard a grinding noise that was getting louder with every corner. On inspection I decided it was just a teething problem from my new design, but while I was taking a right turn at speed the grinding noise came back, louder than ever, with sparks flying past the window. The car sank 12 inches with a great thud. I ground to a halt with a worried look on my face as the two front wheels made their own way home – unattached.

Cool driving blunder

My first serious girlfriend dumped me on Christmas Day. I'd driven to the house she shared with her mother to deliver her presents, and she broke the news in a typically blunt way. Distressed beyond words, I ran out to my car and decided I'd depart in a dramatic and memorable fashion. I jumped into my beaten-up Escort and attempted a fast-moving reverse flick out of her narrow driveway. Unfortunately, instead of flying backwards in a cloud of burning rubber, I deposited my car into her mother's prize flower bed. This was bad enough, but, in my frantic attempt to escape before anyone noticed, the spinning back wheels dug themselves deeper into the soil. My now ex-girlfriend's mother attempted to push the car out. She then remembered she was asthmatic and quietly collapsed on the driveway. To make matters worse, I had to borrow £75 from her to pay for a tow truck – I'd spent all my money on the Christmas presents. It transpired my 'ex' was meeting her new boyfriend that night, and was unable to get her car past the wreckage of mine, which was blocking the driveway.

Hard-to-get blunder

When I was 20, I had no luck with women. Every time I spoke to a prospective girlfriend, I froze. I stuttered, spluttered, and generally made a complete fool of myself. Girls, using the uncanny sixth sense that only they have, sensed my hopelessness and gave me a wide berth. But all that changed when I met Julia. With gorgeous long red hair and snow white skin, she looked like she had just stepped out of a Pre-Raphaelite painting. I was determined not to mess this one up, so I came up with a cunning plan. Having read somewhere that girls liked a challenge and were attracted to the kind of blokes they couldn't have. Unfortunately, I got slightly carried away, and I thought I would be guaranteed success if I played even harder to get. So I told her I was a homosexual.

This didn't put her off. She invited me out the following night, saying she would 'arrange something very special' for me. I'd done it! I pictured the evening: Julia would introduce me to the love of a woman, I'd lie there, pretending to experience for the first time the unexpected pleasures of heterosexual love.

I turned up early, to find Julia already there. I was shaking in anticipation. She looked me in the eye, and said: 'Rick ... meet Gerald.' I froze, confused. Gerald stepped forward, looking like a refugee from the Village People. A leer broke out underneath the bushiest moustache I've ever seen. His shaved head glistened in the moonlight as he strode purposefully towards me, his black leather trousers squeaking. I turned and ran. Needless to say, I never saw Julia again.

Tea with milk?

While in my first year at university, I suddenly found myself extremely hard up, and so were my student housemates. As anyone who has shared a house will know, a certain amount of 'borrowing' of one another's food goes on. Normally I took this stoically, but as I was trying to live on £1.38 per week, I found I could bear it no longer. I had put up with it for several weeks, but the final straw came when someone in my house all but finished my carton of milk. Returning home drunk and looking forward to my evening meal (and lunch and breakfast) of Frosties, I found the milk was almost all gone. I hit the roof. Determined to teach the culprit a lesson, I pissed in the carton and went to sleep, still seething. I was awoken at midday by one of my housemates saying my parents had just arrived to visit. 'I made them a cup of tea, I used your milk,' she said. I had trouble facing my parents after that, especially since my father crashed the car while being violently sick on the drive home.

Dairy produce fiasco

My aunt used to work part time as a typist for the Inland Revenue in Manchester, where she took it in turns with the other girls in the office to buy breakfast. One day she wandered into the butty shop, ordered the usual buttered teacakes and put them into her bag – right on top of a pair of underpants my uncle wanted returning to Marks and Spencer because he didn't like the colour. My aunt then went into M&S and took the pants to the till for exchange. 'Has he tried them on?' the girl on the till asked. My aunt said absolutely not, then looked on in horror as the assistant held the pants up to the light – and a bright yellow streak was plain to see. The assistant refused to give my aunt a refund, saying that it was quite clear the pants had been worn, as they were 'soiled'. In a last, desperate attempt to preserve her dignity, my aunt said in a very timid voice, 'It was only butter, you know...

Names entered

On Remembrance Sunday last February, myself and a few friends decided to attend a small memorial service at a nearby village church. When we arrived, we filled in the visitors' book sitting in the foyer, purely because judging by the neatly printed surnames, everyone else in our small community had already entered their names. The service went very well until the padre began to read out the village dead, and we recognized the book he was reading from. Before he could get to our neatly printed names however, my friend cracked, turned to me and blurted out, 'We are going to hell for this, mark my words!' before bolting for the door. I just followed, shrugging my shoulders and tutting at the padre. We later found out that our names were indeed read out, and not one person noticed.

Sauna saga

About 12 years ago, when I was an innocent 26-year-old, my brother-in-law joined a posh local health club and took me along one evening as a special treat. After a work-out in the gym he suggested a sauna, so I stripped off and followed him in. The sauna was empty and I settled down on the top row, taking the small bowl of water that he handed to me. When I asked what it was for, he explained that the body needs to adjust to the sauna's high temperatures, and that your testicles are susceptible to heat damage. Now this seemed plausible, as I knew from biology 0-level that your balls were the coolest part of your body, so I positioned myself in such a way that I could sit with my nuts floating on the water. After a while, a couple of blokes strolled in, carrying the same bowls, and poured the contents over the hot coals. I was about to suggest that they save a little for their balls, when my brother-in-law suddenly cracked up and left, leaving two smirking men to explain correct sauna etiquette.

Selfish gym-goer

Last April, after completing a strenuous work-out at my local gym, I decided to spend a relaxing half-hour in the sauna. It had a lockable door with a large tinted glass window, the other side of which was the men's showers. Feeling selfish, I put the lock on and lay down to enjoy a bit of solitary sweating. An old chubby man then wandered into the showers and, after trying the sauna door, stood under a jet of water. I left him to it and closed my eyes until it was time to leave. When I opened my eyes however, I couldn't help but notice the old boy having the best wank of his life. Worse, he was marvelling at his reflection in the door window. Then he suddenly waddled straight over and, with only a thin sheet of glass between my head and his angry Jap's eye, unleashed a thick torrent of gentleman's gel all over the window. I waited a good hour before I dared come out.

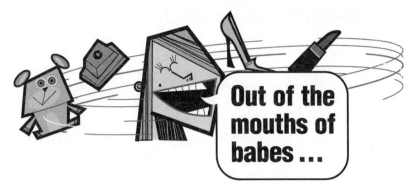

Out of the mouths of babes ...

Preparing for a road trip, my sister looked up from the map to declare, "I didn't know there was a river all the way round London." That'll be the M25.

Watching Saving Private Ryan with a few friends, my sister wandered in, waited patiently for a few minutes then asked, "Which side are the Germans fighting for – the Nazis or the Americans?"

Wedding faux pas

A couple of years ago, I was asked by my flatmate if I would help out at her wedding. My job was simple: all I had to do was pick out a track on a CD, press the button, and watch as the beautiful bride walked down the aisle with her father to be given away. She was due at three o'clock, so at 2.45 I nipped outside for a quick cigarette with a couple of the ushers, all the while keeping an eye on the path to the entrance so that I could rush back in and put on the music when her car pulled up. After about 15 to 20 minutes, I started to get a bit concerned about her lateness, so thought I'd better go inside and check what was going on. As I pushed open what I was later told was the side entrance to the church, I was greeted by the strange sight of my flatmate walking down the aisle with a furious took on her face ... to the tune of Mr Boombastic. Nobody had a clue what track to play, and when they couldn't find me, somebody had just hit the play button. To cap it all, I accidentally caught the bouquet later on in the day.

Blasphemous brother

Last year I visited my sister for the weekend. We were chatting on
Sunday afternoon when she told me that the Jehovah's Witnesses
had been coming round week after week, and just didn't seem to take
no for an answer. As we drank our coffee there was a knock at the
door, and I told my sister I would deal with it. Sure enough, there on
the doorstep was a clean-cut young chap with an armful of books.
Before he could begin to bore me with his chatter I told him, quite
loudly, to fuck right off, and slammed the door in his face. Seconds
later there was another knock at the door, and I went back to answer
it. 'Look, mate,' I said, 'I've told you once. Now do yourself a favour
and fuck off.' The young man remained very calm, although I noticed
he turned rather red, and said: 'I'm the curate of St Cuthbert's
Church, and am just checking to see that Vikki's (my niece)
christening was satisfactory.'

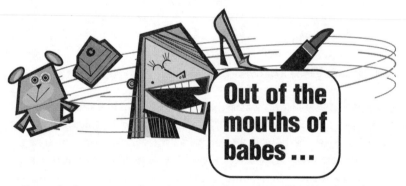

Out of the mouths of babes ...

*Recently, I was cravenly trying to justify to my girlfriend why I was
shelling out for a new car stereo system. I told her it featured a
television, satellite navigation and a DVD player. "Cool," she
replied. "It sounds like the bee's bollocks."*

*On holiday recently in Mexico, we got chatting to a couple in the
bar and discovered they were from Austria. "Oh wow," said my
girlfriend. "Do you speak Ostrich?"*

Hair mishap

My hair was much too long for the hot weather so I heated myself up even more by going to one of those saloons staffed by Claudia Schiffer lookalikes. I was shown to a seat by a luscious blonde. I removed my sunglasses as she put a gown over my shoulders and I started cleaning them, beneath the gown. Before I could say 'short sharp crop' she screamed, 'You dirty bastard!' and yanked off the gown to reveal my now clean pair of sunglasses.

Graffiti victim

When I was a student at music college I took the job of organist at the local church in order to make a few quid at the weekends. The pay for Sunday services was abysmal, but it was easy to make up for this by doing the occasional wedding and funeral service. One Friday night I got completely out of it with my mates down the pub, which ended up in a session that lasted nearly all night. I eventually crashed out at around seven in the morning, with the promise from my mates that they would wake me up in time for a wedding service I had to perform the next day. Being the reliable bastards they are, they woke me up about 15 minutes before the ceremony. I chucked my clothes on and ran down to the church, where – luckily – the procession was only just making its way in. With a big smile I pushed my way through the crowd, saying 'Make way for the organist!' I sat down at my organ and, surprisingly, played the music without fault. Afterwards I went up to the vicar and apologized for being late, but he looked at me with an expression of total horror. 'You played well,' he said with a bright red face. 'It's just that you have the words "EVIL BASTARD" written on your forehead in lipstick.'

Blind date dilemma

After splitting up with my girlfriend, I decided it would be a laugh to reply to some personal ads. One was from a 39-year-old woman after a young man for a fling. After we exchanged several explicit letters and steamy phone calls, she said we should meet. When we finally did I realized I made a big mistake. She'd described herself as slim and attractive, but was short, plump and had more arse than a donkey. After we'd spent about half an hour in a pub, I realized that I must escape. I went into the Gents but all the windows had bars on them. I waited until she went to the toilet, leaving me to took after her expensive coat and designer umbrella. After about a minute, I calmly walked out of the pub, then ran like an Olympic sprinter. Losing my way I asked directions to the nearest tube and felt a huge wave of relief as I saw an Underground sign in the distance. Then horror struck. Across the road was the pub I'd just escaped from. What followed was a scene of complete chaos as I ran through the crowds shouting, 'Get out of the way!' Thankfully, I never saw her again.

Water fear

The last caving expedition that I went on involved an unexpected 'sump' – a point where rock meets water. This particular obstacle was four foot long, and the only way past was to dive into the icy water and pull myself along a permanently fixed length of submerged rope. Easy enough, perhaps – except that I can't swim. Amazingly, however, I managed it, and enjoyed a full day's caving without incident. On the return leg, I again arrived at the ominous sump, and three of my mates dived under before tugging on the rope – the signal for me to go. I held my breath, screwed up my eyes and ducked underwater, frantically pulling my way to safety. As soon as I thought I was clear I raised my head, only to hit rock. I pulled myself further forward and tried again. More rock. Starting to panic, I made one last, desperate effort to save myself from drowning. To my amazement, I burst out of the water – only to be surprised to find that I was 20ft from the sump and completely alone. My mates later told me that when I appeared from under the rock, they had stood either side of me and held a large boulder over my head, keeping pace with me as I dragged myself along the rope – before eventually adopting the 'scatter and divide' method to avoid a serious beating from a very scared caver.

Accidental insult

Recently I moved into a lovely new flat in a really great part of London, and had to find new flatmates. Luckily I found three super people, one of whom was a gentle German giant named Otto. After a few weeks in our new home I got round to putting up some bookshelves, and began the task of carrying all my books down to put them on the nice new shelves. I loaded up my arms and made my way down to the living room, where Otto was enjoying a cup of tea. Unfortunately, I tripped and dropped a couple of volumes at Otto's feet. I couldn't work out why the chap looked so horrified until I looked down at the heavy historic tome nestling against Otto's slipper: a copy of Hitler's Willing Executioners, an academic study about the collective guilt of the German people. Otto moved his stuff out three days later.

Hole undammed

During the early Seventies I found myself in hospital with two broken legs. In the bed next to me lay a fat old man, who was in for chronic constipation. Every day after dinner, some poor nurse would have to stick a hose up his arse so that he could pass solids. Obviously this made him very irritable, so I used to rub salt in the wound with a cheerful announcement of, 'That was a great crap!' whenever I used the bedpan. The time came when I was finally allowed to leave, and I told the old boy that I would miss watching his daily hour of discomfort. He grumpily informed me that he needed a shit, but before I could summon a nurse, someone had a heart attack in the corner, and everyone scooted away to help. All alone, he pushed his generous arse out off the bed, until I was within kissing distance of it, and proceeded to empty his bowels onto the floor in front of me. A humungous pile of brown, black and red shit rose up off the tiles, and when he had finished he pulled his arse back in, turned to me with watering eyes and said, 'What a great crap that was!'

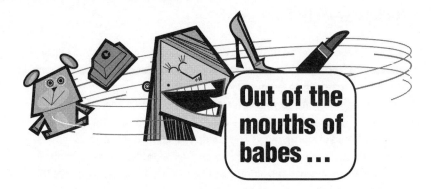

Out of the mouths of babes ...

With news of a cyclone in the Solomon Islands, I suggested to my wife they should build underground shelters. "They can't!" she replied. "They're in the middle of the ocean – dig down and you spring a leak."

Talking about a pet for our new flat, I suggested a tortoise. My flatmate pointed out that tortoises hibernate for half the year. "Why not get two, then?" my girlfriend chipped in.

Library laughs

Last year at university I competed in a practical joke tit-for-tat campaign with my friends. One day, while in the library with my mates Steve, Wayne and his girlfriend Lisa, Steve and I thought it would be amusing to remove a magnetic security strip from a book and plant it on Wayne. This we duly did, slipping it in his jacket pocket, knowing the security alarm and Secret Police-inspired librarians would provide adequate amounts of embarrassment. When the alarm went off and Wayne was asked to empty his bag for inspection, he became agitated and refused. Following a lengthy argument while Wayne proclaimed his innocence, he was finally persuaded to let the librarian look in his bag. She pulled out a magazine, believing it to be a stolen periodical – but the naked girl on the cover confirmed it was Razzle rather than Business Week. Wayne duly turned red and his girlfriend stormed off. They split up later that day and Wayne still hasn't forgiven us.

Kitchen horror

Last year I was lucky enough to meet a beautiful girl at a party. I was even luckier when the girl – a model I had thought to be well out of my league – actually seemed to enjoy my company. Fully seizing the one and only opportunity in my life to make it with a stunner, I spent every second of the evening with her, and was shocked when my invitation to come to supper the following week was accepted. She told me she was a vegetarian and I spent the week devising the perfect meal. But while I was cooking my winter vegetable casserole I realized I didn't have any vegetable stock, so I bunged in a chicken stock cube, seasoned the whole thing heavily and prayed she wouldn't notice my deception. All went well. She ate a huge portion and complimented me on my cooking. When I asked her how long she had been a vegetarian, she told me it had only been for a year and that she actually loved meat but had developed a severe allergy to animal fat, breaking out in hives every time she ate it. Sure enough, as the evening passed her face broke out in blotches and she began to get feverish. In the end I had to confess. Due to her state she missed a modelling assignment the next day, and has never spoken to me since.

Moronic motorist

Last July I was staying with my girlfriend for the weekend when I had a slight problem with my car. This would not have been so much of a drama, except that I only noticed the problem on Sunday afternoon, and I had to be at work, 150 miles away, early on Monday morning. I went into a blind panic when I noticed that fluid had leaked out all over the back wheels, and, taking the car for a careful test I felt that the brakes weren't responding as well as they should. I telephoned my boss, telling him the problem, and he was not at all impressed. On Monday morning I drove the car at a steady 15mph to the nearest garage, and asked them to check the brakes for me. After a couple of hours I noticed the mechanics were laughing at me, then the manager called me over and told me my car was fine. After I'd returned home I received a letter from the garage which did nothing to placate my boss. It read: 'After a lengthy investigation of stripping and checking the front and rear brakes, it was determined that the fault was dog urine on the wheels'.

Laundry slip-up

Until recently, I had managed to enjoy a rather appealing washing arrangement, whereby I would take my work clothes around to my mother to be cleaned while my girlfriend would take care of my everyday stuff. A few weeks ago, however, mum started to visit my flat on an almost daily basis, and began taking all my washing – including my girlfriend's 'share' – when she left. Feeling unneeded, my girlfriend decided to lay down a few ground rules: namely that I should refer to her as 'Mammy' and let her do her fair share of the laundry. Over the next few weeks, she would bring round my clean clothes and say, 'Your Mammy is looking after you, isn't she, love?' 'Yes, Mammy, you are,' I would reply. One morning, after a particularly sordid sex session, I slipped out of bed and went to work without disturbing her. Later that day – at work – the phone rang, and a woman's voice said, 'It's your Mammy.' Smiling, I thanked the caller for the night before and asked her if there was any soreness in her nether regions. There then followed a steady silence, before the caller informed me that she'd decided to have a break from my father, that she was going to stay with my sister and that she wouldn't be able to do my washing for a while.

Store drama

When I was younger I was into motorbikes in a big way, and after yet another strip-down of my 50cc, I headed down to my local dealer to order some parts. While I was standing in the queue, dreamily watching the young girl working behind the counter, one of the shop dummies, complete with helmet, boots, jacket and gloves, fell over. The young shop assistant quickly came over and picked it up, and we had a laugh about it while I ordered my parts. Returning the next day to collect them I took my place behind a mean-looking man, who was dressed as if he had just stepped off the set of Mad Max. Again I soon found myself staring at the shop assistant, completely lost in thought, when suddenly the biker in front of me moved. Unfortunately, I had a sudden flashback to the previous day – and before I knew what I was doing I reached forward and grabbed him tight round the stomach. We wrestled for quite a long time before I came to my senses; all I could muster as I looked into his furious eyes was: 'Sorry, I thought you were a dummy.' Not surprisingly, I've never been back.

Tattoo screw-up

For several years I had wanted a tattoo, but never liked a design enough to make the commitment. Then, last year, a Japanese student attended the college I go to, and we became friends. I introduced him to the lads, and we all had a great year. When he had to leave, he gave each of us a beautifully designed card with the Japanese characters of our names printed on them. My name looked really cool in Japanese script, so I decided to tattoo it on my shoulder. Everyone said how great it looked, and I was really pleased ... until I went to Sicily this April, when I took the opportunity to show off my tat on the beach. We were challenged to a game of volleyball by some Japanese girls who kept screaming 'Sidney!' at me – which was odd, as it's my best friend's name. Yep, the cards had been switched, and I now have my mate's stupid name scrawled across my shoulder.

Bed department violence

I was recently shopping at a large local furniture store with two friends of mine, Jimmy and Dave. We'd previously spent a few hours in the pub and were in a pretty mischievous mood as we made our way around the beds, wardrobes and tables. It was in the bedding department that the mishap occurred. One brand of bed had been running TV ads featuring a hippo lying on a bed next to a tiny chick – the idea was that the bed wouldn't cause two people to 'roll together'. The shop had the bed on display, with a tiny stuffed chick and a giant hippo lying next to each other. Jimmy ran over and booted the chick across the floor, then landed a roundhouse on the side of the hippo's head. Startlingly, the hippo rolled off the bed and cried: 'What the fuck did you do that for?' Jimmy had smacked a man whose job it was to dress up as a semi-aquatic mammal. Luckily, the sight of a blue hippo squaring up to Jimmy was so funny that we all ended up rolling around in laughter.

Filthy kiwi

After leaving university I moved into a flat with a group of friends – one of whom I was pretty keen on. We had been in the flat a couple of weeks and I felt I was making good headway. One night a few of us, including the girl I fancied, were sitting around in my room chatting and having a few drinks. Trying to be laid-back and cool I was wearing an ilavalava – a Samoan version of the kilt, worn by both men and women. After a while we ran out of drinks and I volunteered to go to the local boozer to get more. I figured nobody wanted a shot of my balls as I stood up, so I slid delicately across the bed. On coming back with the beers I saw that the two blokes in the room had tears of mirth running down their faces, while the two girls were ashen-faced. I also noticed a book sitting in the middle of the bed. I picked it up and was shocked and embarrassed to find that, while sliding off the bed, rather than keeping my dignity I managed to lose it all by leaving a 4-inch shit stain on the duvet. I did, eventually, get it on with my flatmate, but it took four weeks of hard work to put the memory of the fudge strip firmly out of her mind.

Samaritan attacks

During a recent lunchbreak, my mate and I nipped out to the local sandwich shop to grab a bite to eat. On the way back we noticed an old lady walking along the busy street with a bit of white paper stuck to her shoe. Ever the gentleman, my mate stepped forward and placed his foot firmly on the paper, the idea being that her next step would pull off the offending article. Unfortunately, it must have been literally nailed into place, because her foot suddenly stopped and she went face first into the pavement. Naturally we legged it, but there were obviously some outraged bystanders, as that weekend the local rag ran an amazing 'old lady attacked in broad daylight' story.

Towerblock shocker

A few months ago I returned from a trip to Australia, and was totally jet-lagged by the time I arrived back at my flat in London. I'd crashed out for no longer than an hour before I was woken by a loud, repeated car horn. I live on the seventh floor of a tower block, so went onto the balcony to investigate. Down on the street below I could make out a Ford Mondeo and its occupant. The man was sitting in the driver's seat, hitting the horn and shouting 'Alfie! Alfie!' over and over again. I shouted down at him to shut up, but he just continued to blow the horn and yell out for his mate Alfie. I was tired and stressed out, so I ran into the kitchen and grabbed a carton of eggs from the fridge. I was so angry, I hurled the whole carton down at the car. The eggs splattered on the Mondeo's windshield, but the man kept up his stream of nonsense. Finally I snapped and chucked a milk bottle down, which smashed on his roof. At last, the noise stopped. I saw two men come and bundle the bloke out of his car: they had obviously been as pissed off as me. I went back to bed and slept for the next 16 hours. Only the next day did the full story emerge in the local press: the man in the car had suffered a heart attack, and was pressing his horn and shouting 'Help me! Help me!'

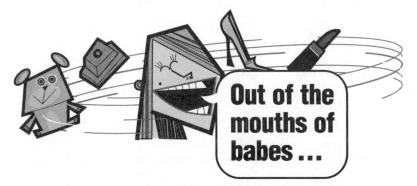

Out of the mouths of babes ...

On a recent trip to the beach my now ex-girlfriend noticed a sign that read, "ALL REFUSE TO BE PUT IN BIN." "That's a stupid sign," she said, puzzled. "Who would agree to be put in a bin?"

My female housemate recently tried to solve a query that had clearly been bothering her for some time. "You know nipples?" she asked, puzzled. "What are they called on men?" This from a woman allegedly studying law!

House arrest

Back in 1993 I purchased my first house, a great open-plan affair with a gallery bedroom overlooking the living room. It had been one of the estate's showhouses, along with the adjoining house, which was still on display. During my first few months of residence I was subjected to countless numbers of people peering through my window, only to realize their mistake when they saw either myself or my girlfriend watching the TV or having dinner. On the odd occasion when I was gardening, people would even walk up to the front door and peek in. Although it was amusing at first, it soon became a bit annoying – until the final straw, which followed a hard night shift. Having crawled into my bed at around 7am, I was woken at 10.30 by my concerned girlfriend who was whispering insistently that someone was downstairs, walking around. Still half asleep, I mumbled something and dozed off, until she pushed me out of the bed, telling me that someone was now coming up the stairs. At the time I had very long ginger hair and a beard, bearing more than a passing resemblance to Catweazle, so I stood there, completely naked, as an inquisitive couple pushed open the door. It was hard to tell who was more terrified. 'It's not a showroom,' I mumbled like a buffoon, and they were gone. Thankfully the showhouse next door was sold fairly soon afterwards and my life is now reasonably normal.

Button pushed

On what seemed like the hottest day of last summer, while on a particularly tedious and potentially relationship-destroying trip around the local shopping centre with my wife, I found myself stuck on a packed escalator, unable to move due to a large group of coffin-dodgers blocking the route ahead. The escalator seemed to be moving exceptionally slowly and, with sweat running off my head and into my eyes, I suddenly reached the end of my tether. Before I could stop myself, my hand reached out and punched the bright red emergency stop button – a move which brought the moving stairway to an immediate halt. People, including the frail old pensioners, crashed forwards into each other, sending bags and packages flying off in all directions. But amazingly, the crime was never pinned on me. The last thing I remember as I trod over the heap of bodies to escape the carnage was a desperate plea from an innocent little boy, who was being soundly thrashed for 'being so bad'.

Happy reunion

Last year I dumped my girlfriend, explaining that I 'just wasn't ready for what she wanted.' Obviously this caused some upset, and for six months we didn't speak. Then we met, seemingly quite by chance, while out shopping. All went well, and to my surprise she invited me to dinner. I accepted, and we had a fantastic meal, before going on to some bars and a club. That week my boss was on holiday, and as his office was in his house, I had the keys to his pad. We had a great night, but in the morning I awoke to find my ex gone, with a note apologizing for the mess. Staggering downstairs, it was obvious I had been set up. The walls, carpet and most of the stairs were covered in green paint. Furious, I called her house, but she was at work, and when I told her mother what had happened, she actually defended her daughter. I lost it, informed the crazy bitch that it was fairly obvious where my ex got her mental behaviour from, and slammed down the phone. After a futile attempt to scrub off the paint, it was time to call my boss. Terrified, I explained what had happened, but he just laughed. He had knocked the tin of paint down the stairs on his way to the airport, and as he was in a rush he decided to leave it until he got back. The ex called that evening, saying that the only mess she had left was a used coffee cup, her mother was in a state of shock, and she never wanted to see me again.

Strange instructions

A few years ago, while working in America, I was struck down with kidney stones and rushed to a plush American hospital for a series of tests. My company was paying the bill, so no expense was spared, and I was appointed my own personal, and attractive, female attendant. I had to lie naked on a table, following instructions such as, 'Tackle to the left please, scrotum to the right,' while my nether-regions were photographed. This was fine until she completely stunned me with the line, 'The doctor would like some of you erect.' She said that she would be back in a few minutes. I then set about raising steam but by the time she came back, the best I had mustered was a lazy lob. She then pointed to another machine standing in the corner. 'I need you to stand up straight for an X-ray,' she said, tears streaming down her face.

Flatmate required

Just over a year ago I had to find a new flatmate, and ended up scanning the university noticeboard. Among the scruffy notes from homeless students was one from a man named 'Jesus'. I proceeded to phone my list of prospective flatmates, but Jesus wasn't in, so I left a message on his answering machine asking him to come around that evening at nine. I then settled down in front of the TV to wait for the other interviewees to turn up, but nobody came – until, at nine, the doorbell rang. Assuming that Jesus had got the message and decided to come round, I buzzed the guy in and stood at the top of the communal stairwell to greet him. Unlike the kindly, bearded chap I had expected, he was a big, mean-looking man, and I nervously stuck out my hand. 'Hello,' I said. 'Are you Jesus?' He must have stared at me for a full minute before slowly replying, 'No, my name is Heinrich.' Convinced that Jesus was on his way up the stairs and unable to lower my arm through sheer nerves, I looked over his shoulder and said quietly, 'Oh, I was expecting Jesus. Never mind, would you like to come in and see my room?' Without taking his eyes off me, the bloke edged down the stairs, one by one, and left. As I found out next day, the girls living above me were also advertising their flat and Heinrich had been on his way up to view it.

Freudian slip

About ten years ago my mum invited the whole family around for Christmas dinner. After we'd eaten I had the urge to do what most teenage boys do, and disappeared up to my room for a quick spank of the monkey. Mission accomplished, I decided to head out for a sneaky cigarette, but to do that I had to tell my mum I was off out for a walk. I trotted downstairs, entered the packed living room and announced, 'I'm just going for a wank.' To this day my grandad bursts out laughing whenever we all get together.

Oldsters taunted

While the last World Cup was on, I invited a couple of mates over to watch an England game. Arriving home late – mere minutes before my pals were due to arrive – I raced around to the shop to purchase the necessary beer and crisps, leaving my glasses at home. On the way back I spied the lads cycling up behind me, so – being the crazy guy that I am – I ran away in a comical manner, shouting: 'Oh no! They're gonna get me! Somebody save me!' When I eventually reached my front garden, I held my arms triumphantly aloft and turned around, hollering, 'Come on, you slow fuckers!' – only for the faces of a nice middle-class couple to swim into focus, staring at me as they cycled past. My mates arrived a minute later, by car.

Stinking fish drama

A short while ago I was taking part in a fishing competition on the River Trent. The match money was fairly serious and I was keen not to leave my rod. I was concentrating on a match it looked like I could win and desperately tried to ignore the effects of the previous night's curry and lager as it applied pressure on my bowel. But eventually the call of nature became too much and I had to give in. I trotted off up the bank, found a quiet stretch of river well secluded in high reeds, dropped my all-in-ones and did the business. I then rushed back to my rod and carried on fishing. About half an hour later a heavy downpour started and I pulled up the hood of my all-in-ones. I couldn't believe what I had done. In my earlier haste I had shit into my hood, and ended up with my own turd in my hair and down my back. Even to this day the lads in our fishing club refer to me, with great wit, as Shithead.

Clear windows

On visiting my mother recently, I discovered that she was having her house altered, placing the bathroom upstairs in what used to be her large front bedroom. There I was, having a morning shit, when the window cleaner arrived and started on the big bathroom window. Now, at this stage of early renovation, the clear glass hadn't been replaced with a frosted version, and so I sat there pretending I couldn't see him for a few minutes, until my bottle went and I ran out into the bedroom with my trousers around my ankles. Once safely behind the wall, I bent down and peeked round the corner so that I could see when he had gone and return to finish the job. And then I heard a noise behind me. Turning around slowly, I found myself looking straight at the cleaner's apprentice doing the other window, staring in wonderment at me bent over, starfish winking, peeking at his boss.

Ballgirl taunted

Many years ago my mate Peter asked if I would like to come and play tennis with him at his local club. Neither of us had played much tennis before, so Pete just hit balls at me as hard as he could, which I tried in vain to smash back. Our amateur attempts didn't go unnoticed by the two women on the court next to us, who spent most of the game giggling. And then it happened. One of them started walking towards us to retrieve a ball, just as Pete hammered back a shot. But instead of coming to me, it shot off to the left, straight into the head of the approaching woman, who went down like a sack of shit. There was a stunned silence as we all stared at her in disbelief, broken only by Peter, who was completely oblivious to what he had done, and without looking up, cheerfully shouted, 'Thanks, lady!' as his ball rolled gently to a halt at his feet.

Scorer mix-up

My first assignment as a budding football reporter on my local rag was to cover a game between Sheffield Wednesday and Blackburn. Things started badly before I even got there, when I became mired in traffic about a mile from the ground. I decided to abandon it, and sprinted towards the floodlights. With seconds to spare I barged into the press room, where my dishevelled appearance caused a ripple of laughter from the seasoned reporters and took a seat next to a man from BBC Radio Lancashire and his guest summarizer. Only then did I realize that I had forgotten my team-sheet, but found it easy to guess what was going on, until a sudden goal caused chaos in the press box as everyone disagreed whose foot had put the ball in the back of the net. Sensing a chance to impress my new media colleagues, I cleared my throat and said confidently, 'It was Kevin Gallagher.' There was a murmur of thanks as the journos jotted the name down, and my proud face must have looked a picture when Radio Lancashire's guest summarizer leaned over, nudged me and said, 'I'm Kevin Gallagher.'

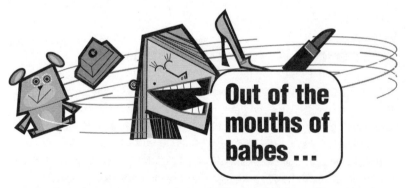

Out of the mouths of babes ...

One of my housemates was preparing for a job interview and read out the list of perks. "Interest-free season ticket loan?" she queried. "But I don't even like football." Hair colour: blonde.

I was telling my girlfriend that I had a mate running the London marathon, and that he was planning to participate in the Belfast one too. "Is that longer than London's?" she asked.

Second-hand purchase

Not too long ago my boyfriend, who is very tall and of a large build, responded to an advert for a second-hand wet suit. We gave them a call and they told us it was still available, so we went around to have a look. When we got there we were greeted by a couple who seemed deadly keen to sell him a ghastly luminous yellow thing, and although it was clearly too small, my boyfriend politely agreed to try it on. Eventually he returned from the bedroom with the suit pulled up as far as it would go, which was only to his chest. The couple then jumped on him and pulled it right up, giving him a colossal wedgy in the process, and forcing the hood right over his head until he was completely trapped in this horrible suit. Looking hot and red-faced, my boyfriend waddled crab-like back into the bedroom to get changed while I made small talk for what seemed like ages. When he finally returned, however, he had the suit rolled up under his arm, blithely said, '£120 was it, mate?', paid the man, and pulled me out of the house, only to ditch the thing in the first bin we walked past. Apparently when he had pulled the material out from between his bum cheeks, he'd left the world's biggest skid mark on the glowing yellow. He never did go scuba diving.

Marathon-runner's mishap

It was the morning of the London Marathon. I was ready to run and there were hundreds of us queuing up to use the portaloos at the start.I squeezed into the cubicle, where the floor was awash with runners' pee. While in there, I decided to apply some more Vaseline to my sensitive areas and accidentally dropped my shirt, soaking it in urine. Just then, I heard the PA system announce one minute to the off, looked in horror at my now soaking T-shirt and made the real-men-don't-care-if-their-kit-smells-of-other-peoples'-urine decision. Holding my breath, I pulled my shirt over my head and for the next 26 miles and 385 yards ran as fast as I could. As I worked up a sweat, everyone gave me a wide berth and at the end no-one rushed to congratulate me on finishing in a respectable time.

Potty training

A couple of years ago I went for a weekend visit to my parents. My wheelchair-bound gran was due to come round for Sunday lunch and, because the toilet was upstairs, we borrowed a commode from the nursing home next door. The old goat decided she needed to use the thing the minute she got through the door, so I went and waited in the garden until the show was over. However, the pot became stuck to gran's flabby arse and, as mum couldn't shift it by herself, I was summoned to give a hand. Mum pulled gran into a standing position (because she didn't want me to see her lady parts) and with a grim face I squatted down and heaved at the heavy bowl. As if the sight of Nan's flabby white arse wasn't bad enough to put me right off my lunch, when the pot's air-tight seal broke, I toppled over backwards and emptied a near-full tub of hot piss all over myself.

Leaking bin trauma

I returned home to my parents' house after a few beers, absolutely bursting for a pee. Running upstairs to the bathroom, I was surprised to find a decorator doing up the tiling. Not wanting to bother him, I went into my bedroom and in my semi-drunken haze, decided to pee in the metal waste-paper bin and empty it out of the bedroom window later on. After a quick kip, I went downstairs to find my parents looking up at a growing yellowish stain on the wallpaper. My father, thinking it must be a burst pipe had called an emergency plumber. I kept quiet and watched nervously. The plumber arrived and when he'd finished examining the tank in the room next to mine, claimed that it was leaking and some parts needed replacing. The bill came to several hundred pounds. I wanted to tell my folks, but the embarrassment would have been too much.

Cheery goodbye

While I was doing basic army training at Pirbright, a friend suggested we stay with his aunt and uncle in Reading. They were a most accommodating couple, and we had a delicious meal before returning to camp. When the time came to leave, I shook my friend's uncle by the hand, then bent forward to kiss the aunt on the cheek. As I did so, she appeared to raise her hand, so I went to shake it, and realized straight away that I had got hold of her right tit. I decided to go ahead as if nothing was wrong, and confidently shook her boob. The next week my mate asked if I wanted to go back but I declined – I couldn't face that old dear again.

Bodypart arrives

Last year, after a crash-course diet, I looked like a beanpole, so I joined the local gym. I decided to wear a loose-fitting Lycra outfit, going on the theory that although it felt baggy now, my impending muscles would soon fill it out. The treadmill was my first port of call, and it wasn't long before I was exchanging pleasantries with a well-built woman next to me. So there I was, jogging away quite happily, when one of her large, firm tits popped straight out of her running-top, giving me the quickest erection of my life. Mercifully she didn't notice, but the old boy on the rowing machine suddenly found himself on eye-level with an exposed penis. He started cursing and waving his fist, and eventually everyone in the gym was aware of my misdemeanour. I was nearly chased out of the place by fuming pensioners, and a week later the gym cancelled my membership. But to be honest, I hadn't planned on going back.

Man on girl's bike

It seems that whenever my mate and I go out, something terrible happens that makes us chuckle. The other day we were on our way to the pub when a big bloke hammered past us on a really old woman's shopping bike. He looked so stupid on the gimmer's vehicle that the pair of us just burst out laughing, and when he turned to scowl at us he was hit by a passing car. We just stood there pissing ourselves while he picked himself up off the floor, but quickly stopped when he turned to face us with an enraged expression across his purple face. Then he charged at us, and as we were rooted to the spot with fear, he would certainly have caught us, had he not suddenly been mown down by a car going in the opposite direction. I obviously felt truly guilty, as the poor chap was hospitalized, but we still gave him the wanker sign as they loaded him into the ambulance.

Hospital chaos

About two months ago, I found myself in the labour ward with my girlfriend. We had been there for about four hours and as I was by now desperate for a piss, I made my excuses and headed out to find the nearest toilet. When I asked where they were, however, I was told that they were in the adjoining ward, so to save time I dived into a nearby cubicle reserved exclusively for hospital patients. Halfway through relieving myself I had the sudden urge to fart, and I let rip with a trump so smelly that my eyes began to water. It was then that I considered the very real possibility that there could be someone outside waiting to use the toilet after me, and I became rooted to the spot with embarrassment. Reaching up, I gave the extractor chain a tug – but instead of a fan roaring into life, a loud siren went off at the hospital reception, accompanied by a flashing red light giving away my location. It was the emergency cord. Panicking, I pulled again, and the siren became even louder. Suddenly my door was unlocked from the outside and three midwives burst in to find me red-faced, stinking of shit and covering my face in shame. Their laughs were stifled only by the sounds of retching.

Car-crime victim

A few months ago I purchased a bright red MG convertible. I spent an absolute fortune on it, adding extras like a pukka stereo and new wheels, and keeping it in tip-top condition. So you can imagine my fury when, after leaving the top down, I caught a man in the act of dragging his keys down my baby's door! Enraged, I shouted at him, and he shot up the street in terror. I ran after him for miles – we went down alleys, ran through traffic and even jumped over some garden fences. He kept on running, but he couldn't shake me. Finally, I chased him into a dead end. I had the bastard. Or so I thought. Only when he turned, panting, to face me, did I realize that he was a big, mean-looking bastard. He had probably only taken flight out of shock; I, on the other hand, hadn't stopped to think what I would do if I caught him. He took out a car stereo (yep, mine) and approached, smashed me over the head with it and knocked me out. I eventually made it back to my scratched, stereoless car with a huge lump on my head.

Post-match incident

A few summers ago, me and my mates regularly climbed over a spiked steel gate into the school opposite my house to play on their tennis court. One evening I was last man off the premises, which meant lugging home all the tennis gear alone. Laden with bags and racquets, I carefully climbed the gate, swung my legs over, and jumped – catching my shorts on a spike and leaving me swinging six feet in the air. Not only was I suffering from an excruciating wedgie, but the seam in my shorts was cutting into my left testicle. And as if that wasn't embarrassment enough, I could only shout as a pair of young rascals wandered over, poked fun at me then stole all the tennis gear I'd dropped. I was dangling for ten minutes before a friend finally came back and helped me down.

Con unloads

Last Saturday afternoon in Aberdeen, I was sitting in a queue of cars at the traffic lights by the harbour. Parked in front of me was a guy in a white Fiesta van with the window wound down, and alongside him was a cattle truck, with some seriously pissed off cows looking out through the slatted sides. The van driver was propping up his head with his hand, clearly enjoying the summer rays, when suddenly, without any warning, a high-pressure jet of pure bovine piss blasted out of the truck, scoring a direct hit on his head. The bloke tried to get the window up, but it jammed, and he took an entire face-load of warm urine. As the truck moved off, the door burst open and, engaging in a lengthy session of projectile vomiting, the driver stood by his van, steam rising from his body, retching for all he was worth. I shook my head as I passed him, my face a picture of genuine concern, and then, much to his annoyance, I absolutely pissed myself.

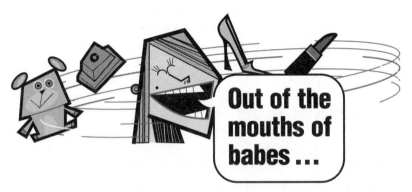

Out of the mouths of babes ...

While staying on the 24th floor of a Las Vegas hotel, my girlfriend was told by her mum to close the curtains whilst getting undressed – so passing aeroplane passengers "couldn't see in".

Alex James, Newport

During a recent conversation with my dear old mum, we stumbled into the subject of homosexuality. "I couldn't be gay," she said. "I just couldn't have one of them things shoved up my arse."

Darren Roberts, via e-mail

Telephone grief

A number of years ago, my hospitalized grandfather was rapidly deteriorating in health, and his daughter (my mum) was getting extremely upset. Having received compassionate leave from work, she spent all her free time at his bedside, and most of her nights crying at home. But things took a turn for the worse when she began getting nuisance phone calls. Worried about my mother's state, I agreed to answer the phone. Each time the thing rang, there was no answer, just silence. Getting more and more annoyed with the situation, I picked up the next call and yelled a stream of abuse at the sod on the other end, then slammed the phone down. The calls ceased. The next day, however, my grandfather's nurse phoned to say that the old man was upset that he couldn't get in contact with us, and would we please call him. It was then, while speaking to gramps, that the situation hit home. The 'crank' was grandad, and he hadn't realized that he had to press 'Answer' on the payphone when his call was picked up. Not only that, but he'd heard me clear as a bell when I'd asked if he wanted to smell my stinking underwear.

Fishing fiasco

The morning after a night on the bevy, my friend's grandfather and his mates decided to go out fishing on Loch Lomond. The group set off in a small boat, but as the choppy water combined with the effects of the previous night's drinking, the grandfather puked his load over the side. His retching was so violent that it dislodged his false teeth and the men watched helplessly as they sunk into the depths of the Loch.

He was livid, but his friends refused to interrupt their fishing trip, and by the time they'd had their lunch he'd calmed down enough to enjoy a short nap. On seeing this, one of the friends took out his false teeth and tied them to a fishing line. When the grandfather awoke, his friend shouted, 'I've got a bite!' and began reeling in his line. To the grandfather's delight, the false teeth were on the end. 'Would you credit it,' he said. 'That must be a one in a million chance.' Giving them a quick clean, he popped the teeth into his mouth. But he gave a puzzled look when he discovered they didn't fit. His friends were in knots of laughter, until he took out the teeth, said, 'They're not mine,' and flung them back into the Loch.

Smell of fear

A friend of mine moved into a house, sharing it with his 40-something, spinster landlady. He was the ideal lodger, and always ready to help with the dishes. One day he woke up late for work and, trying to do three things at once, put the toast on and went upstairs. When he returned to the kitchen, he found to his horror that it was full of smoke. The toast had turned to carbon. Opening windows, he prayed that the landlady wouldn't discover his mistake. Eventually the fumes cleared and he was just about to leave when he spotted a laden clothes horse in the corner. Afraid that it would reek of smoke, he lifted an item of clothing and sniffed. It was fine. At the same moment, his landlady appeared in her dressing gown and gasped in horror. He looked at her, she looked at him, he looked down to see that he'd been sniffing a rather stained pair of old frillies.

Spooky prank

A few years ago, I was staying overnight at a friend's house with a group of mates, when we got talking about the paranormal. One of our group, Mike, consistently told us to stop taking the piss, as 'playing with the Devil' was no laughing matter. Naturally, this just made the rest of us tell stories of a more and more extreme nature. Eventually Mike got so pissed off and upset that he went to bed. The rest of us stayed up talking for a while, then decided to round off the night with a little practical joke. We waited until we thought Mike would be asleep, then snuck downstairs and began scratching at his door, expecting him to tell us to piss off and go to bed. Instead, we heard an almighty smash followed by a loud scream. We opened the bedroom door to see that Mike had hurled a chair through the window and jumped through, slashing his legs severely as he did so. We no longer mess with the Dark Side.

Football terrace shock

I was at a recent Liverpool match where Michael Owen was about to stroll in a hat-trick. As I rose to acknowledge my hero, my world went brown. Screaming in agony, it felt like I'd gone blind in my right eye, and my forehead and ear seemed alight. My first reaction was that I had a brain tumour which had exploded in the excitement. My worst fears appeared to be confirmed as I examined the brown and white matter emanating from my head. As the goal euphoria dissipated, a number of my fellow supporters began to laugh at my hideous condition. 'It's pie lad, pie in yer eye!'

An over-enthusiastic fan to my rear had, at the moment of scoring, ejaculated his lunch up in the air with myself as unlucky recipient. Apart from a pleasant lady from St Helens who provided tissues, the Tarbys of the crowd set about belittling my injuries with talk of dieting and steak and kidney in the sky. Bastards!

Pre-med applied

Last July I found myself in hospital for an operation to straighten my nose. After my pre-med injection, the nurse gave me a green robe and small hat, and left me to get changed. Pulling the curtain around the bed to avoid prying eyes, I was horrified to find that the dressing gown didn't fit, and as the strings were far too short, I had a choice: I could leave the front half of my body exposed, or my arse. I opted for the latter, pulled back the curtains and gently sat on the bed. By now I was starting to feel the effects of the injection, so I put on the hat, and waited for the nurse. I noticed that the man in the bed opposite was staring. Not only that, but everyone in the ward was looking at me, and a nurse walked past, desperately trying not to laugh. Clearly, the joke was on me, but in my confused state I couldn't work out why. Defeated, I scratched my head, only to be surprised that, despite my hat, I could still feel my hair. Further exploration revealed that the garment had two large holes, but before I could do any more, a near hysterical nurse took me into the operating theatre and stuck another needle in me. As I realized what had happened, I gently passed out in the knowledge that there was a pair of pants on my head.

Seedy stargazer

When the Hale-Bop comet was in our skies I spent a lot of my evenings looking at it with my binoculars from my back garden. It was a good place to view because it was dark and nobody could see me. More recently, I heard about the dramas occurring on the Mir space station, which I also heard was visible at night, moving from east to west. One night I thought I would try to see it, and I went into my garden, which faces east, and began to look. It started to cloud over, and without thinking I went to the front of the house and continued to peer through my binoculars. I couldn't see anything, but when I dropped my binoculars from my eyes I noticed that my next-door-neighbours were looking over at me. They thought I had been trying to catch one of them stripping off in the bedroom window, and called me a pervert. To this day I have never had a chance to explain what I was doing, so they probably still think I am some kind of Peeping Tom.

Man down

A few years ago, my girlfriend and I decided to visit a shopping centre on the outskirts of town. It's the type of establishment that claims to provide a great day out for all the family, with cafés, rides, displays and a couple of people in bear costumes. When we got there I followed my girlfriend into the store, and paused to watch two ladies give a First Aid demonstration in a cordoned-off section, which had previously held a display of vintage motorcycles. As the pair rolled the dummy onto its back, however, part of its internal mechanism popped out through its trousers, giving the impression that it had a huge wooden hard-on. Naturally I thought this was brilliant, and I shouted to my girlfriend to come and see the awesome spectacle, but she just ignored me and walked away. Puzzled by her lack of interest, I turned back to the demonstration, only to find that both women were staring at me, clearly furious. It was then that I realized that the 'dummy' was actually an unfortunate lad in his early twenties, suffering from a fit and being resuscitated by two passing shoppers.

Culture shock

About two years ago, while I was living with four friends, I contracted a particularly vicious strain of thrush. The doctor gave me a prescription, but it was proving useless against the fungal onslaught. A friend had told me that natural yogurt was the answer, so off to the supermarket I went, and bought the biggest pot they had. Back home, I placed the afflicted bodypart into the pot and soaked it for an hour or so. Bliss! I put the yogurt in the fridge so that I could treat myself again later – but when I returned to repeat the treatment, the pot had vanished. I was horrified. Who had stolen my yogurt? Eventually one of my flatmates confessed. I never had the balls to tell him where the yogurt had been before he had eaten it, but served him right, thieving bastard! I'm sure he had very bad breath and an unusually aggressive case of plaque over the next week.

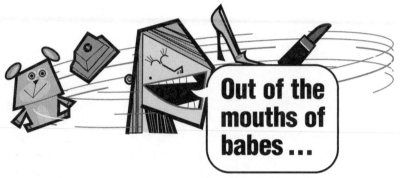

Out of the mouths of babes ...

Reading an article on Princess Di, my girl came to a part about "her brother, Charles Spencer". "I thought her brother's name was Earl," she said.

My lady and I were having a Chinese when we heard people talking about being born in the year of the rat. Asked if she knew what year she'd been born in, she said, "'Course, 1978."

He was framed, guv

When Crimewatch was at its peak some years ago, my friends and I always wished we knew the criminals featured. Until one day when we recognized one of our workmates – or at least someone uncannily like him. Now, we all knew that at the time of the 'transvestite flashing' our workmate was with us. He was an innocent man. But did that stop us? Did it fuck! It just had to be done. Just for a laugh, you understand, I phoned the police ... The ensuing scene was like something out of The Bill. A police van, loaded with coppers, pulled up outside. They burst in, grabbed our poor unsuspecting colleague, and bundled him into the van. The next day, the CID questioned us; had we noticed anything 'suspicious' about our colleague's recent behaviour? Was he a 'washing line thief'? Needless to say, we were too scared to tell the police the truth; someone claimed to have caught him reading a copy of Golden Shower in the toilets. Fortunately our mate was let off through a lack of evidence. He was last heard of living in a hostel in Oldham, after his wife left him.

Kidnap disaster

My brother, a fairly strange mate and I decided to kidnap another pal's three younger brothers whom he babysits on Wednesdays. The plan went like this: having assembled a pick-axe handle, a metal pipe and a length of chain, we'd enter the house with woolly hats over our faces and tie our mate up while one of us ran around shouting, 'Where's the fucking kids?' We'd then leave empty-handed, get changed in the car and go back in to 'rescue' our mate – thus, he'd be eternally in our debt. So, the door opens and we rush in. My brother runs upstairs shouting, 'Where's the fucking kids?' while we grab our mate, Simon, who puts up a fight. A very bad move, as Peter, the strange mate, seems to revel in inflicting pain and starts punching Simon. It all goes horribly wrong. Simon develops breathing problems, so my brother and I take our masks off and tell him it's only a joke. But our apologies are cut short as the house is stormed by police. Unbeknown to us, Simon had been on the blower to his girlfriend and, still on the phone while he answered the door, she'd heard the shouting and called the police. We tried to explain to the coppers why three grown men got their larks by virtually giving another of their mates a heart attack. His girlfriend didn't find it funny either.

Illegal booze

A couple of weeks ago I was walking through Leicester after a night at the pictures when, on the way to the bus station, I was approached by two young girls who wanted me to go to the off licence to buy some alcopops for them. For no good reason, I agreed, and they gave me a fiver. But once inside the offie, the man behind the till asked me if the girls outside were with me, and when I said yes, he refused to serve me. I went out and told the girls this, and they insisted I try the offie across the road. So I went into the second offie, picked up the bottles and went to pay the woman behind the counter, who had some trouble with the till. And by the time I came to pay, the door flew open and two coppers came in and nicked me for buying booze for minors. I was then dragged to the station, kept for three hours and released with a warning. On my release, the two girls were outside the nick, with a big bloke who came over and twatted me for nicking a fiver from his sister.

Tasteless prank

After an all-day drinking session, my mate and I came across a dead cat spread-eagled in the road. My mate, ever the prankster, picked it up and, to my horror, calmly walked into the local Chinese takeaway, threw the recently deceased moggy on the counter and announced, 'Right, that's the LAST you're getting! Until you pay for the last dozen, NO MORE CATS!' Then he left. Five seconds later, the restaurant was emptied of its horrified customers, and the irate takeaway owner was hurling abuse at us. We decided that a tactical withdrawal was necessary, and legged it. After a quarter of a mile, we calmed ourselves down by popping into the offie for a six-pack. Quenching our thirst, we were surprised by the police, complete with the irate owner claiming, 'Those are the bastards who scared off my customers!' We were consequently bunged in the back of the van, interrogated and charged with various offences, from breaching the peace to cruelty to animals – all of which I pleaded not guilty to, especially cruelty to animals, which I argued was somewhat difficult as the creature was already dead. Unimpressed, they chucked us into separate cells until 6am the next day. The case eventually got to court, raising a few laughs from the public gallery. I got a ticking off, but my mate's £250 payout to the takeaway owner for loss of takings meant that we're right off Chinese at the moment.

Worrying football story

On one of my rare trips from North Wales up to Turf Moor, the home of Burnley FC, I had the usual hassles of Saturday afternoon parking near the ground. After a frustrating 20 minutes dashing round nearby housing estates I eventually spotted a place about 100 yards up the road. On approaching the spot, a police squad car passed me from the opposite direction and I noticed the uniformed driver waving his half-clenched fist at me in a long masturbatory gesture. I flashed him a 'V' sign thinking him prejudiced against Burnley fans – I was wearing my claret and blue home shirt. There was a screech of brakes and the car reversed. An angry policeman got out. 'What do you think you're playing at, mate?' he said. 'Well, you called me a wanker,' I replied, sheepishly. 'Actually, sir,' he said, 'I was telling you to put your seatbelt on.'

Car lovers

On a night out with my girlfriend, the only place where we could truly be alone together was in my car, a Mini 1000, which we parked in a deserted lane before getting down to business. As I am 6ft 2in, there was a lack of space and so we continued up against the side of the car. Suddenly we were startled by the glare of oncoming headlights. My date had the presence of mind to dive into the passenger door, but I remained in the road, transfixed like a rabbit. Eventually, I came to my senses and ran to get in the driver's side. But I discovered the door had been locked – not by me, but by my (soon to be ex) girlfriend, who was finding the escapade very amusing. Acting on instinct, I went to the front of the car, lifted the bonnet and pretended to be the victim of a breakdown. What I didn't reckon on was the car being driven by two members of the local constabulary, who had decided to help me out – only to find me with one shoe on, my trousers held up by one hand and my shirt tucked into my boxers. What gave the game away was the huge erection bulging in my pants. I tried to maintain a front by saying it must be a dodgy ignition circuit. 'Can't see what's so exciting about a few spark plugs, sir!' said one policeman as they burst into laughter, looking at the large bulge in my pants.

Breaking the law

I have only broken the law once in my life and, sadly, crime paid. I had
put in for my driving test and was given a date for the nerve-racking
day. Unfortunately, the date the DVLC had given me was one day after
my 18th birthday. I worked out that I would have to stop my birthday
boozing at around 9pm in order to be clear for the test the following
morning. So, on my birthday I went out, promising my girlfriend on
pain of death that I would stick to two or three pints, and be tucked up
in bed by ten o'clock. Needless to say, I got shit-faced. Furthermore, I
stayed out until 6.30 in the morning, deciding that I would cancel my
test due to illness. The following morning, when I'd had only three
hours' sleep, my girlfriend came round, unannounced, and dragged me
out of bed to get me ready for the test. I didn't have the nerve to tell
her I had been on the piss all night, so, fuelled with tea and a packet of
mints, I went down to the test centre. Maybe it was the booze, or
maybe I'm just a great driver, but anyway, I passed. I'm possibly the
only man who qualified to drive while under the influence. And I'm
ashamed of myself.

Car calamity

On the night of my graduation ball, my mate left his keys and car at
my house so we wouldn't do anything foolish. As we were drinking
ourselves under the table, I came across a girl I had lusted after for
several terms, and I charmed the wench in no time. Soon, on a short
stumble back to my place, we started craving a pizza. I suggested
that she drive my friend's car to a take-away. We'd hardly got in
before we were going at it hammer and tongs. Halfway through, we
were shocked to hear, 'What the fuck is going on?' It was my mate –
he'd brought his spare key to the ball and had headed back to his car
for a kip. Within seconds, he'd fallen into an alcoholic slumber, so
the lovely lady and I continued as before. Then, fully sated, we set
off – but women's driving being what it is, she took a bend too
sharply and ended up on the other side of the road up a bank.
Suddenly sober, I got out of the car, and dragged my groaning friend
into the driver's seat. I told my lady friend to go back to the flat

while I moved into the passenger seat, pouring whisky over myself, and waited for a passer-by. Soon the Old Bill were with us. I tried playing the 'pissed-as-a-fart passenger' as me and my still-oblivious pal were dragged off to the local cop shop. He remembers nothing of the night, other than what I told him: that he'd insisted on going to get a pizza. He lost his licence for two years; I got a night in the cells. I have since married that appalling driver – and when I told my one-time friend the truth some years later it earned me a broken nose and six stitches. Still, that was a bloody good piss-up.

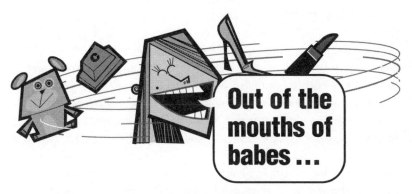

Out of the mouths of babes ...

My mate was recently telling his girlfriend about an acquaintance who'd been badly beaten up and had staples in his head. "Christ," she retorted, obviously shocked. "Why would anyone attack someone with a stapler?"

Doing a crossword last week, my girlfriend asked to join in – so I read out "Biblical Giant" as a clue. "Jolly Green!" she replied, quick as a flash.

Speaker left on

Some years ago I was working for a small business firm in Manchester. On the way home I was just about to drive up onto the M26, when I had to stop at a red light. In front of me was a police car, a Jaguar, then a learner. When the lights turned green the learner started to pull away, stalled, and couldn't restart his car until the lights were red again. When they changed to green, he stalled again, prompting the man in the Jag to get out and walk towards him. Suddenly the police car loudspeaker burst into life: 'Would the gentleman who has just left his vehicle please remember he was once a learner too.' Clearly embarrassed, the man returned to his Jag. As the lights changed, the learner stalled again, when we were treated to, 'Fucking hell, the dozy twat has done it again.'

Stupid boys

A few years ago, during a particularly hot summer, some friends and I visited a local toy store and bought a load of super-powerful water pistols. After several hours of shooting at each other, we got a bit bored and decided to hit the streets in search of new victims. We jumped into my mate's car and began to squirt innocent pedestrians, making good our escape at high speed. Eventually we got bored of this too, and were just about to head for home when we saw a man laden down with shopping bags. We knew that we had to whack him. We slowed to a crawl for the drive-by, lowered the windows, and treated the man to a full-on, four-rifle assault. The poor sod was saturated, and as we sped away we looked back and laughed at him standing soaked and bewildered with his shopping spread out all over the pavement. Later that evening, we were all heading for a night out on the town when we noticed the blue flashing light of the Old Bill in our rear-view mirror. We were rather bemused by this as we hadn't been drinking, and we certainly hadn't been speeding, so we pulled over to the side of the road confident we were safe. The policeman walked up to us, tapped on the window and said, with a smile, 'Alright boys, where's the water pistols?' It was the bloke we had drenched. He then ticketed us for speeding, and made sure we knew he would be keeping a special eye open for our car in the future.

Unlikely auto occurrence

After a very drunken evening at a party, a friend of mine foolishly decided to drive home. After about a mile, he started going round a roundabout, but realized he'd missed his exit. He stopped the car and started reversing. Then, to his horror, a car went into the back of him. His immediate thought was: 'I'm doomed', especially as he's a lorry driver and would almost definitely lose his licence. Things then went from bad to worse as a police car arrived on the scene. My friend watched the policeman talk to the driver in the rear car. His heart dropped when the policemen walked over to his car and motioned for my friend to lower his window. Putting on his most sober voice, my friend said: 'Evening, officer.' 'It's all right, sir,' the policeman replied, 'you can go. That driver must be completely plastered – he said you were reversing round the roundabout!'

Girlfriend rattled by crash

A while back my uncle wanted to impress his girlfriend with a day out in the country, so he borrowed my dad's car – despite not being insured for it. He set off with his girlfriend... and not long into the journey dinged another car. Having no insurance details to swap he sped away from the scene of the accident, hiding the car in a field as the police cruised around, trying to find him. He managed to avoid the rozzers before finally ringing his sister to ask her to come and pick them up from the middle of the countryside. On the way home they stuck to the back roads, and his sister, enjoying all the odours nature has to offer, declared, "Wow, you can really smell that fresh country air.""No," my uncle had to correct her, "I'm afraid that's my girlfriend." She had literally shit herself from fear of being caught by the law.

Lads blag footie freebie

A couple of seasons back, when Barnet FC were sponsored by a well-known lads' mag, it soon looked obvious that the novelty of following these football minnows was wearing off. The mag's once detailed "Barnet Updates" were becoming smaller and smaller, and it was blindingly obvious – to me, anyway – that they weren't going to the games any more. So on learning that my team – Exeter City – were playing Barnet away, some mates and I decided to take advantage of the magazine's apathy. We phoned up the London club claiming to be from the mag in question and asked to attend the Exeter game. Come the day, not only were VIP tickets waiting for us at the gate, but we were treated to a free bar, three-course meal and a round of applause from the chairman and directors at the post-match function arranged in our honour for our "unfailing support" that year. To cap off a perfect day, Exeter won.

Animal lover rebuffed

Wandering home one night the worse for drink, I spotted a hedgehog in the middle of the road. Just as I was thinking that if it didn't start moving it would get flattened, a pair of headlights appeared. I ran into the road, waving frantically at the oncoming vehicle, which stopped a few feet from the poor creature, at which point I mouthed the word, "Hedgehog," and pointed at the road. The driver nodded in acknowledgement and I stepped out to rescue the errant woodland creature – until it became obvious that the hedgehog was, in fact, nothing more endangered than a U-shaped corrugated pipe from a washing machine. Not wanting to look a complete prat I pulled my sleeves over my hands to avoid being "pricked" and gingerly carried the piping to the side of the road, then nodded to the driver, who pulled away. Feeling justly miffed I then drop-kicked the pipe a good 60ft into a neighbouring garden. I should have waited a few seconds more, for the driver obviously saw me in his rear-view mirror and screeched to a halt, leapt out and chased me down the road, shouting and screaming about animal cruelty. He was beyond reason, so I ran. So much for my good deed.

Cold woman punishes visitor

A few winters back, a couple of mates and I were killing time in a park when we stumbled upon an exhibition of ice sculptures, so naturally we had a look around. One of the sculptures was of an attractive naked woman, which caused me to instinctively run up to it, put my hands around her and say, "Give us kiss, love!" before sticking my tongue in her mouth. It was all very funny, until I realised that my tongue had become stuck to the freezing sculpture and I couldn't pull myself away. My friends ran for some warm water to part the pair of us but seemed to take an unfeasibly long time about it, leaving me alone to mumble incoherent excuses at dozens of gawping park-goers.

Air-con betrayal

I'm 24 and a researcher for a car company, which recently sent me to Singapore for some very dull meetings about sales statistics. I went with a female colleague whom I'd been seeing for some time. Towards the end of the trip we found ourselves at a table with 12 other people. As the meeting dragged on my girlfriend kept teasing me by running her hands down her thighs, until I couldn't take any more.

I thumbed my phone ringtone, stepped out to take the "call" then asked my girl to join me so we could escape to the loo for a shag, where I bent her over the toilets while she moaned and talked dirty as usual. Fortified, we rejoined the meeting... until my smug smile turned to panic as I heard the unmistakable sound of a toilet flush over the ventilation system above my head. Searching the faces round the table, I met a mix of admiration and disgust.

Pensioner misses her tipple

My uncle does his bit for society by taking the local pensioners for walks. One Sunday morning he picked up an old girl from her "retirement community". After doing the usual activities – going around the park, feeding the ducks and wandering through the markets – my uncle suggested they go back to his house, where they had lunch with his wife and two children before trooping into the front room to watch TV. The old dear asked my uncle if she could have a brandy but by the time he'd returned with the drink she was fast asleep, so he told the kids to keep it quiet while the oldie had a nice nap. A few hours later it was time to get her back to the home, but she wouldn't wake up. It turned out the family had watched the entire omnibus edition of EastEnders with a corpse on the sofa, while the kids, on their best behaviour, played at her feet.

Stripper asks for it

Many moons ago while on the lash in Belgium, my fellow alcoholics and I popped into a sex club. We took up position next to the stage and watched in disbelief at some of the things the fine ladies were doing to each other. One of the strippers then announced that there was the equivalent of £100 on offer to any man who would (or could) shit on her face. An eager young Belgian leapt on stage and squatted over her as she pursed her lips... but nothing happened. Another guy hopped up, dropped his trousers, and again nothing happened. While the fella next to me was explaining that if someone is blowing on your anus then you can't defecate, one of our group climbed on stage, stood over the young lady and dropped his drawers. Before she'd even had a chance to pucker up and blow, he'd emptied his load on her head. It was in her hair, her mouth, everywhere – the young chap had been suffering from the squirts for days. Our "reward" was to get chucked out. Belgians – you've got to love them.

Soldier pulls hyper Kraut

When I was in the Army I pulled a bird in a German nightclub. She was a little wild but I was the worse for drink, so I let her drag me back to a faceless apartment block on the outskirts of town. After drunkenly negotiating some fiendish locks on the door we headed upstairs to her flat, where we proceeded to have energetic sex well into the small hours. Next morning she was still hyper, dancing around the place, while I needed a piss, so I headed off to find the toilet. It did strike me as odd that her block had a communal bathroom and kitchen, but it was only on the way back to her room – when I passed a man dressed in white and wearing a name-badge – that I realised my companion was more than a few cards short of a full deck, and had in fact taken me back to her mental hospital.

Cream tea for Fido

A few years ago when I lived with my parents I arranged a lift home with an attractive female work colleague, knowing that the house would be empty for a while. I invited her in, and before long we were going at it on the sofa in the lounge. It had been a while since my last spurt, so it didn't take long before I shot my bolt straight up her. Lying there with a smile on my face, I was disturbed to see her stand up in the middle of the room and, saying, "I hate this bit," drop my come all over my parents' rather expensive carpet. As she did this the door opened – although luckily it wasn't my parents but my pet dog, which bounded straight towards my pile and lapped it up. I quickly got rid of the lady, and five minutes later my parents duly arrived home. The first thing my mother did was sit on the sofa, to be greeted by my faithful pooch licking her all over her face.

Spurned ex thwarted

Several months ago my girlfriend needed some bunions removed, leaving her in hospital with a huge plaster cast on her foot. I decided I'd take this opportunity to finish with her, seeing as how she couldn't really chase after me for dumping her! However, a few days later I heard a loud banging and screaming at my door. Looking out of the upstairs window I saw my ex, freshly discharged from hospital, booting the door with her heavy, plaster-encased foot. This went on until the door crashed off its hinges – but mercifully without the expected entry of a crazed harridan barking for my blood. Poking my head into the hall, I could see her lying on the porch, whimpering for help. The subsequent X-ray showed that my psycho ex had kicked the door so hard that she'd broken her right leg, leaving her in plaster for the next three months. Unsurprisingly, we're not back together.

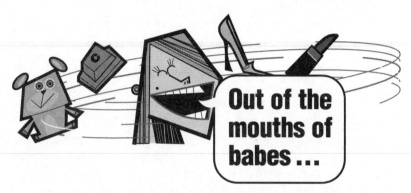

Out of the mouths of babes ...

On a trip to a park, my wife and I joined some schoolkids for a tour of the cow fields, where she raised her hand and asked, "Why do all of your cows have girls' names?"

During a school trip to a small island a few years ago my sister and I ate our packed lunches together, which attracted loads of greedy birds. "How did they get to the island?" my sis blurted out.

Dream date turns sour

A few months ago I got chatting to a fine young thing in the students' union, and was happily surprised when she suggested we go back to her flat. I was even more content when her flat turned out to be an overly flash-looking luxury apartment. I presumed she had wealthy parents and thought no more about it – as no sooner had my jacket hit the designer leather couch than she dropped to her knees in front of me. However, my bliss was shattered by the sound of a key in the front door, whereupon my date turned pale and told me to leg it down the fire escape. Confused and still half-pissed, I did what she said. I was halfway down the external staircase when I heard a posh woman's angry shriek from inside. "Peter!" she screamed. "It's the bloody cleaner!"

Costly call

Driving back from my girlfriend's one night, I spotted a police car lurking ahead. By braking sharply, I managed to get down to 30mph and cruised through without any bother. I hadn't gone more than another mile when I passed my girlfriend's dad hurtling back home well over the speed limit. Eager to earn some brownie points I called him up on his mobile to warn him of the porcine presence, but I'd scarcely exchanged pleasantries before the miserable bugger cut me off. Thinking nothing of it, I continued home. It was later that night when my girlfriend called to warn me to stay clear of the house for a while, since her dad was in a foul mood. He'd just been pulled over by the police, and although his speed wasn't too much in excess of the limit they were going to prosecute, since they saw him holding a mobile to his ear as he tootled past.

Eggy mistake

My mum owns a cockatiel, and one day my mate and I decided to play a trick on her. Taking two white Cadbury's mini-eggs we put them in the bottom of the parrot-like bird's cage, nestling them among the ripped-up newspaper. Knowing my mum would think they were real, I was going to reach into the cage, pick out the eggs and, to her horror, scoff them down! When I returned home from work with my mate that evening, sure enough she'd discovered them, wrapping the speckled baby-birds in cotton wool. Pretending to coo over the little fellas, I plucked the "eggs" out of the cage, popped them in my mouth and crunched down hard. Out of my mouth trickled warm, sticky egg yolk. After I'd yakked up over the kitchen floor, my mate managed to stop laughing for long enough to tell me he'd come clean to my mum, and the pair of them had swapped the fakes for freshly laid ones from the breeder.

Taped knob horror

A few years ago, when I was a virgin of 16, I went out with an older girl. My inexperience was obvious, as every time we so much as kissed I'd get a hard-on. So before our next night out I decided to wrap my snake in surgical gauze, then bound it tightly to my leg using insulating tape. Arriving at her parents' house that evening I found that her mum and dad were out, which meant we were soon swapping spit. I felt the tape straining, but holding, and was even able to smirk, cheesily, when asked, "Where is he tonight?" But with cruel irony this proved to be the occasion I was fated to go all the way. When nimble fingers tugged at my boxers, it was only her shriek of horror as she exposed my bulging, mummified member to the light that brought me back to reality. That, and her sobbing exit from the bedroom. I never heard from her again.

Fart does damage

I was at work when I suffered the onset of a sudden attack of wind caused by the jacket potato and beans I'd had for supper the night before. I could tell that building up was a massive fart that would have both stunk and made an ear-splitting noise, but I was too lazy to slope off to the bogs on the next floor up. So to spare my colleagues – and my shame – I waddled off to a meeting room to release the monster. It was dark as I closed the door behind me and gratefully let rip, before reaching for the light switch. Unfortunately, my plan of hiding in there until the evil gases had dispersed was foiled: to my horror, the light revealed that one of the directors of the company was sitting in front of me, cradling her head in her hands. The poor woman suffered from migraines, and had been quietly sitting in the darkened room waiting for the pain to go away.

Pics show pal up

Some months ago a few friends and I logged on to an Internet chatroom, knowing that another mate of ours would be online at the same time. Registering as "saucysuzy19" we began chatting dirty to him and ended up getting his e-mail address. We must have made a good impression as the next day he could talk of nothing else but the previous night's conversation. Naturally, over the weeks we continued to e-mail him filthy anecdotes. This culminated in us sending him a bunch of amateur porn photos we'd found on the net while asking for some in return. The next day we duly received five pictures of our victim, fully naked, fingers up his arse and covered in his own come. Needless to say his girlfriend didn't appreciate being forwarded them; nor did another 50-odd mutual acquaintances.

Tourist gets runs in public

On a six-week summer trek with my mates around South America, all was going well until I came down with a serious case of the trots. This meant when I had to go... I had to go. Which is exactly how I felt as we were waiting for a bus in some tiny town in the middle of nowhere. The bus station's waiting room was little more than a shack with a man behind a desk, but by using a combination of lousy Spanish and frenzied sign language I managed to convey to him the fact that I needed the toilet. Badly. He grinned and pointed to a bucket in the corner of the room. Thinking this must be normal for a developing country and wracked by cramps, I got my mates to stand in front of me as I tugged at my trousers, squatted down and dumped my foul load in the bucket – to the dismay of the other travellers. I'd almost finished when a door swung open in the wall behind the bucket and a young lady emerged, revealing a sparklingly clean set of toilet facilities behind her.

Plod's plot runs into trouble

I was once a copper, partnered with a character who liked to take out a car on night patrol on his own – meaning that after the pubs had kicked out I wouldn't see him again until 6am. We had to patrol 60 miles every night and my colleague always came back with at least 70 on the clock, but no-one could work out where he'd been – until one night, when I was told a police car had crashed on a local estate. I drove over and there was my colleague's vehicle poking out from a garage wall. It transpired that he'd taken to "patrolling" a local lady's bedroom, parking the police car in her garage, jacking the front wheels up and then, with great skill, placing the car in first gear and delicately balancing a brick on the accelerator. This allowed him to satisfy both her and the Chief Inspector's mileage targets – until some local kids had sneaked in and given the car a push. The rest was history, as was his career.

Improviser loses appetite

I was lucky enough to have a one-night stand with a pretty foxy girl a few years back. I was busily doing said lady from behind when she screamed for me to screw her harder. I suggested a bit of bum sex but she said she didn't have any KY, so in a flash of inspiration I went to the fridge and grabbed a tub of Utterly Butterly. Back in bed I smeared a generous handful round her ring, realised it was a little too much and scooped the excess back into the pot. After a most pleasurable time I awoke the next morning to find my "date" eating breakfast: toast and Utterly Butterly. For some reason I didn't feel very hungry after that.

Fiddler caught out

I recently drew the short straw of being the only person in my department to have to work on a Bank Holiday, but at least I'd be able to fulfill an ambition: to knock one out while sat at my desk. The only danger was a nearby ladies' toilet – there were several women working at the other end of the building. However, confident that I'd spot any ladies heading towards me in plenty of time, I called up a porn website and started stroking. Unfortunately, my meticulous planning had failed to take into account a second entrance to the toilet, and just as I got to the vinegar strokes a sneaky little minx burst out of the entrance by my desk. I span around in my chair to hide my shame, but this movement and the added excitement of a female in close proximity meant I shot my load under the desk, leaving man-paste dripping down my manager's PC. Next day it became obvious my jizz had completely screwed his CD-drive. I then watched in great amusement as Systems chided him for spilling paper glue on it, then downgraded his replacement machine.

Gorilla gaffe

In an attempt to ease my student overdraft I spent some time working behind the bar of one of the seediest pubs in Yorkshire, where they employed no fewer than three gorilla-like doormen in an attempt to contain the inevitable violence. Every Wednesday, however, was "Ladies' Night" – a happy event during which anyone was capable of pulling. At the end of one such evening, while clearing up the broken bottles and glasses, I noticed a single female sat alone in the corner of the pub, her back towards me. Armed with my dustpan I ambled over to check the lonesome lady out, then swaggered to where the bouncers were comparing tattoos and declared that it was no surprise she was on her own as she was rough as a badger's arse and twice as ugly. "That's my fucking wife," one of the Neanderthals informed me. Which concluded my last night at that establishment.

Plod take their time

After a night out, my mates and I were walking past a theatre when we noticed the name of the play was spelled out in large metal letters hanging on wires. Scrambling up, I managed to change The Town Mouse And The Country Mouse into the highly imaginative "wAnCer". Admiring our work, we were interrupted by some coppers. They were hardly able to disguise their amusement as they pointed out the town's biggest police station a few feet away, from where they'd watched the entire episode. Can I also take this opportunity to add that I would have got clean away as the ringleader were it not for my mate, Danny, who squealed like a pig the second his collar was felt? Thank you.

Shuffle in the spotlight

Picture the scene: one night during the Gulf War ceasefire I was stuck on a hill in a trench overlooking Dohuk, a shitty northern Iraqi city, periodically using a night-vision device to check what was going on. After a couple of hours of bugger all, my mind wandered to dirty thoughts. Needless to say the old man started to grow, and soon I was getting rid of some "pent-up aggression". The trench was cramped but as it was pitch black, I stood up and continued merrily shuffling away. Lost in thoughts of ecstasy, I disregarded two thumps from our rear lines. Seconds later the earth literally shook as an A6 Intruder flew mere feet above my position and dropped an aerial flare over the city, and two artillery shells popped out flares of their own (this was the noise I'd heard). I'd carefully timed my self-pleasuring to coincide with an Anglo-US harassment operation, which left me silhouetted and highly visible for miles around, cock in hand.

Betrayed by the box

Having just purchased a new widescreen TV, I had a flash of brilliance in the bath: sell my old one online. Composing a description while soaking, I excitedly towelled off and ran downstairs to take a digital photo of my old telly, then e-mailed the description and picture to an online auction site. It was only when I checked the site the following day that I realised the camera's lens had picked out an item that wasn't included in the sale: me – or more accurately my plums – poking out from under a towel, perfectly reflected in the TV screen. Bids had already been placed, which meant that try as I might, I couldn't remove the photo from the site. Consequently my love-spuds were exposed to millions of internet users for a whole week. At least I sold the telly.

Removal man rushes in

I used to work for a removals company, and the first – come to think of it, the only – rule we had was never to use the customer's toilet. After a particularly heavy night on the lash, however, the tortoise was showing his head just an hour into my starting a job. The car belonging to the family we were moving had disappeared from the drive, so I took a chance and dashed up the stairs four at a time, flung open the door to the loo, spun round and dropped my trousers. There immediately erupted from my arse a thunderous fart, closely pursued by the smelliest cow-pat I had ever laid. As I sat, head in hands, groaning softly to myself, I looked up to see the lady of the house standing in the shower cubicle with a bottle of bathroom cleaner, studiously staring at the tiling. Similarly avoiding eye contact I said that I'd better go, and she could only give a little nod and whimper, "Yes." I didn't venture from the back of the van for the rest of the day.

Lucky mog

My girlfriend used to tell me that it was disgusting I let my cat Valentino lie in bed with me, under the covers. "What's the worst that could happen?" I would scoff. Then I found out. One night I was nodding off to sleep, the cat under the sheets, me stroking her, when I came across a hard lump on her fur. It felt like something tangled in her pelt, so I picked at it. The cat didn't mind, so I continued till I'd got most of it away. Pleased to have done my moggy a favour, it was only then I realised I'd been picking dried lumps of shit from my pet's arse.

Double the fun

One night at uni the lads and I stopped off at the bar to take in a few beers before going to a Man City match. Some girls we knew were there too, and we wasted no time in chatting them up. I ended up going back to one of their places, ditching the lads. We were soon up in her attic room and at it like the clappers. After various positions she wanted to do it doggy-style and I kindly obliged, but the sloping ceiling over the bed was so low that I had to open the skylight to put my head through. To my delight I discovered that her house was next to Maine Road, and I could see the pitch. So I managed to watch most of the second half, while she got the longest-lasting screw of her life.

Oldie gift spurned

My friend is an ambulance driver, transporting the old and infirm to hospital. When management informed them that receiving a gift could lead to dismissal my friend had to tell one of his regulars that he could no longer accept her regular bags of Brazil nuts. Afterwards, the oldster's daughter cornered my mate and explained that her mother couldn't get out on her own, but that every week she brought her a selection of chocolate-covered Brazils. For months, the toothless old bat had been sucking off the choc, bagging the nuts and feeding them to my mate.

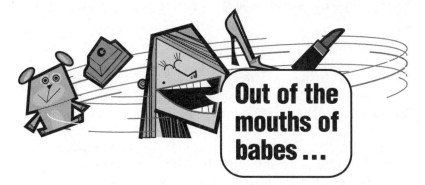

Out of the mouths of babes ...

Driving the old girl down the A5, a motorbike with German registration went flying past. "I wonder if that's left, or right-hand drive?" mused my mum.

Watching the news about the Ark Royal departing for the Gulf, the commentator said that the ship was carrying, amongst other weaponry, Merlin anti-submarine helicopters. "Does that mean they fly underwater?" asked my girlfriend.

Girl regrets club encounter

For a time I worked in a genito-urinary clinic in Glasgow where the patients were mostly young people, so it was no surprise to recognise them in pubs or on the street. Typically they would cross the road or hide in embarrassment – an understandable reaction given that I knew the most intimate details of their sexual escapades, and most likely had probed, prodded and swabbed their genitalia. One night I was with some friends in a nightclub when the girl next to me at the bar started chatting away like we were long-lost friends. It was clear that she recognised me, but had no idea from where. I couldn't resist stringing her along for the best part of ten minutes before the inevitable look of horror spread over her face – as she realised I'd frozen her labial warts just two months previously.

Pear-shaped end to posh night out

When a classy girl at work agreed to go out with me, I knew she had expensive tastes, so I decided to go all out to impress her with a meal in a swanky Italian restaurant and by dressing in my best gear. I had a suit but the problem was that I didn't have a decent tie. However, after phoning a few friends I got a loan of one of those clip-on Homer Simpson jobs. The big night arrived and the meal went amazingly well. She drank loads and started to get frisky, before suggesting that I walk her home – she had her own place on the lower floor of a larger house. The journey back was fast and flirty, and when we got back to her flat she started down the steps, then turned and gave me a passionate kiss. Just like the movies, she next grabbed me by my tie and said in a sexy voice, "Are you coming in?" Needless to say the clip-on immediately came away in her hands, and she sailed backwards down the steps. A long night in A&E waiting to be seen for a badly bruised ankle killed any remaining passion left in the poor girl.

Copper cracks case

Fifteen years ago I was a fresh-faced sprog straight out of police training college, sent to check on an old dear who hadn't been seen for a couple of days. There were milk bottles on the doorstep and unopened post piling up on the welcome mat so, suspecting the worst, I took my size tens to the door and started searching the house. The only room I couldn't get access to was the khazi, so once again I put my Doc Marten's to work. The door flew in then immediately bounced back, hitting me in the face. Opening it a little more carefully this time I entered the room, to find that the poor old lady had obviously died of a heart attack while laying a log, fallen off the shitter and blocked the door with her head. She now also had a nice big dent between the eyes, courtesy of yours truly – a fact I tactfully omitted on returning to the nick to submit my report. Turning up the next day, I had a bit of a shock when I found that a murder incident room had been set up for an old dear whose post-mortem revealed a fractured skull. It was a very nervous young copper who gave a rather more detailed report to the detective superintendent later that morning...

Pet betrays petting

Some time ago I was sort-of seeing a girl I'd met in Tenerife that summer. I say "sort-of" because she was engaged at the time, which meant the only way we could get together was when she was able to make an excuse to her hubby-to-be and hotfoot it across town. As I was still living with my parents, we'd go for a hefty piss-up while waiting for my folks to go to bed, then use the front room as a make-do shag shack and ride the night away. After one of her hasty early-morning departures, my conquest phoned to say she'd lost her knickers and a sock; eager to avoid an embarrassing confrontation with my mum I turned the front room upside down, but couldn't find the missing garments anywhere. Until later, that is, when a pleasant evening's family television viewing was interrupted by my parents' puppy staggering into the lounge and vomiting a black G-string onto the living-room rug. I never did find the sock.

Ball dare backfires

When I was a 14-year-old at boarding school, lights out in the dorm was the cue for a whole bunch of arsing around. One incident involved a game of dare, during which my mate Dave bet he could fit both nads into a Marmite jar. Such a receptacle was produced and Dave soon proved the doubters wrong but, unfortunately, he couldn't extract his testicles. He then walked around for two days with his love-nuts trapped in glassware, before desperation drove him to the design workshop. His plan was to remove the jar by smashing it with a hammer: a foolhardy procedure that resulted in him smacking one plum square-on and cutting the other with broken glass. He lost the bruised bollock and, on visiting him in hospital, I was sworn to secrecy – a vow I have maintained ever since. Er, until now.

Shopping trip turns sour

After a stint working offshore as a welder I gratefully boarded the train from Aberdeen, and proceeded to celebrate my return to dry land with a few beers. Consequently, I soon felt the need to relieve a little gaseous pressure. The carriage was quite full so I cocked my leg and tried to sneak out a quiet one – but disaster struck and I followed through. I could feel the parcel wedged in my crack, so at Edinburgh I gingerly de-trained and went to a shopping precinct, found a clothes shop and hurriedly bought the first size 38 denims I could find, before waddling back to catch the next train. As soon as the train was moving I dived into the toilet, ripped off my old jeans and skiddies and tossed them out of the window. After cleaning myself up I opened the package I'd bought, to find... a Wrangler jacket.

Tile man can't complain

When I worked for a company selling tiles and bathroom suites, a woman a few years my senior came into the showroom for the umpteenth time having finally decided on the tiles she wanted. As on her many previous visits she flirted like mad with me, bending over as I loaded up the car so I could see the tiny thong she was wearing. Consequently, as an act of sheer chivalry, I offered to ride with her and unload the tiles back at her place. The conversation on the drive back was awash with innuendo, so it was no surprise when my fourth tile-laden journey up the stairs was interrupted by the bedroom door opening – and her inside, wearing nothing but the thong. Before I knew it I was getting the ride of my life! Unfortunately, when we were done, I still had to finish unloading the car. Being understandably knackered, on my next haul I slipped on the bathroom mat and tipped a box of tiles into the bath, leaving it with a massive crack. So we ended up going back to the shop, which meant that not only did I get the shag of a lifetime but commission on the sale of a new bath. Result!

Chunderer's chuck lives on

As a fresh-faced first-year at uni, I went on a night out with my new housemates. When we got back to our top-floor flat I was battered, so after polishing off a take-away I stumbled to bed. An hour later I awoke, needing to be sick. However, I could hear my new chums chatting in the living room and I'd have to pass them to get to the lav. So, to save face I stood on my bed, prised the top of the window down and spewed my guts out. Brilliant! Except that next morning I was greeted by a pebble-dashed pane and window ledge, stinking and impossible to clean. That wasn't the end of it, as the next day I was awakened by a knocking sound. For a week this continued until I opened the curtains quickly enough to expose the culprit: a cheeky magpie, happily chipping away at my crusty chunder.

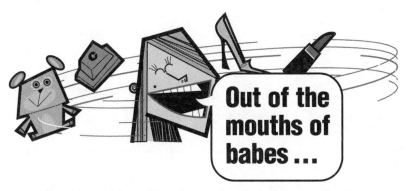

Out of the mouths of babes ...

While taking the last of her three daily inhalers, my girlfriend exclaimed, "I seem to spend half my life just breathing in!"

Playing 20 Questions during a long train journey, my girlfriend had to guess I was thinking of Freddie Mercury. She couldn't even work out what industry he was in, so as a not-so-subtle hint I started playing with my Walkman. "I get it!" she squealed. "Is it the man who invented headphones?"

Face-cloth faux pas

After a night out with pals, I decided to call in on my then-girlfriend for a bit of late-night lovin'. Having quaffed a few bevvies, I slept like a log – until the early hours of the morning, when I woke up with a banging headache. The only immediate cure I could think of was something cold on my forehead, so I stumbled groggily into the bathroom, grabbed the first flannel I could find and stuck it under the tap. I then returned to bed and comforted myself by draping the cloth on my face, enjoying its moist dampness... until I was woken by a shriek from my girl. "What's that doing in here?" she screamed, pointing at the flannel. I soon found that the thing I'd used to soothe my face was in fact her mum's "special cloth" – the fanny flannel she used to wash her muffin. Not the best start to the day, believe me.

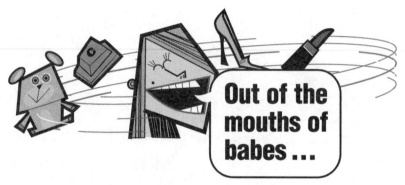

Out of the mouths of babes ...

On a day out in London my girlfriend came out with: "You know the Nelson on Nelson's Column – is it Nelson Mandela?"

My mum had a stroke and was told she would eventually lose her sight. My girlfriend was very upset, but had these words of consolation: "Don't worry – I'll learn Braille so I can read to you when you're blind."

Drinker rues nap

Following an afternoon's drinking, I decided I'd reached my limit at 6pm and tottered off to the bus stop for the 30-minute journey home.

Unfortunately, the combination of lager and the warm top-deck of the bus meant that I immediately fell into a drunken coma. It was a full two hours before a fellow passenger shook me awake, when I saw we were in the centre of Manchester. I stumbled off and went to the station to catch a train home. To kill time I strolled round the station and picked up a paper before catching the train, eventually arriving home about 9pm. It was only 30 minutes later, after I'd taken a piss, that I finally looked in the mirror. To my horror, my nose had been covered in highlighter pen, while my forehead boasted the word "TWAT" in biro – which explains the look I'd got in the newsagent.

Prankster rewarded

A few years ago I worked in a bacon-processing factory. One day, tired of feeding joints of pig meat into the slicer, I decided to relieve my boredom by playing a joke on the girl working further down the conveyor belt. Letting out a scream from behind the machine, I tossed a rubber glove full of piggy off-cuts onto the production line. My high-jinks fell flat, however, when on spotting the "severed hand" my co-worker fainted, falling head-first onto the belt. As her hair wound around the pulleys I managed to hit the emergency stop button, then stuffed the glove into my overalls and shouted for help. I got the rest of the afternoon off as the fire brigade worked to release the poor girl, who luckily had no memory of what had happened. The next day I was called to the MD's office. Expecting a P45, instead the old boy heartily shook my hand and passed over a cheque for £250 as reward for my "prompt actions" which had "probably saved the girl's life".

Hair hacker con

A few years ago I joined the police, which meant going to training college deep in the countryside, where we were continually hassled about our hair being too long. That was lucrative news for the local barber, who would drive to the school once a week and hack the cadets' hair for a fiver. Luckily, one of our course members was a barber before joining the force and would provide the same service at a fraction of the cost – namely his beer and smokes for the 15 weeks of our incarceration. Although he drank like a fish and smoked like an Iraqi oil well, it worked out cheaper, so every Sunday a queue would form while he trimmed our bonces into the requisite thug-like haircut. At the passing-out parade, we got to meet his wife and commented on how his skills had saved us money. Laughing, she revealed he'd never cut hair in his life. Our "barber" had, in fact, been a landscape gardener before joining up, but had wanted to try haircutting because "lawns and heads are pretty much the same".

Oral lover's surprise

In a bid to save some cash, my girlfriend and I once shared a room with a mate in a flat. It was cheap, but the downside was that we didn't get to spend much "quality" time together – until one fateful night when our roommate announced he wouldn't be back till dawn. The moment the door shut we stripped off our clothes and jumped straight into bed. I'd recently had my tongue pierced with a ring; my girlfriend loved for me to go down on her, so, wanting to drive her wild with my new toy, I duly obliged. Ten minutes later she started tugging at me, wanting a little more than tongue, so I began to pull myself up. But a shriek of pain came from my girl and I found I couldn't lift my head – my instrument of pleasure had become entwined in her pubes. I tried to unscrew the ring, but it was too slippery, so after much squirming we realised that pubic trimming was the only option. It was 20 agonising minutes before our flatmates vacated the kitchen and, wrapped in a duvet like some kind of high-tog mutant crab, we could shuffle downstairs to retrieve the household scissors.

Vomit jest backfires

After substantial over-indulgence in the course of a night out, my girlfriend and I returned home feeling quite sick. Being no beginner in the regurgitation stakes, I fetched a basin and left it next to the bed in case one of us needed an emergency throw-up during the night. Next morning I was first to wake up, and glancing down saw that the basin remained uncontaminated. I thought it'd be a laugh to pretend I'd been sick during the night, then throw the "vomit" over the missus. So I gave her a nudge and, when she opened her eyes, picked up the bowl and hurled its contents at her. It was then that I found out she had indeed been sick – the sort of clear-looking, watery variety I'd entirely failed to notice at the bottom of the bowl. It ended up all over her, somewhat spoiling my hilarious joke. And my sex life.

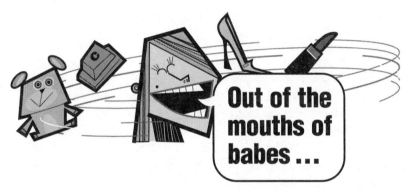

Out of the mouths of babes ...

My ex once got a letter from her bank, informing her she was badly overdrawn. "I'm not!" she wailed, waving her chequebook. "Look – I've got loads of cheques left."

When I asked the woman behind the newsagent's counter recently whether they had any Fisherman's Friends, she made a beeline for the magazine rack. "I can't see it here – but we've got Angler's Week, Trout And Salmon..."

Mate dopes diver

On a diving trip to the Red Sea, my mate Trevor asked me for a "Zantac" for his heartburn. Being in a rush, I legged it down to my cabin, grabbed the pills and threw them to him. After the dive, Trev popped down to his cabin – and wasn't seen again for most of the day.

As the week progressed, I began to get worried about why Trevor was so quiet – he's normally the life and soul of the party. To be honest, it got so bad that some of the females on the trip thought he was suffering from depression, as he spent most of his time alone. At the end of the week, as I packed I came across my Zantacs at the bottom of my bag. It was only at the airport, as Trevor was explaining how out of condition he must be as he'd felt completely knackered for the entire trip, I realised I'd thrown him my prescription sleeping pills that first day.

Drunk performance backfires

Some years ago I dated a 17-year-old, whose parents – while not disapproving – insisted she be back by midnight. One evening, as home time approached, I persuaded my girlfriend to stay over, then phoned her mother to explain that she'd had one too many and passed out on the sofa. I went on to say that I'd drop her off next morning. Unfortunately my cunning plan backfired when her mum immediately rang off, jumped into the car and drove over to pick her up in person. That meant that to save our relationship, my girlfriend had to turn in an Oscar-worthy impression of being slaughtered. So impressive was it that Mum took one look at her little princess then marched her upstairs to my bathroom and bundled the poor lass under a cold shower, fully clothed. Curfew was strictly observed from that day onwards.

Hungry father wades in

While I was courting I'd go to my girl's house for Sunday tea with her folks and we'd always end the meal with tiramisu. One evening, my girlfriend and I retired to her bedroom, taking our desserts to eat in front of the TV. One thing led to another and soon I had dipped my old fella into one of the bowls of gloop. Much fun ensued and within minutes I was dispensing a helping of sticky pudding of my own. Soon afterwards, I could hear the dishes being cleared downstairs, so I picked up the remaining tiramisu and walked onto the landing, to be met by my girl's dad coming up the stairs. Seeing the bowl of pud in my mitt, he said, "Not eating that?", snatched it from my grasp and to my horror began to spoon the gooey, cock-flavoured treat into his mouth. I was horrified to say the least, but he simply smiled at me and said, "Mmm, lovely!" It remains a family secret to this day.

Speedy squaddie

Some years ago, I was a young soldier serving in Belize. It was hot, humid and bloody boring – our only entertainment being wagers involving rounds of beers at Happy Hour each Friday. One of our bets was to see who could get to Punta Gorda airport the fastest. One Friday, I was on duty and got lemoned into taking my boss to the airport. It looked like a good way to win myself a free night's drinking! We were meant to leave at 10.15 for an 11.00 flight, but he kept me waiting for 20 minutes. Finally we climbed into the Land Rover and I floored it. Everything seemed to be going great on the approach and a new record looked like being in the bag – until we came to a hold-up. A bunch of kids were walking down the middle of the road, a couple of adults out in front. The boss told me to beep the horn to get them to move over, so, being a good soldier, I did as ordered. The kids finally shifted, but I drew some evil looks from them as I pulled past. It was only when I drew level with the adults that I realised I'd just forced a child's funeral procession off the road.

Pugilist regrets last bout

Aged 18 I faced a dilemma: pursue my boxing career or become a doctor. Medicine won. It was six months after my last fight when I was sitting in a pub with a couple of cold drinks and got a call from my old coach, desperate and begging me to fill in for an injured fighter at a show later that very night. It was to be one of those exclusive dinner-and-boxing affairs in front of a bunch of prominent people, including the mayor of Belfast, no less. Still, despite the dazzling company I politely declined until my coach told me the name of my opponent. I detested the guy! Spurred on by the thought of having one last pop at him – and, to be honest, by the booze – I caught a cab home, dusted off my gear and an hour later was in the ring, pumped up on adrenalin and ready to go. In the first round I boxed well, bloodying my oppo's nose and humiliating him with my defensive wizardry. However, in the second he caught me flush in the stomach with a right jab. Immediately a tidal wave of half-digested Guinness gushed from my mouth, coating my opponent. Of course, the fight was promptly stopped and I exited the hall to a chorus of hysterical laughter, shame-faced, and with Guinness puke dribbling from my chin. As if that wasn't humiliation enough, it was a sound I was to hear over and over again: the bout had been filmed, and the resulting video in aid of local charities was bought and endlessly replayed by every one of my "friends".

Stag slip-up

On a recent stag trip to Amsterdam, we all loosened our inhibitions herbal-style before migrating to the red-light district. As you do. Before long most of the group had ducked behind one scarlet curtain or another, leaving a moral majority – Dave and I – to think pure thoughts. Dave was the groom-to-be so it was no surprise that he abstained; nor was it a shock when he announced he was popping off "to get a little something for himself", as he'd already smoked his way through a forest of pot and was doubtless off to score some more weed. In his absence, the remainder of the party returned with various smug expressions on their faces. Half an hour later and with no sign of Dave, his delectable but insecure fiancée called my mobile. Was her boy all right? she wanted to know. Could she speak to him? She was asking me because the best man, Stuart, hadn't made the trip. I was running out of small talk when at last Dave reappeared, grinning like a loon. I thought it would be a laugh to have him "confess" his low-level drug abuse to his betrothed, so I shouted that Stu was on the phone and wanted to make sure he'd been a bad boy. Without a second's pause, Dave snatched the mobie and bellowed, "Stu! You'll be so proud of me! I just found the biggest, fattest prossie there is and got her to take it right up the arse! I never get that at home, and it only cost me 30 Euros! You there, Stu?" Amazingly, the wedding still went ahead. Without me.

UV betrays tugger

I once had a girlfriend who still lived with her parents, but generously enough they'd let me crash in her room overnight. After we'd satisfied each other's sexual appetites we'd drop off to sleep, but I was a rampant young teenager then and after a quick nap I'd regularly wake up with my diamond-cutter restored. The girlfriend would be out for the count, so I got into the habit of sticking my manhood out from under the covers and slowly tugging away for anything up to an hour, before letting fly across the room onto her suitably cream-coloured carpet. By morning, all evidence of my stray loin-juice would have evaporated, so the secret of my overactive nuts remained hidden... until the day my girlfriend hired a sunbed. Her father and I lugged the thing into her bedroom and set it up under the watchful eye of her mother, who threw the switch to spark up the eight-tube monster. Like a scene out of CSI, the room was flooded with brilliant blue light – under which my army of long-abandoned little soldiers positively glowed. For a second I was flushed with pride at just how far my muck had flown over the months, until her parents got on their hands and knees, rubbing away at the carpet to try and work out what had caused those mysterious stains...

Lover limbers up

A couple of months after getting together with an air stewardess, the hospitable lass gave me the key to her house with the freedom to pop round unannounced if my night-time urges so dictated. Clearly, her job meant she was often away for days at a time. So when she called one evening to say she'd just landed in Manchester and felt horny, I was on the road within seconds and soon letting myself in, ready for the welcome-home shag of a lifetime. Making myself at home, I "warmed up" naked on the sofa – curtains closed – with one of our Swedish videos. Sure enough, soon I heard the back door opening. My excitement quite literally grew as her footsteps approached the living room, and I threw the door open, cock in hand... to be confronted by her father, holding bread and a carton of milk. Apparently, the old boy always popped round to turn the heating on and stock up on perishables when his little girl was due back home. Thankfully he omitted any mention of the incident from the wedding speech he gave for us last month.

Bag switcher

When we moved in together, my girlfriend and I soon got into a routine: each morning while I was in the shower, she'd make my sandwiches, bundle them up in a plastic carrier bag and leave them on the kitchen table for me to pick up on the way out. My workmates were most impressed at this domestic harmony, and would joke about her secreting chocolate treats and little notes in with my scran. The joking stopped one lunchtime, however, when I emptied out the bag to reveal not tasty sarnies, but a mess of waxy cotton buds, tissue paper and a single used tampon. In my haste I'd picked up the full bathroom swing-bin, which my girl had left for me to drop off in the dustbin.

Boast turns sour

A few years ago I worked in a bar on the north coast of Northern Ireland with my mate, Sparky. This was where we got to know a young lady who was up for the summer. In fact, the pair of us got to know her very well – by shagging her in every way possible. At the end of the summer she left to work in Canada, and that was the last we heard of her... until the following year, when a guy dropped in for a drink. He was a golfer over for the Black Bush amateur tournament, and said he'd been told about the bar by the same young lady. All it took was a vodka and Red Bull and within minutes I was boasting to this bloke about all the sordid activities Sparky and I had got up to with this girl – blow-jobs, DPs, shooting all over her face. Then I asked him how long he'd known her. "About eight months," he told me, "but we've only been engaged for the last two."

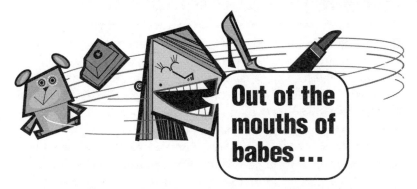

Out of the mouths of babes ...

My (sadly) ex-girlfriend used to delight in watching trashy afternoon TV – until one afternoon when her flow of garbage was replaced by live coverage of a major sporting event. "Not again," she complained. "I'm going to have to buy another telly."

My wife rang me at work to tell me her car had a flat tyre. "But I don't think it's too bad," she said. "It's only flat at the bottom."

Driving lesson ends badly

A few years ago I took driving lessons during my college's summer break. When it came to the end of my fourth lesson, my driving instructor had enough confidence in my abilities to let me drive us home. As I turned into the entrance of my road, he told me to be careful of a man fixing something under his jacked-up car, his legs sticking out. I proceeded to creep down the road as another car came the opposite way. We were touching wing mirrors as we passed... then I felt a crunch under my passenger-side wheels, followed by a blood-curdling scream. My driving instructor looked out of the window, turned back to me with a face of horror and screamed, "Drive! Fast!" I barrelled it to the end of the road before asking the instructor how bad the guy looked. He couldn't tell me because he was laughing so much. Only when he managed to get himself under control did he explain that I hadn't run over the grease monkey's legs but his can of Coke, spraying it all over him.

Thin walls prove tempting

The girlfriend and I had moved into a new flat, followed a couple of weeks later by a couple downstairs, who turned out to be sex-mad – they were at it 24/7, and extremely loudly! One night I came home to find that my girlfriend had gone to visit her parents, so I flicked on the TV. Naturally, this was when my neighbours decided to have a shagging session. As they got louder and louder I decided that if you can't beat them, join them, so I went into the bedroom – which was above theirs – in order to hear better. It was actually quite a turn-on, so I lay down with my ear to the carpet and embarked on a five-knuckle shuffle. Before long, both me and them were getting to the point of no return... when the bedroom door was flung open and there stood my girlfriend with her mum and dad. She'd brought them round so they could hear how noisy the flat was. I can safely say this is the most embarrassing thing that has ever happened to me, and you can imagine the atmosphere each Sunday during dinner at her folks' place, even today.

Beware the Bot

I'd come back to Britain after leading an expedition of 16 students through the jungles of Belize. They'd been half-gnawed to death by mozzies, but I thought I'd got off lightly with just a few bites on my left eyebrow. However, within a week my eye had swollen up. Gentlemen, meet the Bot Fly. This little bastard catches a female mosquito and lays its eggs on it. The eggs drop off when the mosquito bites you, your body heat hatches them out and the larvae burrow into your skin. My local A&E had to perform surgery to extract the things, which had used backwards-pointing barbs to anchor themselves into my eyebrow flesh. End of story? Sadly, no. Three weeks later I was relaxing in a bath when I felt pressure behind my eye. I then squeezed out no less than four 2cm-long squirming maggots from my skull; one popped out so hard that it flew through the air into the bath water. Anyone want some free fishing bait?

Spanish nookie goes awry

The wife and I had rented a villa with my parents, and it wasn't long before the Spanish sun began to induce its usual daytime horniness. One day, after lunch by the pool, my parents announced they were going to the local shop, giving us the perfect opportunity for some alfresco fun. The wife went on her knees under the table to perform her matrimonial duties. Mere minutes later I let my good lady know that I was about to erupt by shouting, "I'm gonna come!" The mood was somewhat spoiled by the sound of my mother saying, "Okay, we'll wait for you." My parents hadn't left yet, and were standing in the doorway to our right! Being at the point of no return I had no option but to let nature take its course. My wife, however, panicked and pulled her head back, leaving me to fly freely – only now did my parents realise what was happening. They were so disgusted that they refused to eat their lunch off the table for the rest of the holiday.

Fireman's bonus

There used to be a cul-de-sac where the local "working girls" would pose in the windows of the houses. One night our fire engine received a call to a flooding there. Sure enough, when we arrived two girls in stockings and suspenders were standing in the doorway, water pouring through the ceiling into the living room. Luckily one of the lads on the truck had worked as a plumber, and diagnosed a burst tank. With this isolated, we drained off the remaining water. Before we left, I joked with the girls that when this kind of incident occurred in a restaurant we got a free meal off-duty, or a free drink if it was a pub. What did they have to offer? To my surprise, hand-jobs for all would be available later! There were five men on that appliance and all of us swore we never went back. But a couple of years later the same house suffered a small fire. Recognising me, the girls said that the same offer was up for grabs – but hopefully more than two of us would take them up on it this time! I never did find out which two...

Bottle's revenge

Driving through the American south-west with some mates, we stopped at a roadside café somewhere in the middle of the desert. After parking the car and working out a touch of deep-vein thrombosis, we spotted some bottles neatly lined up in a row against the base of a nearby wall. Naturally, we started hurling rocks at these targets. Two of the three bottles smashed really quickly, but one just wouldn't succumb from long range. In the end I reasoned that as skill hadn't prevailed, a more direct approach was required – so I found a larger rock and stood right above the bottle, then smashed the thing down. It was only after a spray of rancid liquid had flown all over my jeans and shirt that I realised the bottle had been thoughtfully deposited there by another passing motorist – judging by the smell, a couple of days ago. And what happened to my caring mates? They ran into the caff with the car keys, forcing me to walk through a throng of diners who all too obviously recognised the bitter stench of stale urine.

The luck of the Irish

I was at a house party in Dublin and, as we Irish do, had consumed copious pints of the black stuff before arriving. The house was jammed, and I very quickly proceeded to chat up this lovely lady I met there. Everything appeared to be going well. There was plenty of eye contact and on a couple of occasions she even reached for my face and looked intently into my eyes. I was on to a cracker! She was slurring her words so she was obviously drunk. Maybe she'd lie back and think of Ireland, I thought. Summoning all my charm I asked for her phone number, before staggering off to get a pen and paper. After promising her for ten minutes that, "Of course I'll ring you..." she eventually appeared to give in, and scribbled something on the piece of paper. I sobered up pretty quickly when I unfolded it and read, "How can I ring you – I'm deaf, you GOBSHITE."

Feline felony

I'm a graduate in pharmaceutical science, and a couple of years ago spent some time on work experience with the Forensic Science Service. One night I was taken out by two undercover coppers to a stake-out on the outskirts of a farm, where they suspected the owner was babysitting a consignment of drugs. In the small hours of the morning and bored out of our skulls, we saw the farmer come out, sling a black bag into the boot of his car and drive off. We followed him to a local lake, where he dumped the sack and returned to the house. Thinking he'd dropped off a consignment of Class As I readied my testing kit, as one of the cops waded in to retrieve the sack – but when he opened it he found not drugs, but two dead cats and a couple of bricks. So, disgusted by the farmer, and annoyed by the long stakeout, wet and cold, we barrelled it back, crept up to the farmhouse, leant the dead cats against the front door, paws out, pressed the doorbell and legged it. Savage justice!

Lover not a fighter

During a night on the town, I managed to pull the most amazing-looking girl and take her home, leaving my friends in the club. After a good half-hour of shagging, my stamina failed me. So I could "re-group" I started to go down on her, but before long my flatmate called my mobile. Apparently a fight had started at the club after I left, and my mate was in hospital. I chucked some clothes on and rushed straight to his bedside and by the time I got to casualty, the police were already there. They promptly arrested me and when I protested my innocence, the policeman wouldn't believe I'd only just got to the hospital and knew nothing of the fight. The police kept telling me to stop lying, as it was obvious from my blood-splattered face what I'd been up to that night. Hmm – maybe I should have kept my eyes open when going down on my lady...

Horse on parade

My girlfriend has a horse and I accompany her round the country to horse shows, which I find a bit boring. One day she let me sit on her horse and walk with him between events. I must admit I felt quite good up there – especially as I saw quite a few females smiling at me. I was grinning away at everyone until I got off the horse and my girlfriend shouted, "Look!" I peered underneath and there was a two-foot willy hanging down for all to see!

Mind the dog

Hoping to earn some brownie points, I decided to do some chores round the house for my wife. It was a glorious afternoon so the doors were thrown open and our pet toy poodle was free to roam. After an hour or so I was hanging up the washing when I saw my neighbour staring over the fence. "Lovely morning for it, Mrs Moody," I beamed, to which she replied, "That's disgusting," and stormed off. I was shocked, so I checked for the offending pair of skid-marked pants, but all was clear. It was then I noticed Dotty the poodle running round the garden with my wife's 12-inch vibrator in its mouth.

Student pong nailed

I had good reason to feel smug with myself. It had taken me ages to persuade this really classy girl to go out with me and even longer to get her back to my student flat. We were all set to enjoy tea and toast but I felt I had to apologise for our manky toaster that makes everything smell burnt. My helpful guest joked, "I know what you students are like, but have you tried cleaning it?" She pulled out the bottom crumb tray to reveal the charred but very recognisable body of a mouse burnt to the sort of crisp that only being trapped and repeatedly toasted over a number of weeks can achieve. I never saw my dream girl again... and to be honest I haven't been too keen on toast either!

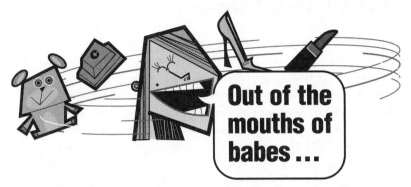

Out of the mouths of babes ...

After watching Japan v Belgium, my friend turned over to the next match on a different channel, which kicked off ten minutes later. "That's amazing!" his girlfriend said. "How did they get the fans from the last game out and the new fans in so fast?"

On the piss late one night in Prague, I needed to find a hole in the wall. "But where are you going to get the money changed this late at night?" pointed out my beloved.

Behold the Claw!

Studying at Heriot-Watt University in Edinburgh, I used to play in an inter-university indoor football competition. One day I went in for a challenge, resulting in an excruciating pain in my left ankle. Hastily excusing myself from the game I hopped to the nearby sports union reception desk, where I sat waiting for an ice-pack and the likely diagnosis of a broken ankle. All of a sudden I felt sick and vomited everywhere, rapidly going into a state of medical shock. My hands then spasmed into a locked, claw-like position and, shaking, I toppled inelegantly into my puddle of spew on the floor. At this precise moment who should stride in through the doors but the entire Tongan rugby squad – in training for a friendly against Scotland on our pitches – along with a camera crew from Sky Sports, who proceeded to film the entire incident. After seeing the footage my so-called mates started calling me "The Claw" – a nickname that persists to this day, made even worse by the knowledge that in reality my injury amounted to no more than a swollen ankle.

Nurse! The screen!

Being a male nurse I get to meet plenty of fit female colleagues and recently pulled a fine filly of a nurse. After spending plenty on wine and flowers I took her back to my place, where we began to undress. She then told me she was untouched by human hands! I was over the moon at having the chance to show this lovely lady my tried-and-tested techniques, and lost no time, expertly stripping her naked as we rolled back and forth across the bed. Just as I was about to inspect her sexy body I noticed a sharp increase in her moaning – followed by a sudden shrieking! She'd only rolled over onto my video's remote control, setting it off and playing back the lesbian porno tape I'd earlier been "sampling". She jumped up and legged it straight out! It's the one and only time I've ever had reason to curse my stash of hot lesbian bongo flicks...

Goth girl gets carried away

One night the lads and I went on the piss at a local rock club, the drinks being cheap as hell. Soon I decided I'd sample a bit of goth for the night. One girl stood out: decent body, clad in PVC with jet black hair, black make-up and those long fake fingernails. So I made my move, got chatting, bought her a few drinks and I was in! We went back to her place and got on with the job. It was great – I could feel her long fingernails going down my back as I worked away, then she grabbed my arse as she reached a climax. Her index finger went straight up my arsehole! I screamed at her to take it out, and as she did the fake fingernail came off in my hole. Every time I moved I could feel the thing digging in, but too embarrassed to go to hospital I asked her to remove it with tweezers. It must have taken the best part of an hour, and for the rest of the weekend I was walking round like I'd just shat myself. No more cheap drinking for me.

Lezza's honour remains intact

A few years ago I was working in London. Ambling through Leicester Square one evening, I became aware that a lesbian couple walking hand-in-hand some yards ahead were receiving a ferocious amount of abuse from a gaggle of beered-up Sunderland fans. I couldn't fathom how the couple had possibly provoked this verbal bombardment – from my vantage point behind them, the only reason I could detect for the jeers and catcalls was that the leggy babe's partner looked to be at least three decades older and had combined a garish snakeskin trouser suit with a streaked blonde quasi-mullet. Eager to demonstrate my sensitive, enlightened side to the lass I was seeing at the time, I commented: "That's awful – have you heard the stick those tossers are giving that lesbian couple, just 'cos one's a bit older than the other?" I must have spoken a little too loudly however, as I was mortified when the aged "lesbian" wheeled around to fix me with a withering stare. It was Peter Stringfellow.

Midnight pisser

Last Christmas I stayed with a friend and his family in their country house. Despite the presence of dozens of grandparents and cousins my mate and I still managed to get pole-axed, crawling into bed in the early hours. Some time later I woke up desperate to piss, but on stumbling out of my bedroom I was surrounded by closed doors. Unwilling to walk in on someone, I decided to relieve myself off the bedroom balcony. Imagine my bewilderment when I came down to breakfast next morning to find paramedics carting my mate's grandfather out on a stretcher. Apparently the old codger had stepped out for his morning constitutional and slipped on a patch of ice, screwing his back. Of course, my bedroom was directly above the accident blackspot: my golden shower had frozen and sent the old bird off to two weeks in hospital. A plumber arrived and spent hours searching for the "leak". I admitted nothing, but did put a little salt on my icy discharge.

Sauna treasure

In order to support myself at university, I used to work as an instructor at a private health gym. One morning while inspecting the saunas before we opened, I made an interesting find: a ten-inch gold vibrator! Carefully sheathing my hand in a carrier bag I took hold of the buzzing beauty, before placing it in the lost property box. Later that day my manager asked me to bring the item to his office for closer inspection. He plunged his hand straight into the bag, took out the tool and waved it in front of the by-now packed office, as the discovery had been the sole object of conversation among the staff all day. A jolly chap, he pointed it at each of the female employees in turn, saying, "Which of you girls left this, then?" before putting the vibe up to his nose and sniffing from one end to the other. "I recognise that smell – is it you, Julie?" he continued. You can imagine the look on his face when, in a stage whisper, I had to inform him that I'd actually found it in the men's sauna.

Carpet mystery solved

Having a reputation as a Mr Fix-It and being the kind-hearted bloke that I am, I agreed to pop round and tune in my elderly next-door neighbour's newly-acquired VCR. While I was lying on my front connecting the necessary cables and tuning to the correct channels using the remote control, I couldn't help but notice the random orangey-brown streaking pattern in the old gimmer's blue carpet, just inches from my nose. It soon became clear what the pattern was when the old boy's poodle came into the room: it was dragging itself along the carpet by its front legs in a sat-upright kind of position, its hind legs and feet pointing to the ceiling. Whether this was a novel way of wiping its arse or it had a bad case of worms, I didn't wait to find out – I was far too busy legging it to the dry cleaners.

Lunchtime gobble turns sour

We were having a new bathroom installed, so I decided to work from home for a couple of days to deal with any problems that might arise. However, bored and with unsupervised access to the internet, I soon started surfing for porn instead – resulting in a phone call to my girlfriend asking her to drop in during her lunch hour. As the builders munched their sandwiches we snuck off to the bedroom, where my young lady gave me an awesome blow-job. Mission complete, I happily headed off to clean myself up – not knowing the bathroom floorboards had been ripped out. I duly went crashing through the kitchen ceiling and ended up hanging on to a supporting joist – ensuring that my flaccid, lipstick-covered member was flopping around in plain view of the builders making themselves a pot of tea.

Slow-burn prank comes off

About a year after graduating from uni, I had a bunch of mates round for the evening, including my on/off girlfriend. As the night wore on I managed to entice her down to the garage for a ciggie and a bit of a flirt, in the hope of her becoming more "on" than "off". There in the corner I saw my trusty old acoustic guitar, which had been gathering dust since my student days. What could be more effective in wooing my good lady than a few chords? But after a quick strum we noticed a rattling noise coming from inside the hollow-bodied instrument. My ladyfriend reached inside, got a grip on a wad of paper and managed to pull it out. A huge wave of panic suddenly hit me, and I was transported back to my student house-sharing days in Birmingham. Like any group of lads living together, we were prone to springing the odd prank, the longest-running being stashing a particularly depraved item of gay porn in each others' rooms, hoping to catch the unfortunate victim out when a ladyfriend ever happened to stay over. And there, 12 months later, was my soon-to-be-ex-girlfriend clutching a well-thumbed copy of Sex Pigs. It was, without doubt, the best – and slowest – stitch-up any of us ever pulled off.

Hound's surprise

The other day I went with a friend to walk his four dogs in the New Forest. One of the hyperactive pups came running up to me with a lovely stick, so, being a dog-friendly person, I patted him on the head, then tugged it out of his mouth. At this point, the lovely lab kept launching himself at me before I could throw it for him to fetch. Insisting on good manners, I had a short battle with said dog, yelling, "Sit!" to him. Eventually, I got him to comply, at which point my friend looked over and asked what the hell I had in my hand? I looked at the "stick", which turned out to be a lovely deer leg, complete with hoof. I dropped it like lightning, shrieking swearwords whilst my doggy friend retrieved it with that lovely labrador smile.

That's not gravy!

Last summer, I was cooking a Sunday roast to impress this hot girl I worked with. Slaving away in the kitchen for an hour before she arrived, I was repeatedly interrupted by the snotty-nosed neighbourhood kids kicking their football into my back garden from the adjoining playing field. After retrieving the ball for about the fifth or sixth time I decided to put a stop to it – told them to, "Fuck off!" and kept their ball. Pretty soon my lady arrived and, realising she'd forgotten to bring any wine, offered to go to the local shop and pick some up. As the cooking was doing alright by itself, I went with her. We returned a few minutes later but now the smell coming from the cooker was so putrid we started retching. The local kids had let themselves in, taken their ball back, crapped in my boiled veg, and then returned the pan to the boil. The little swines.

Ladies' Confessions

Experiment goes wrong

I met this really fit guy in a bar and because I hadn't had sex for a while was very horny and feeling quite experimental. Once we got back to his place foreplay was short and we went straight to some very hard shagging. A little later I thought things were getting a bit tedious and I'd better spice things up. So I slid my hand around to his arse and slipped a couple of fingers inside him. He wasn't shocked at all and we carried on with our rude fun. A bit later we moved on to slower canoodling. Shortly he took my fingers and licked them one by one. However, once he got to my index finger he started to gag and then threw up all over my naked body. It's the worst night I've ever had and I've since given up alcohol.

Pub session leaves evidence

My husband and I used to run a pub. One night after closing we decided to get down and dirty all round the bar. On our way around the rooms we left a trail of discarded clothes, and after a full-on session went to bed. The next morning I went down to open up and at the bottom of the stairs found a neatly piled set of clothes and a pair of shoes. Tucked inside the shoes were a pair of knickers and a bra, the cleaner having done a little extra tidying! She just smiled and said good morning and the incident was never mentioned. Of course, I couldn't look her in the eye for a week.

One-nighter goes pear-shaped

After having a few too many at my local one night I ended up staggering back to this guy's house. We stumbled up the stairs in the dark, both feeling really horny. After a bit of fumbling around on the bed he finally got started. He'd only been pumping away for a few seconds when I felt a warm, wet substance shooting up inside me. At first I thought that maybe he'd come really quickly but then to my horror I realised that it wasn't his ejaculation he couldn't control, but his bladder. I'll never forget the embarrassed look on his face.

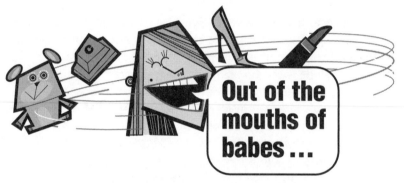

Out of the mouths of babes ...

Discussing the Incredible Hulk TV series one lunchtime, we established that Dr David Banner was played by Bill Bixby and the Hulk by Lou Ferrigno. The office blonde chipped in, "Was it two different actors then?"

On a night flight back from Florida, my wife looked out of the window at the featureless sky and said, "Are we flying above the stars?" D'oh!

Clubber gets surprise

On the way to a nightclub in Manchester with my mate, I simply couldn't wait to go for a piss, so I decided I'd have to go in a market stall which was in the middle of the street. Thinking I was alone, I dropped my knickers to piss on this pile of cardboard inside the stall.

But as I crouched down and began to release my wee I suddenly realised I was pissing on a tramp underneath all the boxes. I nearly died of shock and pulled up my knickers without finishing.

Hungover lady forgets to douche

After getting drunk with a group of friends on a hen night, I got talking to this fit bloke and went back to his for some really great sex. Then I duly left, not wanting the awkward morning-after goodbyes. The following night I had a date with a guy I had just started seeing. Feeling all hungover we just decided to get a video out. Later that night we were getting horny and he decided to put his fingers up my lady flower. Imagine my embarrassment when he pulled out a condom with spunk still in it. It must have slipped off during my sex session the night before! We never went out much after that.

Randy daughter spotted

Years ago when I still lived at home I woke up one morning feeling very horny and decided to have a fiddle under the covers. God knows how long later, but after one fantastic orgasm, I opened my eyes to find my bedroom door ajar. I was horrified as I always slept with it closed and it could only mean one thing – my dad had looked in on me as he occasionally would. The thought of him seeing my hand working furiously under the covers was so shameful that I tried to keep out of his way all day. That night as I was off to bed he said, "Good night – and behave yourself!"

Lezzer reveals truth

At our university there's a girl all the lads love. On Valentine's Day she received something like 40 or so cards, to my pitiful none. She taunts them all the time, dances on the tables, shows her ass and flashes her tits at them. Pity for them that she's a lezzer who's going out with me!

And we have a great plan to eat each other out on the coffee table in the conference room.

Massage does trick

A few years ago my boyfriend surprised me with a holiday to Turkey to mark our anniversary. One day while he was sunbathing at our hotel I decided to go for a massage in the spa, hoping to relax after virtually a whole week of never leaving our hotel room. I settled down on the table and closed my eyes while the masseuse worked her magic. So relaxed was I after 15 minutes of therapeutic rubbing that I didn't flinch when I felt something touch my privates. I opened my legs a bit further and my generous masseuse kept on fingering me, until I had a great orgasm. Now when my husband asks me to talk dirty I know exactly which "fantasy" to tell him about.

Wrong cream daubed

When I shared a house at university I woke up one morning with a bit of an itch around my bits. In my still-groggy state I figured it must be thrush, so I took some cream from my bedside locker and applied it. Pretty soon I realised all was not well as the sensation had turned from a slight itch to a burning pain that made me cry out loud. That's when I took a second look at the cream – it wasn't Canestan as I'd thought, but a tube of Deep Heat left by my ex. My screams woke my housemates who found me squatting in the bath dousing myself with cold water. But it wasn't sympathy all round, because in my dash to the bathroom I'd left my bedroom door open, leaving my housemates to see our married landlord in my bed.

Number called in haste

One morning I got up feeling a tad horny so I thought it'd be a good idea to ring my man on his mobile and give him some action down the line. I got myself positioned, phone in one hand and hot pie in the other. The second the phone answered I went straight into it, proceeding to tell him how I was getting very horny, lying in bed working myself off and imagining that I had another girl naked beside me. Suddenly a voice interrupted me just when I was really starting to enjoy myself. Oh shit – it wasn't Al's voice, it was his dad's. In all the excitement, instead of pressing "Al" on the mobile I had pressed "Al Snr". I didn't wait to hear what he had to say, and up to now he hasn't mentioned it, although now when we call round he seems much friendlier than before...

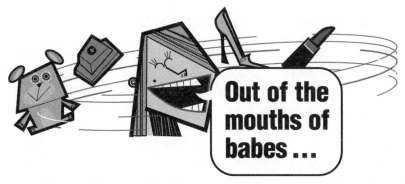

Out of the mouths of babes ...

When my girlfriend was learning to drive, she was asked, "What do you need to watch for falling off the trees in autumn?" Her reply: "Squirrels." She's a copper, by the way.

After hearing that the Pentagon had been attacked on 9/11, my girl assured me that Sheffield would be next on the hit list. "We've got the Octagon..." she explained.

DJ gets caught

On a night out in Blackpool when I was 18, I got speaking to a DJ in a club. After the club (and several Aftershocks) I was unable to walk properly, so the DJ I had been chatting with offered to help. Of course he ended up taking me to his house and telling me it was okay to spend the night. After much kissing and groping, he got his manhood out and asked for a blow-job. Being off my head I happily agreed, despite wearing a brace on the top row of my teeth. After about 10 minutes I got bored but when I went to pull away, a small piece of loose wire on my brace pierced through his foreskin and he grabbed my head in shock. We were stuck because he was too scared to yank my head away quickly. In the end he got on his mobile to his ex-girlfriend to come round and help. When she came in she burst out laughing, pulled out her camera, took a few pictures and left. I was so embarrassed that I pulled away quickly and tore a strip out of his foreskin.

Tourists leave souvenir

Early this year my boyfriend and I went to Fort William in Scotland for a cosy weekend. After taking a cable car, we did some exploring and stumbled across the remains of Inverlochy Castle. My boyfriend started getting all horny, so I pulled up my skirt and bent over so he could take me from behind. After ten minutes or so he came over my bum, then wiped me clean with my panties, which we left there as a souvenir. Only after we emerged from our hideaway did we notice an old woman walking her dog. The old dear paused a moment, looked down and then muttered something about having no respect for a 700-year-old castle.

Kebaberie gets steamy

One day, after an afternoon spent drinking, my boyfriend and I decided to visit our local kebab shop. The man serving us always stares at my 36D breasts, and as it was summer I went in there in a see-through top and pink bra. We ordered two chicken kebabs, and the guy serving said to me in a sexual manner, "Would you like some extra chilli sauce?" "Yes, please," I replied, "and may I use your toilet?" So I went off to the loo, shortly followed by my boyfriend. When I had my knickers round my ankles he began rogering me from behind, when suddenly Mr Kebab turned up with his knob out. My boyfriend said to him, "Do you want to feel her fanny?" which he did and started wanking. In two seconds flat he shot his load all over the floor and ran back to his duties. After my boyfriend finished me off, we went back in to collect our nosh. He charged us full price for two kebabs, but we got home to find only one! We felt so stitched up we haven't been back since.

Boss enjoys morning relief

While at work on a dull Monday morning I began to feel horny, so I went into my boss's office (who I'd been seeing for two months), got under the desk and started sucking him off. It was one of the best blow-jobs I'd ever given. Then suddenly the door opened. The MD came in and said, "We're waiting for you." To which he replied, "I'm coming," seconds later spraying his load down my throat. He'd forgotten about the board meeting he was supposed to be in. For the rest of the day we couldn't stop grinning at each other.

Scarf covers naughtiness

My scroogy ex-boyfriend was so unbelievably tight-fisted, he never once paid for me to go to the pictures. So to get back at him I decided to snog someone behind his back, who, unfortunately, covered my neck in loads of nasty lovebites. The next morning I had to wear a scarf to cover the bites. My ex complimented the stylish scarf and to this day doesn't know the real reason why I wore it.

Horny lady improvises

I was in my final year at uni and having been working hard for my exams, the days I got to spend with my boyfriend were few and far between. One morning, feeling horny, I went to the bathroom to get ready. As I was doing the normal routine I saw that one of my flatmates had invested in an electric toothbrush.

I perched on the edge of the bath and while my other housemates thought I was cleaning my teeth I was having the time of my life with this new vibrating brush. To this day the owner still doesn't know what I got up to – the only person who does is my boyfriend, who can never look at the toothbrush in the same way.

Holidaymaker improvises twice

Last summer in Ibiza I was sooo wild. One night I had a steamy session with a guy I'd picked up in a bar. Afterwards, I needed a cool midnight dip, but he headed to a club – charming! Still, I was determined to go skinny-dipping. Just one problem; nothing to tie my hair back with, so I picked up one of the condoms we'd used, rinsed it out and used it to tie my hair in a ponytail. I wasn't alone for long. A good-looking local lad was swimming nearby and to cut a long story short, a look turned into a snog, a snog turned into a grope, and pretty soon I was back on heat. We dried off but now I had another problem: no condoms. Then I had an idea. I told him I was going for a pee in the bushes and not to look. It was a bit fiddly, but I finally undid the condom from my hair, went back to my Latin lover, pulled it over his cock and used it to shag him senseless! Just doing my bit for recycling.

Jack the lad causes panic

A few years ago, I fancied this lad who goes with anything with a pulse, so inevitably ended up in the sack with him. Our session culminated with him requesting to shoot his load on my tits. Obligingly I lay back and closed my eyes while he started masturbating and sure enough, I soon felt a hot runny liquid on my chest. To make him think I was enjoying it I started rubbing my hands all over my breasts and belly. That was until I opened my eyes and saw my chest covered with blood, as well as the palms of my hands. He hadn't actually come yet and was still wanking, with this blood pumping out his cock! "It's all right," he said. "I shagged this lass a few months ago and she was a bit dry and this has happened ever since." Well needless to say I was no longer in the mood, so I made my excuses and left. See ya, scummer!

Feuding Flatmates share more than just a lover

A few years ago I flat-shared with a real bitch. She would snare blokes, keep them on for a couple of weeks then dump them. She "joked" that I should have her cast-offs as I hadn't had a boyfriend for months. Anyway, one Saturday morning I awoke to find that she'd left a note saying she wouldn't be back until Sunday night and that if John (her current lover) called, to tell him that she'd left for good. She had only been seeing him for a week and even by her standards that was quick. An hour later John knocked at the door. He looked really upset when I told him she had gone so I invited him in. Then I did what any woman would do under those circumstances and decided to make him feel better by shagging him, which was fantastic. Best of all we did it on the bitch's bed. When she returned I feigned concern and badgered her about John and why she'd dumped him. Eventually she just blew up. "If you must know," she screamed, "I found out that I had gonorrhoea and I couldn't face telling him." So my revenge was short-lived: turns out she had given it to him, and he'd given it to me. Moral: always wear a condom.

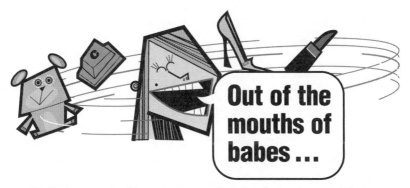

Out of the mouths of babes ...

Walking past a building site, I mused out loud as to how such large cranes were built. My always-helpful girlfriend chipped in with, "If I was building one of those I'd start at the top and work down." Genius.

Me and a few workmates were coming out with various crap double entendres. Listening in, a female colleague blurted out: "I don't know what double entendres are – will one of you fill me in?"

Horny student savours sloppy seconds

Feeling really randy at uni not long ago, I drunkenly ended up with one of the sexy footballers from the university team. Back at mine, we had a pretty rampant session and were just finishing off when I got a call from my ex-boyfriend, a complete tosser who lived above me. Because he was in such an emotional state, I agreed to go up and see him, telling the sexy footballer that I'd be back shortly, but neglecting to mention that it was my ex-boyfriend I was visiting. So, having heard my ex's sob story of what a bad night he'd had, I ended up shagging him, too. You can only imagine the pleasure it gave me knowing that not only had he got sloppy seconds, but that he'd got his mate's man juices all over his cock. All in all, a productive evening.

Pair get sacrilegious

My boyfriend and I hired a church for a party we were due to be having. Not wanting to stay at my mum's house and with no money for a bed and breakfast prior to the bash, my boyfriend suggested we stay in the church as we had already been given the keys. So we bought beer and sat in the aisles. Everything started out very romantically – the church had nice spotlights shining on the altar. But not long later I found myself, legs spread and dress hitched up, being joyfully screwed across an altar. What a sinful night that was!

Lezzer fools mum

My mum doesn't realise I'm a lesbian, and she'd go mad if she found out. A year after meeting my first girlfriend, we're still going strong, though there was almost trouble one night, when after giving her a good licking-out and returning home, my mum said she could smell fish on my breath. I made the excuse that I'd had cod for tea. Close one!

Randy bloke gets shot in the eye

My boyfriend always had a thing about wanting to come on my tits, and one evening, after a seriously heavy night on the town, I finally gave in to his wish. I lay on the bed tossing him off while he sat over me. Just as he was about to come, he looked down at his proud manhood to get the full view, only to receive a hot wad of his own love wee in his eye!

Lush leaves mark

A few years ago I was in my local celebrating my 20th birthday, getting absolutely wrecked. I somehow got home and really needed to be sick. I made it to the bathroom and stuck my head down the pan, but then the urge to shit came over me. There was nothing I could do but shit in the position I was in. Wearing only a G-string, and with the poo being of a semi-solid consistency, you can imagine what happened. I left the bathroom with what could only be described as a cow-pat on the new bathroom carpet.

Foodie fills up

While living at my parents' house, my boyfriend and I regularly ordered Chinese takeaways. We then locked ourselves in my room and ate it away from the prying eyes of my sister. One evening, though, I'd been reading tips on how to give an extra-special blow-job, so I was keen to try out my new tips on my man. We soon got down to business, making lots of amorous noises and slurps. I was just getting him there when my sister knocked at the door and asked, "What are you eating?" Little did she know I had a mouthful of dick!

Boss goes everywhere

Managing to attract my gorgeous-but-married boss, we took to shagging at every opportunity. While working one dull Saturday, he came into the office unexpectedly, desperate for some of my personal skills, so we nipped off to the loo. Time was precious so – with trousers round ankles and thong round bum-cheeks – we went at it, him behind as I hung on to the door handles. As he was about to come, I jumped off and whipped around in an attempt to catch his juice in my mouth. Alas, I mistimed and ended up covered in the stuff! Hastily cleaning up, I returned to the office. It was only at the end of the day that my workmates told me that my hair was covered in sticky jizz – the humiliation!

Cops get eyeful

After a night out clubbing, me and my fella headed home. On the way back, however, things got horny and we ended up having sex on a traffic island surrounded by bushes. They concealed us, or so we thought. Mid-shag, I looked up to see a copper peering over the bushes! I got up, covered in mud, thinking this was the worst moment ever. But it got worse, as there by the side of the road was not one cop but a whole van of them. I could hear their cheers as we scurried off down the road, shame-faced.

Bride enjoys lesbian pre-nups

The night before my friend's wedding, the bride-to-be decided to handcuff herself to me for the rest of the night. While in the toilet of a nightclub, she told me how sexy I was and started to kiss and fondle me. Fuelled by alcohol, I didn't stop her and soon we were on the floor, fingers and tongues everywhere until I had the best orgasm ever. The next day, sitting in the church, I couldn't help but smile at her new husband, knowing that just 12 hours earlier I had my tongue between his lovely wife's legs.

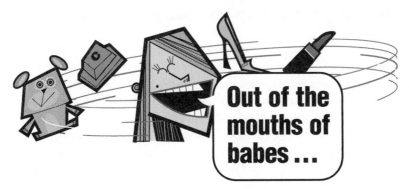

Out of the mouths of babes ...

On The Life Of Mammals, David Attenborough closed with: "Next week the story of the apes, and how one large primate took over the world." My watching girlfriend replied with, "Who's that, King Kong?"

After telling my mum that a mate was on holiday in Kuala Lumpur, she replied, "Aren't they the little people in Charlie And The Chocolate Factory?"

Lovers damage pride and joy

Every Christmas back home in Australia, I travel down south with my boyfriend's family to stay in their beach house. Last Christmas my boyfriend and I were desperate for some time alone so we took off in his dad's utility truck. We found a nice spot in the middle of the bush where we knew we were completely alone. We climbed onto the back of the truck and my boyfriend stood on the tray while I sat on the roof of the car with my legs wrapped around his waist. We had the most amazing shag and were getting quite rough with one another. When we arrived back at the beach house the whole family were sitting on the balcony. My boyfriend's father (who loves his truck), jumped out of his seat and stared at the roof of the car. Not only did he discover that my arse and hands had made perfect indents in the roof, but also that I had left my semen-soggy panties in the tray at the back. After that it was a very awkward Christmas dinner!

Skinnydipping leads to bra jiggery

On a boozy night out me and my mates met some really hot blokes and went back to their hotel, where we all went swimming – naked. After some time, we decided to go back to their rooms to continue the fun so went to get dressed. I could hear sniggering and one of the blokes held up a bra with padded tissues stuffed down it. They joked about whose it could be. My friends all retrieved their bras and I picked one up too, and we all said it definitely wasn't ours! Off we went to their rooms for some jiggery. But I never did admit that the bra was mine – and to the poor lady whose bra I pinched I'm very sorry, but I just couldn't lose face in front of everyone!

Horny temp caught at it

I used to work as a temp a few years back and ended up being posted to a firm of solicitors for a week. On my second day I was feeling really horny and thought no-one would notice if I slipped off to the toilet for five minutes. So I got to the loo, took off my skirt and panties and went for it. Just at the point of climax the toilet door burst open and stood in front of me was my manageress. In my hurry to relieve myself I'd forgotten to lock the door! I was so embarrassed I left the same day.

Sleeping hubby gets shower

My husband has this annoying habit after visiting the loo in the middle of the night. He returns to bed, starkers, snuggles up to me to warm up, and then I feel a small trickle of piss down my thigh. I figured revenge was in order so one night I crept to the loo and purposefully didn't wipe myself. I then proceeded to crouch over his sleeping face and shake myself dry. On feeling the urine trickle onto his face, my husband, still fast asleep, stuck out his tongue and lapped up the wee.

Couple give show

When I was younger I had this fantasy about having sex with other people watching. So one drunken night me and my boyfriend got naked, opened the curtains and with the lights on really went for it. Cue instant abandonment as we spotted a small child opposite watching.

Dullard's girl does dirty in front of him

I was going out with this guy for about a year, and to be honest he was not the most exciting of men. One day we decided to spend the day in together and I thought this would be the ideal opportunity to spice up our sex life. How wrong I was. Within minutes of arriving at his house he started working on his computer, plus his mate Nick was there. So much for us being alone. But Nick was cute and we got on like a house on fire. We got on so well that when he came into my boyfriend's (freezing) room and got under the duvet, my fella didn't even bat an eyelid. That's when the fun began. My man didn't even notice my quiet little moans caused by his best friend flicking my bean under the duvet! At one point my bloke did turn round but only to see me pretending to be asleep, while the truth was his mate was giving me a fantastic rogering in the spoon position!

Mum improvises for odd-job man

A few years ago we had a visit from a bloke at our local furniture store to fix a broken chest of drawers. I asked him if he would like a drink and he said he'd love a cup of tea. Unfortunately when I opened the fridge, I found we had no milk except, innocently sitting there, a bottle of my recently expressed breast milk ready for my new-born son. There was only one thing for it... I gave him his drink and he chucked it down quick as a flash. He then told me it was the best cup of tea he'd had all day! When I see him in the local furniture store I always have to smile.

Out of the mouths of babes ...

Watching George Foreman flogging his "lean, mean, grilling machine" on TV, my girlfriend chipped in with: "What does he know about cooking? He plays the banjo."

During a visit to Chessington World of Adventures with my girlfriend, we found ourselves watching a lion. I jokingly mentioned that it looked like the roaring one at the beginning of MGM films. "That's the most famous lion in the world," replied my girlfriend. "Except for Tony the Tiger, of course."

Couple make good use of hussy

A couple of years ago my fella and I lived above a right man-eater – every weekend we'd hear her at it with a different fella. Secretly this used to be a bit of a turn-on and I'd often end up jumping my man to the sexy sounds. One evening, after we'd indulged in a Saturday afternoon's drinking I saw our neighbour getting a pizza delivered. Figuring that was her in for the night and feeling a bit outrageous thanks to the booze, I bet my man he couldn't get into her knickers. Half an hour later, and after feeding her a bullshit story about going out for some wine and locking himself out, I was lying in bed frigging myself off while listening to my man give her the screwing of her life. Pretty soon after – and all that night – I was on the receiving end, too.

Lady takes chance

Weeks ago at work a very cute chap, who I knew fancied me, asked me out for a drink. He always seemed lost and lonely, so I thought, why not? We met at a bar and he was actually very amusing, so we soon began meeting regularly. What I noticed was how often he complimented me on my make-up, and always asked where I'd bought a particular outfit. One evening he asked if I'd like to go to his flat for dinner the next Saturday and I accepted. When the day came I made sure I looked pretty hot. But when the door opened at Charles's flat, I was greeted by a stunning girl. It was only when she said, "Hello Rosemary," that I realised that it was in fact Charles! All our meetings suddenly made sense! For a moment I thought of leaving but decided to stay and was glad I did. We had a great evening – "Camilla" cooked us a perfect meal and of course there was very interesting conversation. And then at the end of the night, having sex with a beautiful transvestite was an amazing experience!

Sex experiment gets tricky

After a boozy session my boyfriend and I got frisky and decided to put objects inside my pussy. After a cucumber and a wine bottle we grabbed a marble egg off my mum's mantelpiece. Imagine my horror when my fanny sucked it up! After much pleasurable fingering we had to get a spoon to scoop it out – the ultimate egg and spoon race...

Sportsman seeks memories

In my first year at university I had been chasing the captain of the football team for weeks when finally (and under the influence of lots of booze), he showed an interest in me. Not long later we were back at my place shagging as if our lives depended on it. After a few hours the alcohol was wearing off and my juices were drying up, but this guy was absolutely insatiable. Eventually I went fairly numb down below. But then all of a sudden I yelped in pain and shouted, "What the hell are you doing?" It turned out that this bloke had a very strange sexual deviancy – it seems that he got off on shoving his watch up my fanny. His reasoning for this timepiece intrusion was "so that I can smell this and think of you". Needless to say, I didn't go back for more!

Mum soothes row

During a blazing row my daughter walked out and left her boyfriend at our house. She later called to say that they'd split up but he could sleep over as planned in her room, while she stayed over at her friend's. So he went to buy some beer, returned to her room and watched telly all night. I popped in about midnight as the TV was still on and to my surprise he was spread across the bed asleep and naked, sporting a large erection. Being a single mum and my sex life somewhat on the slow side, temptation got the better of me and I slowly leaned over the bed and began to suck him off. After a while he began to stir so I grabbed a scarf and wrapped it around his head, saying, "Sorry I was angry," (pretending to be my daughter). I then straddled him, making sure that I pleasured myself good and proper. The next morning, I overheard my daughter and the boyfriend talking about how real an erotic dream felt last night. It got worse when later on she apologised for all the rowing the night before and said she'd decided to stay with him after all. Oops.

Swimmer gives an eyeful

Recently I went to stay at my rich boyfriend's house. I'd been keeping myself trim for him all summer by swimming each morning, so when his dad told me about the pool at the end of the garden I was gutted that I'd left my bikini at home. I didn't catch exactly what he said next, something like, "...no-one's around, so don't worry." The next morning I went down to the pool, bright and early, left my kit by the pool-side and did 20 lengths, au naturel. But after my exercise came two horrific shocks. The first was discovering a row of his sisters' spare swimmers in the pool house – obviously his dad meant they weren't around, and I was not to worry about borrowing them! The second shock came when I learnt that the old man next door had been pruning his prize roses...

Lady exposes bad boyfriend

When my best friend told me that my boyfriend was sleeping around I plotted revenge. He had been hassling me for anal sex, so one evening I told him I would only let him if he dressed in women's clothes and let me tie him to the bed. After I gave him a makeover, I tied him up with my stockings, then told him I had to go and get the lubricant. He didn't know, but I'd invited our mates round for a party, so went to let them in and told them to go into the room where my boyfriend was lying on the bed with an erection, make-up, stockings and suspenders!

Office girl treats boss

One weekend, my boyfriend and I had to go into my office to pick something up. Of course, it was deserted, and both feeling horny we decided to get down to it on my desk. After the deed was done we realised we'd left a sizeable pool of love juices next to my computer, so we grabbed a nearby sponge and cleared it up. The following Monday at work it gave me great satisfaction to kindly volunteer to wash up my cretin of a boss's mug and serve him up some special protein-rich tea!

Jiggy couple park up

After a hot and heavy trip to the movies, my bloke suggested we go for a drive. I happily agreed as I was gagging for it. We drove out to what we thought was a secluded spot down a woodland road, turned the engine off and moved to the back seat. Immediately I unzipped his jeans and started sucking his cock; he happily returned the favour, putting one leg on the parcel shelf and licking me out. After I came he leaned me over the rear seat and took me from behind. We were at it for five minutes when some headlights approached. I didn't stop pushing on to his cock but the lights seemed to stay on for ages. Suddenly there was a tap on the window. My boyfriend wound it down and an embarrassed old lady said, "Excuse me, but could you move as you're blocking my driveway?" I couldn't stop giggling as we hastily drove away.

Ladies get familiar

The other day I went to my boyfriend's house but his 24-year-old sister answered the door and told me he wouldn't be in until later because he was playing football. She asked me if I wanted to stay for a few drinks while I waited so I said yes and went inside. Pretty soon we'd gone through two bottles of wine and she was asking me if my sex life was any good. At first I was embarrassed but decided, mainly thanks to the alcohol, to tell her every dirty detail of sex with her brother. After hearing my filth she said out of the blue that she bet she could give me multiple orgasms if I let her. I giggled and said okay. We made our way to her bed and slowly took each other's clothes off. After much feverish kissing and fondling I went down on her, pulling the bed quilt over me, and proceeded to lick her clit while sliding three fingers into her soaking wet pussy. However, to our horror, my boyfriend had returned home without either of us knowing. He knocked on his sister's door and before she could say anything he came in and witnessed a mysterious figure going down on her under the covers. He apologised and quickly shut the door. I sneaked out the house and the next day he told me what he'd seen, calling his sister a "dirty cow". If only he knew...

Girl interrupted

One day I got home from work early, the first time in months that I'd arrived there before my boyfriend. Relishing some time on my own I decided to pleasure myself on the sofa. During a luscious naked frig I was almost reaching climax when I heard my boyfriend arrive home. Hoping that he'd continue the fun I shouted for him to come in and join me, only to get a little more than I'd bargained for. He'd brought back a load of his workmates to have beer and watch football. Oops.

Couple borrow more than bed

One night, me and my then-boyfriend were keeping a friend company while her mum and dad were away. After shitloads to drink, we decided to call it a night. My friend gave me and my fella her room while she slept in her parents' bed. When we got to the room, after all the vodka, we were both as horny as hell and got down to some serious shagging. Then my bloke grabbed the nearest thing to him to "insert" into me for pleasure. It turned out to be my mate's hairbrush which got covered in my hot love juices. We didn't think anything of it until the next morning when she came into the room, grabbed the brush to do her hair, and stuck it, handle first, in her mouth while she tied her hair back! Yummy for her!

Exercise beneficial

In the last couple of months I've realised how much fun going to the gym can be. That's because I've discovered that there are two things that can give me an amazing orgasm – sit-ups and doing my calf muscles on the machine! I wonder if anyone has noticed yet – perhaps they think those groans are of pain and not pure pleasure! Should get down the gym more often...

Convent girl ruder than ever

As a teenager I went to a Catholic school and it was those years that taught me all I know about being a naughty girl. Anyway, a few weeks ago my bloke was out, so I organised for my old schoolmate, Hannah, to come round. Soon we were legless! Remembering "old times", we stripped down to our underwear, got out my old camcorder and stumbled into bed. We began sensually touching each other, but soon it was a lot more. When we couldn't find my dildo, Han began fucking me with the nearest thing to hand – my crucifix! Phew! Some weeks after these disgraceful scenes my boyfriend found the tape. To his surprise there were two naked chicks on his video – he was well chuffed and thanked me for a massive turn-on. Don't mention it!

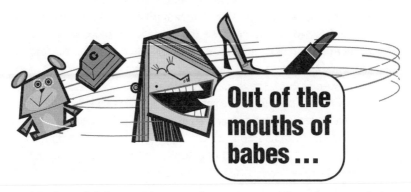

Out of the mouths of babes ...

Watching dolphins in Singapore last year, my girlfriend was mightily impressed by their ability to perform complex tricks. "Well, they are the second most intelligent creatures on Earth," I replied, sagely. "What's the first?" she said, then pondered the answer for a moment: "the dog?" It appears so.

When the Ireland vs Spain World Cup game went to penalties, my girlfriend asked what would happen if both teams kept scoring. I told her that they go through all the players – even the goalkeepers. "Then who would save it?" she asked.

FHM e-mail ruins life

I'd been planning to send FHM my confession involving lingerie, a champagne bottle and an orgasm for a while, but it's ended up causing me grief. I originally tried to e-mail my confession from my home computer at my parents' house. Due to a spelling error in the address the e-mail was returned as undelivered into the family inbox, which I later discovered my father read. I'm sending this from my boyfriend's computer.

Technology aids lust

When my husband was sent off to Bosnia for six months we prepared
for the separation by investing in a pair of picture phones. The "private"
pictures we exchanged were good, but they didn't replace everything I
was missing. After two months of my man's absence, I met a guy from
work I quite fancied. He came round to my place one night, and after a
while we got down to sex. While we were doing the deed he suggested
I take some pics. The closest thing to hand was the phone, so I took 10
shots of really steamy stuff. Chatting to my hubby the next day, he
asked me to send him some "nice" snaps of myself. When I did, he
sent me back some of him wanking, asking me to send him some more.
It was then I realised that I'd inadvertently sent a couple of pics of me
and my work colleague at it. But my hubby loved it! Phew!

Lady makes filth tape

The city-centre studio I run has an exit in a small alley that we cover
with CCTV. Whenever friends talk about spicing up their sex lives I
always suggest an outdoor session in the alley behind where I work
because "it's very secluded and I've done it loads of times". Every
morning I fast forward through the tape and make a copy of any open-
air sessions – currently I've over two hours of friends and complete
strangers getting a seeing-to, completely oblivious to the camera and
even more oblivious to the fact my late nights at work usually consist of
masturbating to said tape.

Girls get lesbo

For ages my boyfriend has been asking me to fulfill his fantasy – lesbian
sex. Anyway, one night while at a party at his mate's, I had this girl
coming on to me. Shortly after my fella asked me if I fancied her. After a
few more drinks I'd had enough and stomped off to the toilet. While in
the loo, the same girl walked in and started chatting. I told her I knew
my boyfriend had set me up and we both had a laugh about it. It was

then I decided to teach my man a lesson. I slid my hand between her legs and started fingering her. Before I knew it we ended up doing each other all around the bathroom – it was the best sex ever. But the best bit is that I've now split up with him and am moving in with Shelly in a fortnight! Thanks for everything, mate, you were right – I didn't know what I was missing.

Sister gets eyeful

Many years ago, when I was a teenager and still living at home, I went to ask my brother if I could borrow an album of his. I dutifully knocked on his bedroom door and upon the shouted reply, "Come in," went in, only to see him shoot his load all over his girlfriend who lay, spread out naked, underneath his bouncing form. I quickly realised that what he'd shouted was his intentions to his girlfriend and not instructions to me! I quietly left without either of them ever knowing.

Lezzers give priceless show

One night, after a particularly drunken uni evening, me and my girlfriend decided to retire to my boudoir for a little rough and tumble. As soon as the door shut we were on the bed, 69-ing the night away. Suddenly I heard a funny noise from the next room. Being that our walls are about as thick as toilet roll, I soon realised the gimpy guy next door was beating himself off at the sounds of our furious orgasms. My girlfriend then suggested we should visit our neighbour. So off we went, stark naked, to knock on his door. With jaw on the floor and a lump in his trousers, we pushed the spotty freak onto the bed and stripped him down. Unfortunately, being an obviously inexperienced chappy, it was only a few seconds before he'd shot his load, so me and my girlfriend decided to finish each other off, to a thunderous climax. Now we can't help but smirk as the pizza-faced fool tries in vain to boast about his conquest to all and sundry, who merely scoff and call him a lying twat. If only they knew...

Sex toy vengeance

My ex-boyfriend and I decided to spice up our sex life so we bought a "Tickler Set" from our local sex shop. When it arrived I eagerly opened the box but my dog thought it was a toy and kept trying to snatch it out of my hand. In the end I had to put it away in a drawer. Later that week I found out that my bloke had been sleeping with my mate, so when he next came round I took him upstairs to try on one of the Tickler thingies. I waited until he'd put it on his cock and then let my dog into the bedroom. She took one look at it, and thinking it was some sort of toy for her to rip to shreds, jumped up and bit him on his cock! Ahh, revenge...

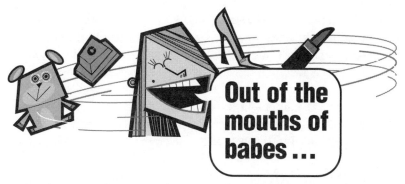

Out of the mouths of babes ...

Overhearing a discussion about the supermarket chain Iceland changing its name to The Big Food Group, our female admin clerk at work commented, "That's a strange name for a country."

Chilling at my mate's house, one of his sister's friends asked to see the new conservatory. On viewing she exclaimed, "Wow! It's like a whole different room!"

Lush reveals a little too much

It was my second year at university and a boozy Freshers' week. One night I reached my full potential by beating the lads' rugby team in a drinking competition on stage. Later on I somehow found my way home to discover my (mostly male) flatmates in the lounge. As I slumped in the corner, one asked me what I'd done to my knee. This confused me, but when I looked down what I saw made me sprint to the toilet. What had happened was that my sanitary towel had slipped down inside my tights and was resting on my knee. The worst thing is that I still don't know whether or not it was there while I was on stage in front of hundreds of fellow students!

Cousins do more than kiss

For a while now, I've been fantasising about anal sex. However, as my husband isn't brave enough to explore the "other passage", I had resigned myself to life as an anal virgin. Then, at a drunken family get-together, my younger cousin was telling me how he'd never managed to persuade any girlfriend to let him try anal. My eyes lit up, and I persuaded him to walk me home that night, as my husband was away. Once home, I explained that we shared a similar predicament, and, after a little persuasion, got him to bugger me on the couch. It was well worth waiting for, and the fact that we were related only added to the excitement. We now meet up regularly for anal sessions.

Gamblers go for it

My boyfriend and I have our little thing called "the one-minute gamble", which means, when we're in my flat, say in the kitchen, and my flatmates are in the house, we time ourselves doing something rude for exactly one minute. It's an amazing turn-on! He might hoist me onto a bench, pull my panties aside and lick me out, or just give me a quick knobbing from behind. I think he's gutted that we haven't been caught yet! I'm pretty sure we'll soon be doing "the two-minute gamble"...

Naughty lady improvises

My now ex-boyfriend came to my works do with me. We were sitting on a table of about 30 people when I noticed a guy I fancied in the office at the opposite end making eyes at me. I like to tease so I discreetly played along. Between courses I excused myself and went to the ladies. However, the guy followed me and pulled me – willingly, I might add – into a cubicle in the gents. He bent me over and lifted my dress, ripping off my G-string. We started going at it like rabbits when through the crack of the door I saw someone come into the toilet. To my shock – and excitement – it was my boyfriend! Luckily the guy put his hand over my mouth, as I then had a great orgasm while watching my oblivious boyfriend! After he left, we waited a few minutes and then made our exit. I joined my boyfriend at the table looking a little flushed! The guy followed a few minutes later and as I glanced up I could see him wiping his mouth with what appeared to be a table napkin. But it was my very moist G-string! Later on I had to make something up, so told my boyfriend that just to tease him I hadn't worn any knickers. He was so horny thinking about it that I had his cock in me on the way home!

Saucy tale gets girl going

I went to stay with my best girl mate and one night we went out clubbing where I met this really nice guy. After a couple of hours of "getting to know each other" he and I sneaked into the loos and I wanked him off. When I was walking home with my mate later (just slightly tipsy), she admitted she'd got really wet when thinking about what my guy and I had got up to. By the time we got to her place we were so horny we 69'd on the floor in her living room. First time with another girl, but I'm certainly ready to put on a show with her for any guy who asks...

Angry girlfriend suits herself

A few years back I was going out with a guy who loved every type of sex going. After trying almost everything there was only one thing left to do – a threesome! I was more than willing so we went everywhere to get another woman, but no joy. Then I received a phone call from his sister saying he'd been seeing other women behind my back. So as I was down in the dumps I went to my friend's house and we started getting drunk. Then her boyfriend turned up, and as the night went on we started talking about sex and all got horny. So she suggested a threesome! We were all willing and it was fantastic. But the best of it was a week later when my so-called boyfriend turned up. My friend stood up and said, "Have you told him about the other night?" I was shocked at first by what she said but then I told him everything – his face was a picture. It felt great. Then I slept with his brother, but that's another story.

Endowed helper bops victim

While on holiday with my then-boyfriend in Greece we were sitting by the pool when the man next to us fell down and started having a fit. I knew first aid, so jumped out my seat and started to move stuff out of the way so he didn't injure himself. Just as I bent over, the catch on my bikini top came undone and my FFs fell out and hit him in the face. I was so embarrassed I made a run for it!

Bloke takes sleepy sex too far

My ex-boyfriend and I were going through a bit of a sexual drought, mostly because he was always too stoned to do anything. One night, when my fella thought I was asleep, he started going down on me. I was too pissed off with him to stir, so pretended to be still asleep. Next thing I know, he's on top of me, having sex. I'm ashamed to admit I found it a bit of a turn-on, so didn't say anything. This happened for a few nights – I just pretended to be asleep, he shagged me silly and we were both happy. Obviously, though, the novelty soon wore off. I had to put an end to it after one night, when he thought I was asleep, he shoved my finger up his arse and began wanking... Had to say enough is enough then, I'm afraid.

Spouse gets it very wrong

My husband and I were at a party and he was accusing me of making eyes at every guy that was there. I went to the toilet to calm down and on leaving saw a girl I used to know from school. I told her what had happened and she dried my tears, then gave me a kiss on the cheek which turned into a full-on snog with her tongue. We returned to the ladies where I had the most fantastic oral sex with tongues and even fingers probing my little starfish. I still haven't told my husband that it's not the guys he has to worry about.

Quickie goes yucky

On a Saturday night out with some mates I was approached by a really sexy guy in a bar. After some polite chit-chat we stumbled into a taxi back to his pad where very soon we began humping like wild animals in his bed. After some time he went down on me and gave me some full-on, mind-blowing tongue action. Losing control I accidentally broke wind in his face, causing him to throw up all over me. I was so mortified and humiliated that I decided not to stick around to wipe his chin...

Camping gets super-rude

I went on this camping trip with my girlfriends and some blokes. One night we all got drunk around the campfire and after a while me and my friend invited my boyfriend and his mate into a tent. It soon got a bit steamy and my mate asked the guys if they'd all fancy a kissing three-way. They readily agreed and tongues were soon everywhere, with my boyfriend making out with my best mate. I was just watching when his friend invited me in – I thought, Payback! Thirty minutes later my boyfriend was passed out pissed on the floor of the tent. Seeing the opportunity, his friend asked me to strip, so I did, nice and slowly to tease him. First he fingered me, then he started giving it to me doggy style as I screamed with pleasure. I thought this was great – cheating on my boyfriend with his best friend while he's two feet away. In the morning I asked him if he remembered anything. He replied, "I can remember two people shagging close by, but I don't know who they were." Perfect.

Sexed-up minx causes mischief

One evening I was waiting for my boyfriend to return home from a few days working away, so I thought I'd get myself in the mood ready for his return. I decided to watch one of his "special videos" and test out the new vibrator he'd kindly bought me for Christmas. After several intense orgasms I heard his car pull into the drive. As he came in the door I didn't give him the chance to refuse and, completely naked, pushed him to the floor, undid his trousers and jumped straight on top of him. Then as I was leaping up and down in ecstasy I heard this almighty crack. My boyfriend screamed and I leapt off to discover I'd broken his ribs with my exertions. He then had to go around telling everyone he'd done it at football training.

Lady mishears lover

During a hot one-night stand, the bloke I was with breathlessly asked me to do a "waterfall". Being more than happy to experiment I smiled, asked him to roll on to his front and then pissed all over his back. Turns out he actually just said I was "beautiful"...

Holiday love gets sticky

Last summer, I went back to this guy's apartment in Faliraki for sex. After a couple of shags he started wanking, then came all over my stomach. Which would have been okay, but he then started licking it all up! And then licked my face with his spunky tongue!
Bye bye Mr Weirdo...

Soldier does damage

Me and my fiancé wanted to have some spicy sex as he was being sent to Iraq for God knows how long. A friend had told us about her boyfriend putting one of those mint things that melt on your tongue onto her clit while he licked her pussy. So, one night during a session, my bloke placed the mint strip on my love button. At first it felt cold, then hot, but I was enjoying the tongue action that I was receiving. Then it started to burn... a lot. I screamed and attempted to move away from his thrusting tongue but he misunderstood and thought that I was really enjoying it, saying things like, "You love it, you dirty little minx!" In the end I had to push him off me just to get him to stop! I've never been in so much pain – I couldn't sit down for a week. All I can say is that my mate must have a clit made out of leather!

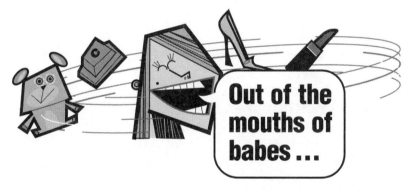

Out of the mouths of babes ...

Out for a meal, my mother-in-law was asked by the waiter whether she wanted her pizza cut into four or six slices. "Four," she said. "I couldn't possibly manage six."

My housemate read a fashion feature about how everyone was wearing crosses these days. "I've worn one for ages!" she exclaimed. I pointed out that it was because of her religious beliefs, not for fashion. "Not true," she replied. "If I wanted to do that, I'd wear one with a little man on it."

Girl gets acquainted with dad

I'd been seeing this guy for two months and although he bought me everything I wanted, he was a real bore. His dad, on the other hand, was very different and much more sexually attractive. So I thought I'd try it on with him when my boyfriend was out getting us a take-away. I crept upstairs and into his room. Seconds later he came in and before he said anything I told him to be quiet, shut the door and lick my pussy. Without protest he did as he was told and was soon taking me from behind and in all my pleasure I didn't see my boyfriend standing there in front of me! Expecting tantrums and accepting the fact that I would have to pay for my own stuff from now on, I was surprised when he got his todger out and urged me to take it in my mouth. During the double whamming I realised that maybe I had been wrong, because, in this respect at least, it certainly was like father, like son.

... and another gets acquainted with mum

My then-boyfriend and I were out for his birthday and I had plans to take him home for a real birthday treat – but he wanted to continue drinking with his mates. I stormed off, but on the way home decided to go to his house, where he lived with his mum, to wait for him. She let me in and offered a sympathetic ear and a drink. After a few glasses of wine I was pretty drunk, so when his mum's hand started working its way up my leg I didn't complain and soon enjoyed the best oral sex I have ever had. To this day, he still doesn't know what happened.

Relaxing night ends in chaos

After a hard day at work, I wanted to get back to my boyfriend's house, have a long bath and go to sleep. After the bath things got heated, and my boyfriend decided it would be a good idea to use an after shave bottle on me. Not only did the lid come off inside off me, but his little brother and his friend walked in when he was trying to fish it out. Bugger...

Hapless husband gets welcome-home "present"

Me and my husband's sex life was pretty boring until the time I got home from work early. My husband came back on time, but I'd decided to have a little fun by myself. He caught me ramming my dildo in myself – with a nappy and bonnet on! Which surprised him.

Horny holidaymaker has double the fun

On holiday in the Balearics last summer, I was with my boyfriend but I'd been flirting with a group of German lads who were staying in our hotel. One afternoon as my boyfriend lay by the pool, I decided to hit the shops. As I left our room I met two of the German guys. They were laden with sangria and asked if I'd join them on their balcony for a drink. After a couple of strong sangrias I was feeling a little drunk and horny as the guys were lying naked on either side of me. I thought, What the hell, I'm on holiday, go for it! So there I was, on a balcony, 15 stories above the pool where my man was laying – being spit-roasted! I was in so much ecstasy that I couldn't help howling like a dog as the guys rammed me from all directions! Returning to the pool my fella was eager to tell me I missed the funniest thing. Apparently while I was away everybody was in hysterics listening to some tart being given a good seeing-to and barking like a dog on heat somewhere up above.

Beau shown the red card

My boyfriend has a fetish for feet. One evening my mother invited us round for tea but made the mistake of taking her sandals off. My boyfriend couldn't take his eyes off her feet, so after tea when we were washing up, I told him off. A little later I went upstairs to use the loo and as I was a bit horny spent a while there. When I eventually returned, my boyfriend had gone. I asked my mum why and she replied he'd told her what lovely feet she had and asked her to have a threesome with the two of us! She'd slapped him and kicked him out, and I ain't heard from him since.

Waiter provides solid service

During a girls' weekend in Amsterdam, we went to a really dubious nightclub featuring naked waiters and waitresses. One waiter took a fancy to me and as the demon drink began to take hold I started to get more daring with him. As we were sat in a poorly lit corner I took a chance and made a gentle grab for his cock. He didn't bat an eyelid and just stood there while I continued to stroke it. It didn't take long before he became aroused. It was obvious he didn't want me to stop so he turned around to face the wall and soon reached orgasm and left a sizeable deposit on the wall. He quickly composed himself and walked away to continue waiting on others. It took me considerably longer to stop shaking.

Weekend worker is given secret treat

While at uni, I worked weekends at an estate agents. I was often left alone, which I saw as an ideal opportunity for spending on my boss's desk in the back room while my boyfriend gave me a good shagging. I'll never forget the time when we moved into the main office, where he sat himself between my legs under my desk and proceeded to give my pussy a licking as I went about making phone calls. All was fine until my boss walked in – we both froze! She didn't stay for long, but it was the most mortifying, but strangely arousing, five minutes of my life, what with the cheeky bugger flicking my pussy with his tongue as I talked to her.

Embarrassment for horny couple

One night me and my ex-bloke stayed at his parents' to look after their house. After a while we got bored so I unzipped him and started to give him a juicy blow-job. We didn't realise how late it was so when the door opened and his parents walked in on us I jolted up in shock, only to find my boyfriend jumping up as well, forcing my top lip into the zipper of his jeans. It got much worse. His mother then had to try and free my lip away from the zip, with her son's limp cock still in my mouth, unable to be taken out until my lip was free. Funnily enough I was never invited round again!

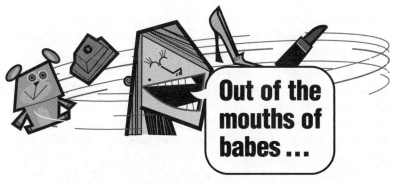

Out of the mouths of babes ...

While discussing how shit Big Brother was, my flatmate quipped, "If only it were more like the 1984 version..." His girlfriend replied, "Was that the first series, then?"

While working as an office temp my sister had to type up an illegible handwritten letter which came from the County Chief Executive. Unfortunately, she used her "initiative" – and signed off his title as "Country Chef Executioner".

Swinger surprised

My husband and I used to enjoy swinging. One time we hooked up with a guy called Mike, who was pretty nervous about the whole thing.

We tried to make Mike comfortable and offered him some wine and nibbles. After a while he perked up a bit, so casually unbuttoning his trousers, I released his throbbing hard-on. My lips were soon tracing his cock with supple kisses. My partner leaned over Mike's shoulder taking Polaroids, then went to recline on the sofa. I carried on dragging my lips down Mike's shaft, then felt something lightly brush my cheek. I opened my eyes to see what it was. I did a double take – Mike was casually eating Pringles while I sucked him off! My husband was in stitches – I was furious. Mike was soon shown the door...

Lady lives fantasy

One of my fantasies is to be taken by two cocks at the same time, so knowing how liberal-minded my man is I let him into my secret. The next night I turned up at his place to find him and his best mate waiting for me, pants bulging. Neither of them could take their eyes off me as I stripped down to my G-string and told them to wrestle each other for my snatch. The sight of their rock-hard cocks pressed against straining muscles soon had my pussy dripping wet. Desperate for cock I squeezed in between them, straddling my man while he pulled apart my butt cheeks for his friend to enter me from behind. It was the best ride of my life. Now I'm looking for a hot woman to help fulfill my man's fantasy... the two of us oiled up in thongs wrestling over his cock.

After-hours shenanigans caught on film

I used to work in an agency in the City. One night after a leaving party, my boss, who I fancied, shared a cab home with me. We stopped off at the office on the way back because he needed to pick something up. As we were leaving he said he really fancied me, so I took the opportunity and kissed him. I then started undoing his trousers, got on my knees and gave him a wicked blow-job. When I arrived at work the next morning there were police everywhere – some drunk had smashed the front window of the office. The CCTV footage was next to be checked;

to my horror the video was played and there I was, butt-naked spread across the table on all fours, noshing my boss off!

Sex toy mishap

A few months back my boyfriend and I decided to have a hot, horny night in. After taking turns at teasing and pleasing he handcuffed me to the spindles on the staircase and took control, using old faithful Rampant Rabbit. Sitting naked and hard between my legs, he pumped the vibrator into my pussy. He was then hit by a few drops of liquid, and thinking that I was on the verge of exploding he kept going. Unfortunately it wasn't me about to explode but the battery. The drops were the acid from inside which had landed smack on the head of his member! As he rushed to the bathroom to wash it off I was left helpless and laughing, still handcuffed.

Lewd lad taught lesson

A few months ago I was in a club with my then boyfriend and his mates. I was on my fifth JD and Coke when my boyfriend's only good-looking mate started flirting with me. Feeling very horny I told my bloke to meet me in the ladies in five minutes for a treat. As soon as he was in the cubicle I was on my knees giving him a terrific blow-job. After a few minutes I heard a muffled laugh, and looking up I saw two of his goons laughing like mad. The prick had told them to come and watch his dirty woman in action. With me feeling very pissed-off back at the bar, the good-looking friend told me how he tried to talk them out of it. Seizing the opportunity to get back at my shitty boyfriend, I took his mate to the same cubicle where he proceeded to bend me over and give me the best shag of my life!

Country girl has special day

This summer I woke up one morning and in my horny state thought, I'm going to spend the whole day in the nude! My parents were away and we live in a remote part of the countryside, so it wasn't going to be too much of a problem. And so I cooked naked, sunbathed naked, watched telly naked... and frigged myself silly naked – lots! Towards the end of the day I wanted to take a risk, so did the short walk to the local postbox without wearing a single stitch. Just as I was returning I heard a car approaching, so slowed down a wee bit and made sure the driver, whoever he might be, saw my cute bum before I disappeared inside! Cue a lot more wanking indoors. I'll have to do this again next summer...

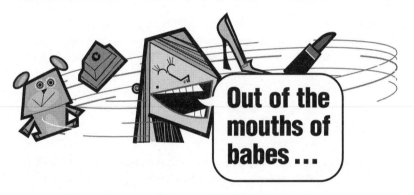

Out of the mouths of babes ...

A former girlfriend was always trying to take a photo of the beautiful sunsets on Ascension Island, but most evenings was foiled by the weather. "Doesn't the sun ever set in front of the clouds?" she asked me eventually.

Visiting the place where Irish martyr Michael Collins was shot, my sister asked why he didn't take cover behind the memorial when they were shooting at him.

Daughter keeps family traditions going

I live with my parents, and recently my boyfriend came to spend the day with me. We soon escaped into my room to watch films. Not long into the movie I felt very horny and it wasn't long before we were having great, passionate sex. But just before my bloke came... my mum walked in! He jumped off me, pulling up his jeans as my mum asked what the hell was going on. At this point I jumped on top of my man and began tickling him, making out that was what we'd been up to all along. For the next few days my mum gave us some horrible glares. To be frank I don't see her problem. We all know about the stash of porn videos, luminous condoms and vibrator under her bed.

Bathtime gets yucky

When I was ill once, my boyfriend suggested we have a nice bath together, which would "make me feel better". So we both got in, me with my back to him in between his legs. We were in there for quite some while and it started to get cold so I lent forward to turn on the hot tap, when I let out the biggest fart you could possibly imagine. I expected my boyfriend to laugh but instead he leapt up with a loud yell and jumped out of the bath. To my horror I realised I hadn't just farted but in my ill state I had also followed through and it was now floating all around me! We weren't a couple for long after that.

Bubble-bath cleverness

My boyfriend and I were taking a bath and I just couldn't keep my hands off his cock. So after a few gentle strokes I got it exactly how I like it, rock hard. I love giving him blow-jobs, so in he went! I'd emptied my fella the previous night but when he came there was a bucketload. Proud of the overflowing contents I had just taken into my mouth, I opened my gob to reveal all. With that, I coughed and blew a huge bubble of come through my nose. Thankfully there was plenty left to swallow.

Holiday shag disaster

My friend and I went on a girlie holiday to Torquay. After a cocktail-fuelled night I pulled this bloke who was also the worse for wear. As I was feeling horny I decided to go for it, so he led me to a grotty stairwell in a car park where he gave me the worst 15-second shag of my life. Then, to my horror, I discovered the condom was "lost" inside me! It took a lot longer to fish out than he'd spent shagging me. And after all my contortions I looked up to see a security camera pointing straight at me. It then actually moved and followed my descent down the stairs.

Chambermaid gets double surprise

I am a chambermaid in a city-centre hotel. One morning I was servicing a bedroom when I found a dirty magazine, so I had a flick through and started touching myself. Suddenly the door opened and the guest walked in. To my surprise he shut the door and joined in. He was well equipped and was soon skillfully spearing me with his hefty cock. I later confessed to my now ex-boyfriend, who was not too impressed.

Loo shenanigans halted

For our anniversary my boyfriend and I decided to have a romantic meal out. Once we got to the restaurant, we couldn't keep our hands off each other and a tingle rose inside me, tickling my pussy. I couldn't control myself and had to rush to the toilets, telling my boyfriend to follow shortly. As I burst through the toilet to check the all clear, I pulled him in and he pushed me into the nearest cubicle. We were getting down to it, when I heard a familiar voice. It was the voice of my mother, pulling my father seductively into the toilets! They'd obviously had the same idea when out for a meal. Sure enough it killed the passion and we left extremely unsatisfied.

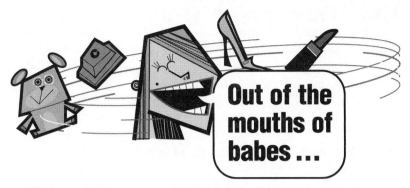

Out of the mouths of babes ...

After remarking to my mate's bird that it was nice to see the sun and the moon in the sky at the same time, she told me: "Don't be stupid! How can that happen? They're the same thing."

During the Jubilee weekend my girlfriend piped up, "Why does Prince Charles always hang around with the Queen?" When I'd picked myself off the floor, she confirmed that she hadn't realised the two were related.

Bus journey brightened up

One day my boyfriend called me when I was on the back seat of the bus and started talking really dirty. It'd been a pretty boring ride before that, but now I unbuttoned some of the buttons on my dress and started to play with myself. I fiddled with my clit for a good half hour and came heaps of times. It was a great feeling knowing I could get caught at any time! My boyfriend loved what I was doing and shortly after came round my house and gave me a damn good shagging.

Couple vary things

One night me and my husband decided to attempt something different – a spot of anal sex. With both our children sleeping in the next room we thought it'd be safe. After my husband got me really horny it was time to insert the python. It took a great deal of time trying to get it in, but finally we managed, with me on all fours on the bed. We were at it for ages groaning and moaning, then my eye caught something at the side of me. It was my six-year-old just standing there! I had to explain myself by saying that daddy and I were playing cowboys and Indians. Thankfully he wasn't traumatised, but the next morning he asked me who won the game of cowboys and Indians.

Underwear encounter

A few months ago I was out shopping with my bloke for some naughty new underwear. I was trying on a really sexy bra but needed the straps adjusting. As there was no one else in the changing rooms I asked the shop assistant to help. As she was adjusting the straps she started gently touching my breasts. Feeling horny I turned round, we started kissing and one thing led to another. With one leg on a stool she gently slid my thong off and started licking me out. After giving me a truly ground-shaking orgasm, we got dressed and walked out. My bloke who was waiting outside was none the wiser!

Lady takes dare

Last month my boyfriend dared me to go to the shops with my mini-vibro in me. I had it in all afternoon, even having an orgasm in McDonald's! But in the next shop, I felt it pop out, slide down my leg and by a miracle lodge in the top of my boot instead of rolling across the floor! The dares continue...

Model gets well into things

I'm a glamour model and the other week went on a shoot, this time at a guy's house. It went really well, with me getting turned on exposing all my bits to the fit photographer, while the house owner looked on with a bulge in his trousers. When all the shots had been done the three of us headed to a nearby pub to unwind. After a little booze I was getting frisky and dying to shag the photographer. So I thought I may as well come out with it. I said to the bloke whose house it was, "I'll give you £20 if you let me and him have use of your bedroom for an hour." He accepted! So we all headed back to his, and me and the snapper disappeared into the guy's room. After some even naughtier photos we had a fantastic sex session. God I love porno shoots!

Novelty party leads to bathtime fun

Recently it was my friend's birthday party, and it was decreed that it would be a themed Rubik's Cube party. What this means is that every guest wears one of each of the six colours of the Rubik's Cube and during the night you swap clothes, so by the end of the evening you're in one colour. The idea is that you have to persuade a member of the opposite sex to swap an item of clothing, whether it be trousers, top – or underwear! It promised to be great, sexy fun as we had a mixed crew of good-looking guys and gals. Sure enough, it soon got heated as the clothes were coming off and going on and the drink was flowing. I swapped my red panties for a guy's blue boxers and felt incredibly horny showing him my pussy as we exchanged smalls. I could see from his swelling cock he enjoyed it too! To cut a long story short, a load of us ended up in a big bath together, where I had my pussy licked by a girl with a tongue stud and my tits sucked by some bloke while his brother had a wank over us. A birthday party to remember!

Knickerless student teases college lecturer

I am a history student and for a bet with my girlfriends I agreed to wear a short shirt and no panties for a full day. I attended my morning lecture which was being taken by our particularly hunky tutor. I sat near the front and, very briefly, kept opening my legs a small way. I soon noticed that he kept looking over, unsure whether he was really seeing my pussy or not. This went on for the whole hour – by the end he was a stuttering, flustered wreck! On the way out I gave him a little bonus, giving him a cheeky flash of my arse. Boy, am I a tease!

Passionate cries heard all around

I was in my new boyfriend's flat and things started to get really hot and steamy on his leather sofa. Soon it escalated into raunchy, filthy sex and as always I got really noisy. After we finished, the phone rang. He answered it and started laughing hysterically. The intercom to his flat had broken and when his mate rang the buzzer my passionate screams were broadcast to the street outside. When a shocked old lady walked past he proudly announced, "That's my mate doing that, that is!" I still haven't lived it down!

House guest outstays welcome

During the summer I had one of my male "friends" staying with me for a few days. I already had a boyfriend, so my mum was not in the least suspicious. One night me and him went out for a few drinks and, sure enough, on the way home had a little fool around before reaching my house. We went up to my room where things started to get heated. I ripped off his boxer shorts, rolled up my tiny skirt and straddled him on the bed. Next thing I knew I heard my bedroom door open. He threw me off him, pulled the blankets over him and pretended to be asleep before my mum came in to ask where all the noise was coming from. I told her that my friend had drunk a little too much and was feeling sick. Then, before I could do anything, she whipped back the bed clothes. She found him naked from the waist down with a throbbing hard-on wearing nothing but a strawberry-flavoured condom. Oh dear. He went home first thing the next morning.

Paddlers give great show

Me and my boyfriend Lee will have sex pretty much anywhere. So when we went on holiday to Spain we thought we'd try it in the sea. We figured that if we went out far enough people wouldn't see. Anyway, as we were fucking and were both really turned on, I heard people's voices. I turned around and saw that we weren't the only two turned on – there were two lads wanking while watching us. Incredibly, they were obviously more embarrassed than us, as they then swam off so we could finish what we'd started!

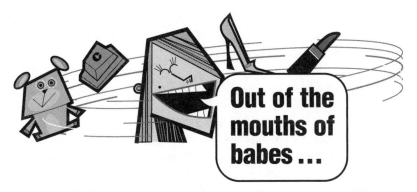

Out of the mouths of babes …

While I was sanding down a piece of wood my girlfriend watched, amazed. "I didn't know that wood was made from little pieces of dust," she explained afterwards.

I took my girlfriend for her first experience of watching football at the pub. The place was packed and all was going well, until Tony Adams put his hand on the mascot's shoulder. "What position does that little man play in?" she asked, loudly.

Roman strip-search leads to airport friskiness

My boyfriend and I were returning from a naughty weekend in Rome, having to get up early for our flight. Scrambling to get clothes on and still a bit drunk from the night before, I just put on what I'd had on then, a black mini, black boots and a top. We made it in time but going through passports noticed the Italian police giving me a good eyeing up. Luckily, the boyfriend found this funny until I was pulled to one side and taken off to a room where I was searched. The fact that it was two gorgeous Italian policemen stopped me from protesting. One said they were looking for drugs, a feeble excuse I thought and let them carry on. Before long, I was stood in black boots, panties and bra with four hands exploring everywhere you can imagine. I emerged 20 minutes later, red-faced but very horny! On the flight back, I told my guy what had happened and as we had a row to ourselves, he was soon getting his first mile-high hand-job.

Teen gets educated

When I was 17 I went out with a boy of about the same age. One day I went to his house but he wasn't in, so his older sister invited me in to wait. She got some wine out and we giggled about girly stuff, and when I mentioned I was worried about being a crap kisser she suggested we kiss. I decided what the heck! She said it was great and could we try it again. She ran her hands all over my body and then squeezed my boobs! Soon in our underwear, she took my hand to lead me upstairs. My heart was pounding, but I was also dripping from all the foreplay. Upstairs, she began by going down on me. But just then the cupboard door flew open revealing a man with his trousers round his ankles and a huge hard-on. He also had a video camera in his other hand. I screamed and my boyfriend's sister jumped up and yelled at him. It turned out he was her boyfriend and he was meant to be just watching, not videoing. After a row they started kissing and then looked at me – I couldn't take my eyes off his huge knob! They both got on the bed and he started kissing me while she was busy fingering herself. He put his cock in my mouth, and she began licking me out. I had an amazing orgasm and after he came in my mouth she kissed me and swallowed it all. We ended up having sex another four times, and I got a taste of everything. It made me realise what a crap shag my bloke really was!

Sex toys offered for testing

Before last Christmas I went on a shopping trip in Cologne with my mum. We were in a market when we spotted a sex shop, so in true FHM fashion we thought, Why not? We duly went inside, only to find that half the shop was discounted goods – because they were second-hand! We found this out because as I was looking at some of the sex toys the shop assistant asked me if I would like to "sample one of them"! I asked her what she meant and was told, "You can go in that room and have a try. There are some wipes to clean it after you've used it"! I promptly grabbed my mum and we left in fits of laughter.

Accidental threesome gets too much for some

It was one of the most drunken nights that me and my best friend have ever had, and when we got home we carried on drinking, getting louder and louder until my boyfriend came down complaining that we were making too much noise. Trouble is, he hadn't done the front of his boxers up and everything he had was on display. At this point my sloshed, turned-on mate suggested a threesome, so, feeling well up for it – and the fact that my boyfriend's dick had just gone up faster than a Frenchman's hands – we were off. All was going well until, just as me and my mate were pleasuring him orally, he coughed and farted and came all at the same time. Both of us just fell about laughing as he stormed off.

Road trip gets squidgy

The annual Bank Holiday weekend break to Skegness was upon us and my mum, dad, my boyfriend and myself were cooped up inside the family Astra. After about four hours of non-stop driving I was rudely awoken by my man's erect love length digging into my waist. Checking in front I found my ma was dozing and dad engrossed in Five Live, so proceeded to resolve the "problem" in no time. However, not getting caught in the act wasn't enough to satisfy my lover's fantasies and being the daredevil that he is, he tapped my mum on the shoulder and asked her if she had a spare tissue...

Twins have fun

I have an identical twin sister. We are exactly the same in every way: looks, personality, laugh, smile, voice, everything. One night we thought we'd play a trick on her boyfriend. We swapped clothes – even underwear – and I went to meet her fella pretending to be her. She was meant to come out later and surprise him, but texted and cancelled. He was none the wiser so I ended up staying out and getting stupidly drunk with him. One thing led to another and before I knew it we were at his flat shagging away.

He told me it was the best and filthiest sex we'd had "so far"!

Summer heat dampened

Last summer I had a barbecue. My boyfriend and I had been together for seven months, but I'd recently started seeing his sexier best mate, so invited him along rather than my boyfriend. But annoyingly, my boyfriend turned up! He started sulking when he saw his mate there so I decided to "cheer him up" before getting his best mate back for a proper shag after my boyfriend had left. Once everyone started leaving, my boyfriend tempted me into a corner in the garden and ripped off my skirt. He started fumbling with my clit but wasn't getting it right, while all the time my bladder was aching. I was still desperate to come so I helped him out by guiding him to the right spot. But this unfortunately relaxed me so much I pissed on his hand! He was well pleased – until I told him it was wee! I'm now with his best mate.

Shopper relieves boredom

One Bank Holiday Monday my parents dragged me around a furniture superstore. Bored to tears I sat myself down and let them get on with it. It turned out the chair I'd chosen had a remote control and after pushing a few buttons it began to quietly vibrate. One turn of a dial later and the vibrating sped up – plus I had my legs crossed and a tight pair of jeans on. In a few minutes I was having an orgasm while the rest of middle England shopped around me totally unawares.

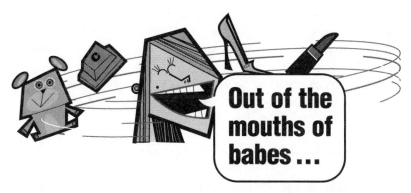

Out of the mouths of babes ...

Trying to impress a female colleague with the wonders of the internet, I popped her postcode into an aerial mapping website and zoomed down onto her house. Bemused, she asked how come she could see her car sitting in the drive when it was clearly parked in our car park. Laugh? I nearly sacked her.

Watching the Stallone movie Cliffhanger on TV the other night, we came to the part where a man is hanging from a tree as a pack of hungry hounds nibble on his shoe. My lovely girlfriend innocently asked, "Are they rescue wolves?"

Lady pens gratitude

I was recently reading *FHM*'s High Street Honeys booklet and as I'm secretly bi-curious, started to feel really horny. As I was all alone in the house I started to play with myself. I came three times in a row and by the time I'd finished my fingers were soaking! So I just wanted to say thanks FHM for the best wank of my life!

Who done it?

Last summer, I went back to this guy's flat for some no-strings sex. After about 15 minutes of shagging he moaned as he blew his load and proceeded to roll over and go to sleep. As I was drunk I didn't complain and joined him in catching 40 winks. The next day as I woke I was greeted with the most disgusting smell. To my horror I realised that during shagging the night before I had shit myself! I nipped off to the bathroom to clean myself up. When I returned I gently rolled my one-night stand over to the other side of the bed. When he woke to find what he believed to be his bedtime mess he came over all embarrassed and apologetic. I assured him it was fine and then saw myself to the door.

Nightlife is blinding

I was out for a drink with some mates in Manchester when this horny guy started chatting me up. It wasn't long before we were rushing to find a quiet spot to get down to some frisky business. Kissing and groping, we both made a grab for each other's rude bits. He pushed my head down so I would blow him, but I just started off by wanking him slowly and playing with his balls. It was all going well but suddenly he creamed into my right eye! To hide the shame, I had to pretend to my friends that I was crying because I'd hurt my foot rather than simply being jizzed on.

Cunning plan

My fella and I were on the verge of breaking up although we still lived together. One night I was out on the tiles with my friends and met up with a hunk I knew from the gym. Things between gym hunk and me started hotting up and I thought, "What the hell?" and took him back to my house. We got down and dirty on my bed when I heard a taxi pull up, and to my horror, it was the ex. Panic ensued but as the ex had no key, he obviously couldn't get in. So, he started trying to prise open the window while ringing my mobile. Crafty as I am though, I thought up a plan; I rang his mobile and when he answered he started shouting, "Open the door, I'm outside!" to which I replied, "I'm at my friend's house and can't get a taxi home, walk down and meet me halfway." Bearing in mind this is four in the morning, the ex then dutifully walked away from the house to my friend's to make sure I got home safely. My gym hunk and I got dressed and left the house, he flagged down a taxi, dropped me off near the friend's house I'm meant to be at and I then proceeded to walk up to meet my ex. Genius!

Car trouble

I was at home with my boyfriend, feeling very horny. Unfortunately my mum was also in. So we had the idea of going for a little drive! It didn't take me long to begin sucking on his cock. The pleasure was so great for my boyfriend, he just couldn't control his speed and drove through a speed camera without even noticing. Two weeks later, his mother received a letter with a fine for speeding and included was the picture from the speed camera with my head clearly sucking his lolly!

Suspenders cause suspense

After receiving a rather sexy bra and thong set from my boyfriend for Christmas, I decided to supplement it with the matching suspender belt. The ensemble produced the desired effect on my boyfriend and we both had a very satisfying night together. But about a week later, feeling a little broke, I decided to return the suspender belt in order to raise some extra cash. As I removed it from the bag, the efficient shop assistant asked if it had been worn. "Oh no," I responded confidently, "it's just that it's completely unsuitable." Then, to my horror, under the bright store lights I spotted a wiry, spiralling pubic hair standing to attention in the sheer net fabric. Beginning to glow, I stood my ground hoping she wouldn't notice. It wasn't until the assistant used her long, perfectly manicured nail to scratch away at a newly visible, white crusty patch that I cut my losses, grabbed the lingerie and ran out!

Gondola gets steamy

Last Christmas my bloke and I were snowboarding in Austria. One afternoon a whiteout forced us to leave the mountain early and we got a gondola all to ourselves. Not ones to waste an opportunity like this we started snogging as soon as the doors closed. It wasn't long till his board pants were around his ankles and his cock was in my mouth. It wasn't until he'd finished emptying his load that we noticed the gondola had a CCTV camera. Sure enough, as we left the gondola we were greeted by three sniggering lifties, the last of whom shook my boyfriend's hand...

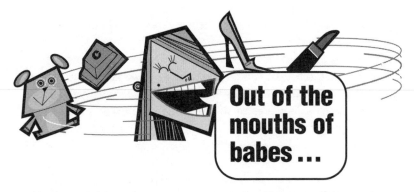

Out of the mouths of babes ...

On our descent into Dublin airport at 25,000ft, my wife pointed down at the bay. "You can see the fish jumping!" she said with girlish glee. Sadly, I had to inform her that she was looking at ferries.

Riveted by the Grand Prix live on telly the other week, my girlfriend sent the entire room into hysterics by commenting, "Do they stop racing when the adverts come on?"
Sad but true.

Danger: odd female

One of my secret sex fantasies has always been to get kidnapped for a steamy sex session.
I mentioned this to my boyfriend, but never thought he would act

on it. Then one day I was walking down to the supermarket when a van pulled up and a masked man grabbed me and dragged me inside. Not knowing what was happening, I started screaming. Then the man let me know he was actually my fella and he wanted sex. I felt myself getting wet almost instantly and we started ripping off each other's clothes. A few moments later he was taking me from behind and I was screaming to make him go even harder and deeper. Just when we were about to climax, the door was violently opened and we were both dragged out. Apparently someone saw what happened and called the police, who thought I was being raped. I've never been so embarrassed in my life, but fortunately the police laughed about it. And I made sure my ex came around later to finish off what he'd started.

Hell hath no fury...

After finding out the man I was with had been unfaithful I was – unsurprisingly – pissed off. I went round to his place while he was at work to get my stuff and found his very dishy flatmate shirtless and looking very horny. I decided my revenge should be to shag said flatmate on my ex's bed, leaving the mess for him to clean up. When my ex found out, he trashed my car, so I decided to ring the police to inform them of the little illegal plants growing in his basement! Revenge is sweet.

Pierced bliss

One day, for no apparent reason other than I was bored, I decided to go and get my clit hood pierced. I put on a nice lacy thong and off I went. I got to the studios and it all went without a hitch. Afterwards it felt really sensitive, plus it didn't help that my jeans were a tad tight. The constant rubbing was seriously turning me on, but it was only when I got on the bus that things really started happening. It was a bit old and rickety and the seat I chose happened to be over a wheel. About halfway home, the vibrations were really getting me hot and bothered. I was having an orgasm on the bus, and it's sooo hard to keep quiet doing that! Let's just say, it was the best bus ride of my life, and I love that piercing!

Twisted sisters

I thought it would a nice idea to surprise my fella, so I went out and bought some bondage gear and a vibro. When I got back home I was really horny, and when I got talking to my sister, we decided to devise a little game. When my bloke got home I took him up to our bedroom while my sister hid. I tied him up to the bed naked, blindfolded him, then started to give him oral. Just as he was about to come I stopped and told him to wait a moment. I moved out of the way and my sister came in with some whipping cream, which she dripped all over his body and slowly licked off. She worked her way down and begun giving him oral until he exploded. She then crept out of the room, which is when I returned and finished the night off for him. He'll never ever know that he got a double helping that night!

Season's greetings

Over the Christmas period I was going through a bad patch as I'd just split from my boyfriend and during the last two months of our relationship we hadn't had any sex at all. Come Christmas Eve I was sitting in my parents' home all alone. The artificial Christmas tree was looking rather inviting, so with myself feeling sexually frustrated and gagging for it, I grabbed the tree and turned it on its side, removing the Angel to reveal a smooth plastic top. Then I slowly inserted the top of the tree into my vagina and pleasured myself. And to be honest it was the best Christmas present I've ever had.

Back door confusion

My husband has been pestering me to let him pop my little brown cherry for three years now and last week I finally agreed to anal sex.

That evening he was lying on the bed waiting, so I began by massaging him. He loved it when I started kneading his bum cheeks and didn't even protest when I slipped a finger in. The next thing he felt after I had readied him was the head of a strap-on! I gave him a thorough pounding which he eventually enjoyed. The only drawback was he walked like John Wayne for two days. I guess it was his fault for not asking which way round the anal was going to be going!

Changing room chancer

I'm the captain of a girls' hockey team and last week a hunky male was standing in for our usual coach who was injured. Before practice I popped into the male changing room to discuss team selection, little expecting to see the new guy lathered up in the shower. I gasped with excitement as he turned to face me, revealing his impressive manhood. Implausible as it sounds, but within minutes I was bent over a nearby table with my arse in the air. My pleated skirt was up, my lacy knickers were down and his big, stiff cock was inside me. He unhooked my bra and began fondling my tits as he pounded my pussy. As he reached climax I span round, knelt down and took his prick in my mouth, gulping down his spunk while watching his face contort with pleasure. Who'd have thought playing with a long stick and some balls could be so much fun!

Lady quick to stray

Recently, me, my boyfriend, his best mate and his girlfriend booked a table at a fancy restaurant. A week before the date we got a call from my bloke's mate, saying that he had split from his girlfriend. However, the three of us still went to the restaurant and the evening was going well until my boyfriend got up and shot to the toilet. He came back complaining that he must have a stomach bug. He kept on going to the toilet throughout the night, leaving me and his best mate alone to talk. The mate knew that I fancied him, and he told me he liked me, too. Eventually we left, and while we were on our way home my boyfriend had to stop off at a public loo – that stomach bug again. Drunk and excited by the evening's flirting, I pulled down my boyfriend's mate's trousers and started sucking him off. I did all my tricks to make him come as quickly as possible and when he came, there was a bucketload. Then I heard my boyfriend open the toilet door. I didn't want to swallow the come, so I pretended to be sick. My boyfriend comforted me all the way home, but what he didn't know was that I had just given head to his best friend!

A sort of revenge

One night I was meant to meet my now ex at a pub which just happens to be in a sleazy part of town. It was his birthday and he was there with his mates as usual. I dressed myself up to the nines and went to meet him but by the time I got there he was pissed and being a prick. Not in the mood for this I said that I was leaving. I left the pub and was walking up the street when a car pulled up beside me (and at this stage I would have done anything to get back at my boyfriend for not giving a shit about me). The window rolled down and the man asked me if I was new to the area, and then it clicked that he thought I was a prostitute! I felt a little tingle in my knickers and gave him the impression that I was. He asked me did I want to get in. I duly obliged and we had some wicked sex back at his – and as a parting present I left him with my naughty little knickers! That'll teach my fella.

FHM helps out

Last night me and my boyfriend had the most amazing sex session! There was come in my hair, come on my tits and, of course, come in my pussy. Know what set us off? Him taking snaps of me in panties for your High Street Honeys competition. Cheers FHM!

Al fresco couple bothered

The sunny weather inspired me and my man to track down new places to have sex, so we went for a cycle to find a spot to get down to it. Kneeling down near a fence I pulled out Tom's cock and and began sucking away. I then ordered him to screw me from behind. Halfway through I heard a voice that wasn't Tom's. Some scabby farmer had tapped him on the shoulder and said, "Just wondered if you need another cock." Mortified doesn't come close.

Balloons cover jiggery

After enjoying a birthday meal out with my boyfriend, his friends and my parents left the restaurant and boarded the minibus we'd hired with lots of red balloons the staff had given me as a gift. It proved tricky to fit them on board but after some rearrangement we all got on. My man and I squeezed onto the back seat, hidden from everyone behind the curtain of balloons. Soon things got a bit steamy when my bloke started caressing me under my skirt. With nobody able to see what we were doing he hitched aside my knickers and I sat on his stiff cock. Our friends were oblivious as they chatted away to us – we did well to reply as things came to a head...

Sexy plan spoiled by coppers

One night I thought I'd give my work-stressed boyfriend a treat by indulging him in one of his fantasies, going to his wearing my full-length black coat and nothing else. Getting-ready time reduced, I jumped in my car and set off to his. Disaster! I saw blue flashing lights in my mirror. I pulled over, praying that the lecture could be administered through the window. This wasn't the case, as the two young policemen asked me to step out the car. Trying to button my coat up while getting out of the car proved difficult, with the officers getting great views of all my naughty bits. Unsurprisingly, they were more interested in where I was off to "on such a chilly night", than giving me a ticking off. The embarrassment!

Mile Highers seduce stewardess

My bloke and I are keen travellers – and happily also sex experimenters. We recently flew back from the United States and got chatting to our fantastically sexy stewardess, deliberately steering the conversation towards sex and threesomes. At around midnight, most of the passengers were sound asleep so the three of us met up in the rear galley. After some lingering kisses to break the ice we started to really go for it. Whilst my fella was busy enjoying her fantastic tits, I rode up her tight skirt and peeled off her thong. After a good ten minutes of three-way action we were busted by none other than the clearly gay purser, him catching his team-mate with my boyfriend's cock in her mouth and a couple of my fingers inside her. She was reprimanded and we made the Washington Press. I've kept the newspaper as a souvenir – and of course the thong.

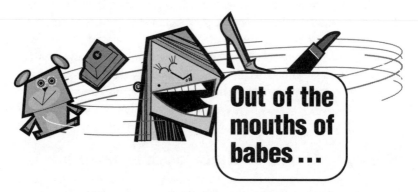

Out of the mouths of babes ...

Approaching Glasgow Airport in the car last year, my wife was getting excited at the prospect of flying. "Wow!" she exclaimed. "Aren't the planes low when they're coming in to land!"

While at a friend's house, her mate came in, unplugged the phone and jacked her own phone in. "I'm expecting an important phone call," she explained.

Nurse 'assists' sperm donor

I work as a nurse in a sperm bank, which is pretty dull most of the time, but has its moments. Recently this sexy guy came in and I proceeded to flirt with him outrageously, asking him questions like, "How often do you wank?" I felt myself getting wet down below as he said things like, "Yeah, I really love wanking over tall, sexy blondes." Shortly I led him to one of our rooms with his little cup. At first I left him there by himself but the thought of him pleasing himself made me even more wet and I couldn't contain myself. I practically ran into the room and said something like, "Thought it'd be best to give you a hand..." Straight away we started kissing and he ran his hands all over my body, stopping between my legs. I climaxed within seconds, then dropped to my knees and gave him a blow-job. When he was finished, I spat the contents into his cup – after all, he was there to donate!

Cheat plays risky game

Sex with my bloke was getting a bit boring, so I started an affair with someone from the office. After a while we got more daring and started doing it in our bed while my man was out. One Sunday my lover and I were getting frisky when I heard the door open! My bloke's footie game had been called off and he had come home. To his surprise there I was in bed, horny and dressed up in my schoolies! My lover was hiding in the wardrobe so I said to my bloke that it was about time he got home and why didn't he get down there and give me a good licking! While he was busy under the duvet my lover had a chance to sneak out but thought it'd be a giggle to wave his cock in my face. What the hell, I played along for a bit, keeping my boyfriend's head firmly on my cooch while I sucked my lover's cock!

Private dancer treat

I used to dance naked in a club, partly because I needed the cash, and also because I enjoy getting my kit off. One evening a couple asked me for a private dance in the back. The club was strict on this, so I had to say no, but they offered me 200 quid, so I said I'd go to their house at the end of the night if they were still interested. Sure enough I went along and was soon on all fours getting a good seeing to, with a mouthful of cock and being shagged from behind by a woman with a dildo! She had the most filthy mouth I'd ever heard, which made me even hornier. They screwed me until I was exhausted – it was mind-blowing! I don't dance any more, but I did move in with them two months ago, (rent free!) and we have the most amazing sex sessions ever.

Dare not Truth

A few months ago I was having a party at my house because my parents had gone out and weren't expected home till the early hours. Me and my mates were all getting drunk and so we decided to play Truth Or Dare. Everyone was choosing truth and it was getting boring, so I asked my boyfriend to think of a good dare to give me. When it came to my turn I chose a dare and it was for me to get it on with my best female mate. So we were in the middle of the room having a good snogging, me with my tits out, when suddenly all went quiet. I stood up to see my parents standing at the door! I have never been allowed a party since, and they think I am in denial about being a lesbian because I am still with my boyfriend.

Swimming pool sauce

I was on holiday with friends, and we were having the time of our lives getting well and truly bladdered. One booze-soaked night, we decided to go skinny-dipping in the hotel pool. One of the guys in our party was obviously enjoying the sight of me and the other sexy girls a little too much, because he had the stiffest cock I'd seen all month! Feeling drunk and horny, me and the girls decided to surprise him by diving underwater and sucking hard on his hot tool. Needless to say, he was thoroughly appreciative and shot his juicy load all over the pool! Feeling indebted to me (having been the last to suck him off) he paid me back by giving me the best bum-bang I've ever had! When I walked to the pool the next day (with some difficulty!) I was horrified to discover the come still floating in the water. Yuk!

Cleaner's big entrance

After a night of amazing sex with a guy I picked up at the Student Union, I got the usual bout of mid morning horniness. My guy started taking me in the ass while massaging my tits. Then, just as he was about to come, his sexy 29-year-old cleaner came barging into the room, with my man just managing to whip his cock out in time. The cleaner then calmly proceeded to slip his still hard cock in her mouth while I looked on, watching as she milked his man juice into her mouth. Little did she know where it had been, and she was so surprised when my guy threw her out of his room when she tried to kiss him!

Underachiever loses date

I was shagging this bloke who I just met, back at his place. He really was the shittest lay I'd ever had – the guy was barely moving, flopped on top of me like a limp fish. Five minutes in I realised I couldn't cope with another minute of this, so I told him to get out of me because I was desperate for a wee. He rolled off and I got out of bed, slipped my dress on and left the room. Then I went straight to the lounge, picked up my bag and shoes and headed for the front door. See ya!

Newcomer proves credentials

I'd just started a new job and there was a "Welcome to the team," night out. Everyone got absolutely hammered on shots and started performing their party tricks – doing impressions or juggling with the ashtrays. So for mine, I got my tits out, right in front of my thirtysomething boss, and showed all my new colleagues how I could get them in my own mouth. It was the shortest job I ever had.

Couple perform for gathering

It was a works summer ball and I met this guy from the other office. We got on like a house on fire – due to the fact that I'd been downing red wine all night and had my beer goggles well and truly in place. It was nearing the end of the night when I challenged him that he dare not shag me outside. But he dared, so off we went. There was a big swing in the grounds out front, he sat down and I hitched up my posh dress and climbed aboard. There I was, bouncing up and down on him, just as an announcement was made inside the venue for everyone to start making their way onto the waiting coaches to go home. We ended up surrounded by cheering, pissed blokes, asking if they could have a go, too!

Ward enjoys sound effects

When I was 17 I was going out with a man ten years older than me who'd ended up breaking his leg in a motorbike accident. I went to hospital, pulled the curtains around us and without saying a word, gave him the best blow-job I'd ever performed then left feeling as if I was the biggest temptress in the world. Only looking back do I realise that the rest of the ward would have heard every slurp and smack of my lips.

Lotion causes discomfort

I'd been seeing my boyfriend for about two years when I found out the double-crossing bastard had been cheating on me with some woman from his office. So one night I invited him round to my flat, got the candles out, put the romantic music on and suggestively lured him into a massage. I'd got hold of my male flatmate's Deep Heat lotion and started rubbing it seductively onto his knob. His screams haunt me even today.

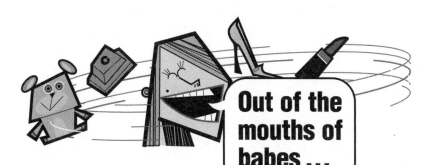

Out of the mouths of babes ...

My girlfriend and I were talking about doing a bungee jump. I wondered whether they lowered the rope down when the jump was over, or winched you back to the top. My girl replied, "Don't you jump, bounce up and land on the platform again?"

One of my lovely girlfriend's colleagues was reviewing a book by immobile computer-voiced physicist Stephen Hawking. Stumped on the first sentence, she asked my girlfriend, "Is he American?" He's English, she replied. The girl wasn't sure, and said, "I've seen him on TV and he's got an American accent."

Dinnertime shenanigans end abruptly

I went out for a meal with my boyfriend and his great-looking best mate, Gareth. I was next to my man while the best mate sat opposite, so I slipped my shoes off and started massaging his balls with my toes. Then my boyfriend piped up, "Gareth, why are you stroking my leg?" Gareth's jaw dropped, and the rest of the meal was eaten in silence. I mean, what could the poor boy reply? "Sorry, mate. I was trying to grope your bird's inner thigh!"